Spectacles of Empire

DIVINATIONS: REREADING LATE ANCIENT
RELIGION

Series Editors: Daniel Boyarin, Virginia Burrus, Charlotte Fonrobert,
Robert Gregg

A complete listing of books in the series is available from the publisher

Spectacles of Empire

Monsters, Martyrs, and the Book of Revelation

Christopher A. Frilingos

PENN

UNIVERSITY OF PENNSYLVANIA PRESS

Philadelphia

10 9 8 7 6 5 4 3 2 1

Published by
University of Pennsylvania Press
Philadelphia, Pennsylvania 19104-4011

Library of Congress Cataloging-in-Publication Data
Frilingos, Christopher A.
   Spectacles of empire : monsters, martyrs, and the book of Revelation / Christopher A.
Frilingos.
      p.   cm. (Divinations)
   ISBN 0-8122-3822-2 (cloth : alk. paper)
   Includes bibliographical references and index.
   1. Bible. N.T. Revelation—Social scientific criticism. 2. Rome in the Bible. I. Title.
II. Series.
BS2825.6.R65 F75   2004
228'.06—dc22   2004049615

For Amy, Emma, and Joseph
ἡ ἀγάπη οὐδέποτε πίπτει

Contents

I

Gods, Monsters, and Martyrs

WHAT DID ANCIENT CHRISTIANS FIND APPEALING about the book of Revelation, a story about the end of the world? To be sure, this text, also known as the Apocalypse, includes some of the Western world's most enduring images. In its visions clash the "gods and monsters" of Christianity: the four riders on horseback who visit famine and disaster upon a dying world; the final battle between a multiheaded beast and the armies of heaven; and the great day of cosmic judgment that gives way to the blinding glory of a "new heaven and a new earth" (Rev. 21:1). The poetical force of the book is unquestionable, great enough to obscure for many readers the details of its disturbing plot, in which the earth and its inhabitants are systematically destroyed to make room for a universe of Christian "conquerors": "Those who conquer will inherit these things [a new heaven and a new earth]" (Rev. 21:7). A frankly imperialist narrative, Revelation predicts the end of the Roman Empire and the beginning of a Christian one.[1]

Many scholars, seeking to understand the book in its original context, have concluded that the shrill tone and misanthropic outlook of the Apocalypse reflected the fears of early Christians, a beleaguered minority in an environment hostile to the new religious movement. By promising an imminent reversal of fortunes, the book's visions, like apocalyptic ideology and literature generally, responded to a collective sense of alienation. Indeed, a scholarly consensus has formed around the notion that Revelation rejects the Roman world because it speaks for a community that has cut itself off from this world: Christ and Caesar have nothing in common.[2]

The present study approaches the Apocalypse from a different angle, finding in its visions of monsters and martyrs desires that were formed and caught fire in the spectacles of the Roman Empire. Revelation, I shall argue, permitted its audience to do what Mediterranean populations under the empire had already been trained to do: gaze on a threatening "Other," figured as the distant barbarians on imperial sculpture or, alternatively, as the unseemly fear that fell like a shadow over the face of a cowardly gladiator. To adapt Edward Said's treatment of "Orientalism": the public displays of Rome made the "Other" knowable and "To have such knowledge of such a thing is to dominate it, to have authority over it."[3] But there are further considerations, for Revelation, no less than other expressions of Roman culture, calls attention to both the allure *and* the risk of "taking in" a show in a society that emphasized the careful scrutiny of one's friends, one's enemies, and oneself. Ancient spectators, seated in an arena or "standing far off" as "Babylon" burns (Rev. 18:9), frequently discovered that they had themselves become part of the performance.

Far from being thoroughly critiqued and excluded, the values and institutions of ancient Rome left an indelible imprint upon the visions of the Apocalypse. Tradition and biblical scholarship make this a controversial proposal. That Revelation has inspired marginal groups is a matter of historical record. The book has persuaded Christians of all kinds that the world would end with a whimper *and* a bang, but it has proven especially attractive to antiestablishment movements. The Apocalypse was first venerated by a religious movement that suffered violent persecution under the Roman emperors. Much later, galvanized by Joachim of Fiore's *Exposition on Revelation*, members of the medieval Apostolic Brethren opposed papal power and died at the stake for their insolence. In the modern era, liberation theologians have used the book to protest capitalism and globalization, while "Generation X" will long remember the siege and fiery destruction of the Waco compound of Revelation-interpreter David Koresh.[4]

To this association with radical groups biblical scholars have added the weight of their scientific findings. For much of the twentieth century, it was common for historians to situate Revelation in the context of severe Roman oppression of Christians. This setting offered a plausible explanation of the lust for revenge expressed in the book; otherwise, one scholar observed, Revelation could only be "the product of a perfervid and psychotic imagination."[5] Some, looking for a specific instance of persecution and finding little evidence of it under Domitian, have argued that the Christian heresiologist Irenaeus was wrong to assign the book to Domitian's reign, and have instead pushed it back thirty years, to the days of Nero.[6] According to Tacitus, Nero blamed Christians for the great fire of Rome, punishing some by burning them as torches to light his games.[7]

The vitriol Revelation spews against the Roman Empire is thus made comprehensible: John's prophecy of a day when the beastly Nero would be tossed into the lake of fire expressed the outrage of early Christians.[8]

Since the 1970s, however, scholars have largely abandoned this assessment of Revelation's purpose and the model of causality it implies. The language and imagery of the book, most scholars now agree, is far too rich to have arisen from any single moment of persecution, no matter the intensity. Attention to the genre of Revelation, in part, prompted the shift. According to a well-known scholarly definition, first published in 1979, Revelation and other ancient apocalypses belong to "a genre of revelatory literature within a narrative framework, in which a revelation is mediated by an otherworldly being to a human recipient, disclosing a transcendent reality which is both temporal insofar as it envisages eschatological salvation, and spatial insofar as it involves another supernatural world."[9] In this view, the symbols of Revelation make reference to more than actual Roman emperors; they connect Roman authority with an evil of cosmic proportions. The book was not a response to a specific episode of persecution but a translation of all human history into a struggle between the forces of good and the forces of evil. The Apocalypse is literally a "revelation," an uncovering of the mundane world that discloses a supernatural actuality—what is really at stake. As such, the book represents a concrete, written articulation of an ancient apocalyptic worldview that enveloped nascent Christianity.

With the appreciation of genre came a different understanding about the relationship of the book to its ancient surroundings. In the span of nine years, two influential investigations would deeply affect all subsequent research on Revelation. Neither offered a straightforward, historical-critical assessment of the book, but both introduced instead models and perspectives from the social sciences to explain the power of the Apocalypse. In a brief discussion of Revelation in *Kingdom and Community*, John Gager suggested that the narrative structure of the book transported early Christians out of a present experience of suffering and into a universe of power and control.[10] The book accomplished a temporary "suppression of time" by presenting to its readers a series of binary oppositions, pairing images of despair, the seven bowls of wrath (Rev. 16:1–20), for example, with images of hope, in this case, worship in heaven (Rev. 19:1–16). The "rhythmic oscillation" between these images exposed the transitory nature of the "here and now," enabling the audience to rise above the conflicts of the present and to pass for a moment into the millennial bliss of the future. The effect, though, was short-lived: the "real world" stubbornly asserted itself again into the lives of early Christians. In sum, Gager argued that the book of Revelation offered to early Christians a myth that temporarily eased the tension between "what ought to be and what is."

In *Crisis and Catharsis: The Power of the Apocalypse*, Adela Yarbro Collins likewise maintained that the driving force behind Revelation was the tension between "what was and what ought to have been."[11] But where Gager insisted on Roman persecution as the main source of this tension, Collins introduced the remarkably supple notion of "relative deprivation": whether or not the officials of Rome arrested, tortured, or killed Christians, John and his readers *felt* oppressed, and this perspective colored every aspect of life.[12] She argued that Revelation created a "crisis" out of widespread exasperation with Rome, enhanced this rancor, and then resolved it.[13] Like Gager, Collins paid close attention to the structure of Revelation; but unlike Gager, Collins eschewed structuralism and employed a model of "recapitulation" to make plain the "power of the Apocalypse." Revelation, she argued, used different images in a series of repetitions: the breaking of the seven seals (Rev. 6:1–8:5) is recapitulated in the seven trumpets (Rev. 8:6–11:19), and again, in the seven bowls of wrath (Rev. 15:1–16:21). The purpose of these violent repetitions was to sharpen the deep-seated resentment of the audience by playing upon the community's hatred of Rome, Jews, and rival Christian groups. "Catharsis" was delivered to the audience through Revelation's final visions of judgment and a "new glorious mode of existence" for the faithful, ameliorating the disquiet evoked elsewhere in the narrative.[14]

Other scholars have offered their own versions of "crisis and catharsis." According to Elizabeth Schüssler Fiorenza, early Christians faced not governmental persecution but social ostracization, which the book's "symbolic universe" enabled readers to transcend.[15] For Leonard Thompson, the Apocalypse established boundaries between the "deviant knowledge" of his Christian community and the pagan "cognitive majority," boundaries that did not yet exist in the urban environment of Asia Minor.[16] More recently, scholars have focused on sectarian rivalry as the principal force behind Revelation's strange images: "The crisis of the Apocalypse is a crisis of authority within Christian circles," contends Robert Royalty, a thesis echoed by the recent work of Paul Duff.[17] The book opens with messages to churches in seven cities in Roman Asia Minor, and in these communities, Christians such as "Jezebel" in Thyatira

(Rev. 2:20) and the "Nicolaitans" in Pergamum (2:15), stood at odds with John's understanding of Christianity.[18] John's hatred of Rome was secondary; his hatred of his opponents was primary.[19]

A range of solutions has thus been put forward to explain the apparent alienation of John's community. Yet, underneath this diversity lies a common *modus operandi*: nearly all recent treatments of the book have first identified the circumstances that led to the composition of Revelation and have then interpreted the book in light of these circumstances. Each has proceeded, in other words, from motivation to meaning, linking the appeal of the book to external or internal points of stress that the book somehow resolved. In an unlikely development, "crisis" has served as the therapy for an anxiety (lurking, we might say, in the unconscious of critical scholarship), namely, the fear that Revelation was indeed the "product of a perfervid and psychotic imagination." What else could be responsible for this strange text but "relative deprivation," "deviant knowledge," or, more recently, a "crisis of authority"?

This is not at all to suggest that these explanations are without merit.[20] On the contrary, these and other models of social interaction have greatly advanced the study of Revelation. But the net effect of theories such as "relative deprivation" and "deviant knowledge" has been to isolate John and his community, separating Revelation from the Roman world. Thompson, for example, concluded that Revelation reflects a "minority that continuously encounters and attacks the larger Christian community and the even larger Roman social order."[21] So too other suggestions for tethering the text to the ancient Mediterranean world have paradoxically driven a wedge between Revelation and the society of the early empire, a setting that has often been described according to fairly narrow categories or been made subordinate to other concerns.[22] The present study, by contrast, does not undertake a new quest for the ideological, psychological, and sociological factors that compelled the seer John to pen Revelation. Rather than developing a theory of origins, I attempt to read the book of Revelation as a cultural product of the Roman Empire, a book that shared with contemporaneous texts and institutions specific techniques for defining world and self.

Symmetry in the treatment of Revelation and the Roman Empire is a primary methodological objective of the present study. It seeks to describe the ambiguities of life under the Roman Principate and to read Revelation as a narrative exploration of these ambiguities. I assume that texts are participants in the fashioning of culture and subjectivity and not

merely statements of preexisting ideologies or worldviews. I do not challenge the hypothesis that John resented Roman rule, nor the argument
that John wished to construct or maintain "high" boundaries between
nascent Christianity and paganism. Nor do I dispute the thesis that apocalypticism served as an ideology of resistance for ancient Jews and Christians, including John.[23] In sum, I do not wish to contest the notion that
apocalyptic elements were part and parcel of early Christianity, but I do
contest the idea that these are the *only* elements that matter for grasping
the appeal of Revelation. Rather than cast the relationship between this
text and Roman culture in oppositional terms, I seek to discern the power
of the Apocalypse for subjects of the Roman Empire by embedding the
book in this empire, more specifically, by relating the appeal of the book
to ancient preoccupations with viewing and the achievement of masculinity. To the further elaboration of the key terms and theoretical underpinnings of this study we now turn.

Figures and Focus

"Monsters and martyrs" here designates two (sometimes overlapping)
character types in the book of Revelation. "Monsters" covers a wide range
of grotesque characters, from the evil dragon to the beasts to the prostitute Babylon. For the early Christian audience, we shall see, one monster
rose above the others, the Lamb "standing as if slain."[24] "Martyr" (ὁ
μάρτυς), or "witness," holds diverse connotations in the Apocalypse. It is
associated with figures whose sufferings are linked—by narrative proximity, at least—to their "witness" to Christ and God, as in the reference to
Antipas, "my martyr" (Rev. 2:13) and in the story of the two prophets,
"my two martyrs" (Rev. 11:1–14). Yet, as Adela Yarbro Collins observes,
"*martys* is not yet a technical term meaning 'martyr' in Revelation."[25] In
this study, μάρτυς relates chiefly to examples of viewing in the narrative.
The many characters of Revelation repeatedly act as spectators: here "wit-
nessing" the demise of Babylon, there gazing at the wonders of the beast.
If the Lamb was the most compelling monster for ancient Christian audiences, Christ, "the faithful witness" (Rev. 1:5), in various guises (including
the Lamb), I will argue, surfaced as the most important spectator in the
Apocalypse.

The monsters of Revelation have attracted far more attention from
commentators than the martyrs: one of its most famous readers, Carl Gus-

tav Jung, focused on the book's strange creatures.[26] In the course of a psychoanalysis of Job, Jung paused to consider the Apocalypse: its beasts—
"the horrid progeny of the deep"—he argued, revealed "an unusual
tension between conscious and unconscious" in John's psyche. Further,
Jung maintained, the violence of the book is the shadow of the seer's
Christianity, a religion of love and forgiveness. Rather than show mercy,
Revelation's righteous deities and semideities wreak havoc, causing
plagues and famines to be visited upon the earth. Revelation's hatred was
the polar opposite of John's religious self: "This apocalyptic 'Christ' be-
haves rather like a bad-tempered, power-conscious, 'boss' who very much
resembles the 'shadow' of a love-preaching bishop." There is more here,
however, than just the repressed resentment of one man: Revelation un-
leashes nothing less than "a veritable orgy of hatred, wrath, vindictiveness,
and blind destructive fury," Jung explained, expressing the darkness of the
collective unconscious. The unconscious produced that which is impossi-
ble for John to comprehend consciously, "that very darkness from which
God had split himself off when he became man." The "horrid progeny of
the deep," the monsters of Revelation, remained unfathomable to the
seer, an unintelligibility that gave birth to fear.

Jung's analysis, while ingenious, is a psychologizing portrait, and few
biblical scholars have found it helpful for the historical study of Revelation.[27] The essay serves nevertheless as a salutary starting point for the
present investigation because it foregrounds the perplexing images that
inhabit John's visions. To mention a few examples: two beasts, a dragon,
a prostitute drunk on blood, a lamb with horns, and winged creatures full
of eyes all inhabit the Apocalypse. What do these monsters mean?[28] One
influential answer was formulated at the beginning of the twentieth century by the German *religionsgeschichtliche Schule*.[29] Hermann Gunkel and
Wilhelm Bousset, leading figures in this school, found in the book's monsters a test case for their methods.[30] Both accepted a "textual law" that the
Jewish and Christian authors were not creative agents in the composition
of apocalypses, but had access to "an unbroken chain of traditions"
stretching back to a primeval age.[31] For Gunkel, Revelation's beasts represented God's primordial enemies, Leviathan and Behemoth; further, the
tradition also lured beasts from the tales of ancient Near Eastern mythology, such as Kingu and Tiâmat of Babylonian myth.[32] Bousset, in *The Antichrist Myth*, argued that the same "unbroken chain" continues in "the
early Christian eschatological tradition," a tradition that "stands in a position of independence in respect of the New Testament."[33] In their

hands, Revelation became one more telling of an ancient myth about a battle between "gods and monsters."[34]

By focusing on a "chain of tradition," Gunkel and, to a lesser extent, Bousset neglected Revelation's contemporary context, a world that bears down hard on the text.[35] Instead of Roman society, sources from the distant past were invoked to interpret Revelation. In a parallel development, some scholars continue to treat Revelation as "the 'Grand Central Station' of the whole Bible," looking for meaning in the book's allusions to the Jewish Scriptures.[36] Since the images of Revelation derive from passages in the Jewish Scriptures, it is argued, the book can only be interpreted in relation to these passages.[37] I do not dispute that the Jewish Scriptures provided John with a cache of images, but these images take on new meanings when they are extracted from their original context and placed in a different one.[38] As Morton Smith has remarked, "The preacher who comes to the Bible looking for a proof text happens to find a good one, one which really says what he wants said. But this does not alter the fact that *he finds it because he looks for it, and he looks for it because of the practices or ideas which have become important in the world around him.*"[39] Whether or not John viewed the Jewish Scriptures as a collection of "proof texts" remains an open question: unlike other early Christian texts, Revelation appropriates images from these Scriptures but never explicitly cites them, leading some commentators to suggest that John understood his own revelation to supercede them.[40] We will not attempt to determine precise referents in this study, but will attend instead to the strategic use that John makes of biblical imagery and language, especially as this usage relates to the production of knowledge about the "Other."

To the extent that this study understands the diverse institutions and texts of the Roman Empire, including Revelation, to be joined together, "networked," in the production of knowledge, its findings will contribute not only to the study of Revelation but also to the cultural historiography of the Roman world. Rather than distancing the book from the Roman world, the grotesque visions of Revelation surprisingly implicate it in the specific practices of viewing that had "become important," to quote Morton Smith, in the creation and maintenance of identity in the Roman Empire.[41] Rome's was a society of spectacle, and one does not have to look far to find monsters on display in the Roman Empire. In the Roman arena, for example, exotic animals from around the empire were exhibited and hunted; and paradoxographies, literary collections of "wonders," recorded accounts of fabulous creatures that lived on the borders of civilization. As Carlin Barton has observed, "the ambiguous, the paradoxical, the puzzling, the obscure and difficult to categorize—in short, the monster—was the great and final temptation" for ancient Romans.[42] The link between temptation and monsters will be investigated; for the moment, though, it is enough to note that Barton's description of Roman society lays out a viewing relationship between a monster, the temptation, and the viewer, who is tempted. More than even specific manifestations of the monstrous in the Roman world, it is the dynamism of the viewing relation itself that throws into high relief the significance of monsters in Revelation. Roman spectacles, this study suggests, not only captured the imagination, they also simultaneously constructed and expressed a subjectivity of the viewing self for Roman audiences. Revelation likewise narrated spectacles for its ancient Christian audience, thus participating in discursive formations already available in the Roman Empire.

Critical Orientation

The critical orientation of this book has already been indicated by the use of certain key terms: production of knowledge, subjectivity, discourse. These terms are part of the legacy of Michel Foucault, whose collected works, according to Patricia O'Brien, piece together nothing less than "an alternative model for writing the history of culture, a model that embodies a fundamental critique of Marxist and Annaliste analysis, of social history itself," and even "a new history of Western civilization."[43] The state, family, sexuality are not "givens" in Foucault's anaylsis but discourses, which enmesh individuals and groups in relations of power.[44] For Foucault discourses are not "more or less distorted by ideology," not more or less accurate depictions of a "real" world, but in fact engender the very quality of "realness" that inheres in formations such as the state, family, and sexuality.[45] In this way, discourses govern the production of truth in a society and determine what will count as knowledge.

In his seminal study *Orientalism*, Said appropriated Foucault's conceptualization of discourse to study the effects of representation in the context of imperialism. As one highly influential example of postcolonial studies, *Orientalism* examined the substantial amount of energy that was expended in the creation and perpetuation of a discourse on the "Orient."[46] This labor, Said concluded, ultimately related back to the Western society, for which the "Orient" was invented: "Orientalism responded more to the culture that produced it than to its putative object, which was also produced by the West."[47] Said's study severed all connections between Orientalism and the reality of the "putative object." As the quotation suggests, it is not chiefly the content of the discourse that matters, much less its accuracy, but the investment of the colonizer in the representation of the colonized that makes the representation potent.

Hence, the *production* of the "Orient" is the subject of Said's study. He argued that the "knowledge" of the East, disseminated by a diverse collection of Western sources—scholars, schools, governmental offices— has always been "impressed with political fact."[48] Further, this representation enabled Western scholars to maintain "flexible *positional* superiority" over the object of analysis.[49] By "knowing" the Orient, by repeatedly exposing its irrational and chaotic existence, Said argues, the West exercised control over the East. Further, Orientalism as a discourse acquired authority in part because its sources were so widespread: the "facts" of the Orient were collected and reported from disparate institutional locations, diverse texts.

Yet, for its many accomplishments, *Orientalism* was plagued by some significant flaws.[50] The most serious concerns the place of the West in Said's analysis. As noted by many critics, Said tended to grant complete stability and authority to the colonizer, attributing to Orientalism an "always successfully realized intention."[51] Other postcolonial critics such as Homi K. Bhabha have problematized the projection of an imperial will to power by calling attention to the ambivalence that characterizes relations of power in an imperial context.[52] A key term in the Bhabhian vocabulary is mimicry: "the desire for a reformed, recognizable Other, *as a subject of difference that is almost the same, but not quite*."[53] With "mimicry," Bhabha adds nuance to Said's model of imperialist discourse: under this rubric falls not only the colonized, the subaltern, but also the colonizer. On the one hand, colonial mimicry is an expression of imperial intention: "the civilizing mission to transform the colonial culture by making it copy or 'repeat' the colonizer's culture."[54] At the same time, however, mimicry is a "menace," since it reveals the limits of the realization of imperialist intentions: the colonized are always "almost the same, but not quite," or, as Bhabha has memorably rearticulated the problem, "*almost the same but not white*."[55] Mimicry is thus a "double vision which in disclosing the ambivalence of colonial discourse also disrupts its authority."[56] In this way mimicry makes apparent the conflicted nature of imperial relations of power.[57] More important, perhaps, is that Bhabha's approach outlines, in a way that Said's *Orientalism* could not, the interdependence of dominant and subaltern and the fragmenting effect that this relationship has upon the formation of identities in both. This is not to suggest that Bhabha is somehow disinterested in the asymmetry of power relations under empire, but that Bhabha points the way to a better understanding of the continual negotiation of authority upon which imperialism precariously rests.[58]

By briefly reviewing some of the points of contact and disjuncture in the arguments of Said and Bhabha, I have attempted to highlight those elements—the production of knowledge, the ambivalence of imperial discourse—that will bear most directly on the present analysis. I have not done so in order to outline a formal "postcolonial method" for approaching the Roman Empire. This book has instead sought to employ the insights of postcolonial theorists to address, for example, the topic of cultural authority, a concern that Said shares with Foucault: what produces, what counts for, and what sanctions knowledge in a given society? By showing the manifold ways that imperialism inflects such questions, the work of postcolonial theorists can bring to the surface aspects of Roman culture that might otherwise go unnoticed. The Roman Empire was not maintained by raw strength alone: of equal or greater significance were the countless moments of interaction and negotiation in which the subjects of Rome, from the elite pagans of the Greek East to the seemingly marginalized Christians of John's community, struggled to grasp for themselves the truth of their society and their place in it.

Spectacle—used here in a broad sense to designate a striking display and one or more observers—was central to this work. I shall argue that spectacle was a particularly effective mode for the production of authoritative knowledge about other and self under the Roman Empire: even in its most stylized forms, spectacle provided a framework for the delineation of the real in Roman society and for the forging of identity. Further, this book contends that a myriad of institutions and texts gave rise to a particular subjectivity, a self-understanding, under the Roman Empire: the "viewing self," as I will label it. As Bhabha's investigations of the ambivalence of imperialism would lead us to expect, this subjectivity was fraught with instability, specifically in the slippage from being the viewer to becoming the viewed. This slippage and its relation to the performance of gender surfaced during this period as a significant cultural problem, worked out in the arenas of the Roman Empire as well as in the book of Revelation. As this investigation will show, the viewing self held enormous

potential, both for undermining, or, alternatively, for supporting the acquisition of masculinity.

At this point it might be helpful to contrast my approach with another recent treatment of Revelation and Roman society, one which similarly appropriates aspects of postcolonial studies. In *Imperial Cults and
the Apocalypse of John: Reading Revelation in the Ruins*, Steven J. Friesen
employs a method of "contrapuntal interpretation" that he adapts from
the work of Edward Said.[59] Placing the Apocalypse and the Roman Empire in a contrapuntal relationship allows Friesen "to draw connections
between the early Christian text and its first-century setting" and to "in-
tegrate materials and voices normally confined to separate studies." In
practice, however, Friesen's approach results in a dichotomy between
book and culture that the present study eschews.[60] While sharing a key
concern—"the proper ordering of human society"—the institutions of
the Roman world, Friesen argues, especially imperial cults, were engaged
in the production of an "imperial discourse" that maintained Roman
hegemony; Revelation instead let loose the Lamb, an "image that cannot
speak for the world of Roman imperialism."[61] Friesen ascribes to Revelation an "in the world, but not of the world" posture: in the parlance of
postcolonial studies, the Apocalypse is a subaltern text that has rejected
entirely the culture of the dominant.[62]

Rather than posit Rome and Revelation as distinct, stable entities,
this book presents Revelation as an expression of Roman culture, possessed of the same ambiguities and ambivalence to which a variety of contemporaneous cultural products—the Greek romance, the Roman arena,
and even the imperial cult—attest. It was precisely through these sites
that negotiation and instability entered the world of ancient Rome. Separating out Revelation as "subaltern" or as "resistance literature" obscures,
I think, the multiplicity of power relations in the structure of Roman imperialism.

For the sake of clarity, I wish to reiterate the point that what follows
does not seek to apply "a postcolonial methodology" to ancient texts and
cultures.[63] Indeed, much of the analysis draws from various schools of
"theory" besides postcolonial studies in an effort to track the networks of
meaning that were spread throughout the Roman Empire.[64] If anything,
my use of postcolonial theory amounts to an "internalized" appropriation
that is meant to sharpen the focus of what are largely historical and literary interests. Nevertheless, this study does treat "empire" as a key topic of
inquiry, and, more important, it identifies shifting "relations of domina-

tion and subordination" as a leading theme of Roman cultural products, which in turn, both underwrite and fracture the formation of subjectivity.[65] Further, while it does not make repeated reference to Said in the footnotes, his unveiling of the vast array of disciplines, genres, and techniques employed in the service of "Orientalism" (and, hence, in the service of Occidental "superiority,") is a model I attempt to emulate throughout the work. Moreover, Bhabha's attention to the fragmenting effects of colonialism in the culture and selves of colonized *and* colonizer guides my efforts to "complicate" nearly all of the hierarchical pairs — emperor/God and subjects, masculinity and effeminacy, viewed and viewer — that surface in the pages of this book.

To conclude, this is not a book about critical theory but one about the pulsing rhythms of Roman culture at play in the book of Revelation. This study in no way means to avoid the obvious, that the Apocalypse repeatedly positions itself and its audience over against the monstrous Roman Empire. But the strategies that were employed to make this point were strictly bound to a cultural context and a historical moment. By relating the appeal of Revelation to the spectacles of Rome, I intend to surround this revelation of a new world with the cultural framework that made the "old" world of the Roman Empire almost inescapably real, even to John of Patmos.

2

Merely Players

> On the day that he died, Augustus frequently inquired
> whether rumors of his illness were causing any popular
> disturbance. He called for a mirror, and had his hair
> combed and his lower jaw, which had fallen from weak-
> ness, propped up. Presently he summoned a group of
> friends and asked: "Have I played my part in the farce of
> life creditably enough?" adding the theatrical tag: "If I
> have pleased you, kindly signify / Appreciation with a
> warm goodbye."
>
> —Suetonius, *Divus Augustus* 99[1]

GAZING UPON THE ARA PACIS AUGUSTAE, reconstructed and isolated, Ben-
ito Mussolini realized something was missing. So upon this "altar to
peace" the Italian premier commissioned the engraving of the *Res Gestae
Divi Augusti*, a chronicle of achievements Mussolini deemed to be unparalleled in the history of ancient Rome. The inscription, composed by
an elderly Augustus in his seventy-sixth year, is the Roman emperor's own
account of his conquests, his munificent gestures, and his *pietas*—that is,
his devotion to the gods and to the state.[2] Though produced well after
Octavian's victory at Actium in 31 B.C.E., this document marks the end of
the ancient Republic and the advent of the Roman principate, a political
and cultural transition famously tagged the "Roman Revolution" by Sir
Ronald Syme.[3] For Il Duce, the ancient "autobiography" was a tangible
expression of his own aspirations, to become the modern *princeps* who
would preside over a reborn Roman Empire. At least one interested on-
looker perceived these ambitions: Adolf Hitler declared that "the Roman
Empire begins to breathe again" in Mussolini's Italy.[4] With the aid of this
inscription, the Italian dictator hoped to conjure the spirit of an ancient
empire.

Mussolini's manipulation of antiquities calls attention to the *Res Gestae* as a *monument*, intended for public view. Further, to the extent that

the ancient inscription's themes of conquest and expansion seem to have coincided with his own political agenda, the Italian dictator proved himself, in Jaś Elsner's words, "a more subtle and accurate interpreter of the *Res Gestae* than many of its more scholarly and less politically motivated editors." The significance of this Augustan artifact for fascist Italy would not be lost on those who saw it: the graffiti of supremacist slogans and swastikas now scrawled upon this modern rendering of the *Res Gestae* seem to support Elsner's judgment of Mussolini's exegetical acumen.[5] The "restored" relic summoned a specter, an imperial ghost that took shape in the propaganda of the Axis forces. As an homage to the Roman power of the distant past, the Ara Pacis, emblazoned on its base with the bronze letters of the *Res Gestae*, "invented *imperium*" before twentieth-century Italian eyes, as it had for ancient audiences.[6]

The power of images to promote the ascendancy of the Roman Empire, however, reflects only one dimension of relations of viewing in antiquity. As Augustus poignantly reveals in the epigraph to this chapter, ancient Romans were aware that viewing was not unidirectional: the institutions and texts of ancient Rome seem to concede that Roman imperialism was a performance. Being seen was part of seeing, and even the emperor—especially the emperor—was included in this dynamic relationship. Fault lines in the geography of Roman authority, like the venation of marble monuments, were perceptible to those living under the empire: the subjects of ancient Rome, we shall see, were afforded diverse public opportunities to "talk back" to power, to cheer or deride the imperial performance. If imperial authority was viewed in this way, then other aspects of Roman life were also accepted under these terms, catching the persons of the Roman Empire, from smallest to greatest, in a worldwide spectacle.[7] Like the comical Jacques in Shakespeare's *As You Like It*, the Augustus of Suetonius affirms, in so many words, that "all the world's a stage / and all the men and women merely players."

Shadi Bartsch's work on "theatricality" under the Roman Empire has provided a framework for exploring imperial authority and the nature of power. According to Bartsch, ancient accounts of Nero's reign reveal it as a formative moment in Roman imperial culture that exposed the "permeability" of the line between "stage and life."[8] When the emperor himself took the stage to play music or to perform tragedy, new pressures were put on the audience: no longer (if they ever were) *passive* spectators, they became "actors in the audience," compelled to show a proper amount of enthusiasm for their emperor's thespian stylings. Cassius Dio reports that "the gestures, nods, and cheers [of the audience] were always keenly observed": those that applauded were honored, while others were punished.[9] Theatricality, "a reversal of the normal one-way direction of the spectators' gaze," undermines the conventional opposition between viewed and viewer that theater calls into existence.[10]

A model that accents the slippage between viewer and viewed, theatricality can add depth to the exploration of regimes of public viewing in the Roman Empire. For the present discussion, it calls attention to the manner in which Roman spectacles often folded reality into representation, eliding the line between the two. What happened in the Roman arena was a particular kind of reality, which made no apologies for occasionally drawing back the curtain to reveal the machinations of empire. By exploring these and other forms of public display in the urban spaces of the Roman Empire, I seek to describe the viewing relations that positioned imperial subjects as spectators. The institutions surveyed in this chapter were sites for the production of knowledge, determining, even engendering, the difference between other and self. At the same time, I shall contend, exhibitions of various sorts also provoked reflection on the instability of this subjectivity of the viewing self: Rome's was a public society in which everything, everyone was at all times on display. There was no place from which to stare with impunity. Two institutions will prove especially important to this analysis: the imperial cult and the public shows. Under Roman rule, imperial shrines and spectacles—the gladiatorial combats, beast-hunts, and public executions of the amphitheater—pervaded the cities of Asia Minor, the provenance of the book of Revelation. Before turning to shrine and arena, the chapter outlines on a general level the interaction between visual images and identity in the Roman Empire.

The Power of Images

In antiquity, the Ara Pacis was viewed by only a small percentage of the people who lived under the Roman emperors. It remains nevertheless a useful starting point for understanding "the power of images" throughout the Roman Empire. According to the *Res Gestae*, in 9 B.C.E. the Senate erected the monument on the occasion of Augustus's safe return from battles waged in Spain and Gaul.[11] The value of the piece does not lie in its connection to these campaigns but in its sculptured display of a "beneficial ideology" of empire under the principate.[12] To grasp the meanings generated by the subtle exploitation of mythological and artistic motifs in the Ara Pacis is both to catch a glimpse of the face of Roman might and to begin to understand the relationship between viewing and identity in the days of John the seer.

Themes of peace and power overlap in the material remains of Augustan Rome, and the Ara Pacis has been a focal point of attention of recent research into the relationship between culture and politics in the empire. As one part of his watershed treatment of images and power under Augustus, Paul Zanker argues that the Ara Pacis frieze expressed a "new visual language," an innovation apparent in the carved figures of the altar that associates Roman rule with stability, prosperity, and moral renewal.[13] This constellation of themes and symbols constituted a "new mythology" of Rome.[14] As an example, Zanker directs readers to the panel that depicts a mother goddess holding a baby in each arm, a cow resting at her feet. On either side of the goddess recline divine personifications of the winds on land and sea—the former sits atop a swan, the latter a sea dragon—who gaze serenely and reverentially at the divine mother.[15] The object of their devotion—Italy, Tellus, or, according to Zanker, Pax Augustus—conducts a placid cosmos; earth and sea work in concord, creating a harmony of nature in which livestock thrive and the monsters of the deep are brought into submission.

A tranquil landscape, this panel of the Ara Pacis turns the mind away from the brutality and repression associated with certain aspects of life under the emperors and invites contemplation instead of the order and increase wrought by the coming of Rome. To many provincial writers in the eastern Mediterranean, the benefits of empire were very appealing. Plutarch praises Rome for quelling local unrest and skirmishes among the Greeks; and Aelius Aristides admires Rome for, among other things, constructing an impermeable border around its vast holdings, preserving it against encroaching barbarians: "But like the enclosure of a courtyard, cleansed of every disturbance, a circle encompasses your empire."[16]

But these positive statements from writers who belonged to the subjugated Greek East must be balanced by less enthusiastic assessments from the same region.[17] Specific worldviews came to the aid of elite Greeks in particular, as they struggled to negotiate their position in relation to Rome. Brent Shaw argues that the popularity of Stoicism under the

Roman Empire could be attributed in part to the way it satisfied the needs of aristocratic Greeks who no longer could depend on classical processes of self-definition:

> On the one hand, the Greeks had to abandon their parochial divisions of insider and outsider (e.g., the narrow definition of citizenship in the *polis* or, more important, the polarity of "civilized" men and "barbarians," especially as regarded the Romans). On the other hand, the Romans were to treat their imperial subjects humanely, within a rational structure of imperial ideology and administration where the subjects themselves had an important role to play.[18]

In the "divine economy" of Stoicism, identity was acquired in relation not to a local community, but to the cosmos.[19] At the same time, other Greeks were looking to the classical past in order to define the self, as the surviving examples of the Greek romance confirm. The contents of these novels will be discussed further in following chapters, but the conspicuous absence of Rome from their narrative settings must be mentioned here. It has been asserted that "most often . . . the past was resorted to as an alternative to rather than a reflection on the present" for audiences in the Greek East.[20] In other words, casting the stories back to a time before the rise of Rome was a strategy for avoiding the reality of the loss of autonomy under Roman ascendancy. As likely a reading, however, is that the Greek elites who composed and heard these romances used the past as a strategy for *contesting* the present: in these tales, "a world without Rome" came into focus, enabling Greek audiences to have "their social and ethical concerns . . . played out in a world entirely of their own."[21]

Further consideration of the Ara Pacis brings to light another motif in ancient writing and modern scholarship about the relationship between Rome and Greece: the rivalry that pitted the artistic and philosophical heritage of Greece against the unmatched political success of Rome.[22] Horace's famous line suggests that the "dominance" of Greek high culture resulted in Roman artistic productivity: "Greece, the captive, took her savage victor captive, and brought the arts into rustic Latium."[23] Indeed, Greek art forms provided Rome with some of the "raw materials" for constructing the facade of imperial benevolence. On the Ara Pacis, babies reach for the breasts of the doting goddess on the frieze, itself richly decorated with fruits and flowers in bloom against a lush and tidy background of vine clusters. The iconography seems to have been taken by the altar's Roman (or Italian) creators from Greek models. A series of Hellenistic reliefs discovered at Pergamum employ, in a far more baroque fashion, this vegetation motif, as do numerous bowls and mosaics located elsewhere in Asia Minor and Greece.[24]

For Zanker, the Roman adaptation of Greek style forms part of a message about a wholesale transformation, a renewal of "traditional" values that Dionysius of Halicarnassus in the preface to *De antiquis oratoribus* labels a "revolution" (μεταβολή) in what was (in his view) a rapidly degenerating society.[25] Augustan Rome returned the people to religion and morality, and prosperity followed: the Ara Pacis, which includes a scene of divine fecundity framed by an orderly version of the Hellenistic vines—a "Romanized" version—joins Roman sobriety and abundance.[26] A brave, new fashion, perhaps, but the Roman Empire was not to be a "brave new world." Rather, the style of Augustan Rome forged a complex alliance between aesthetics, politics, and morality that was cemented by a connection to "ancient" traditions and conservatism. The Ara Pacis survives today as a representative of the artistic vanguard in ancient Rome that favored a "good" Greece or "Attic Classicism," over the "bad" Greece or "Asian Hellenism," a stylistic opposition that reflected the political efforts of the "Apolline" Augustus to distance himself from the legacy of the "Dionysiac" Marc Antony. The emperor, according to Zanker, did not simply ride a wave of conservatism; he led the parade: "The new style of Augustan rule was beginning to prevail. The pyramid that was Roman society had a clear and undisputed pinnacle. The emperor and his family set the standard in every aspect of life, from moral values to hairstyles. And this was true not only for the upper classes, but for the whole of society."[27] In sum, argues Zanker, it was not propaganda but a spontaneous combination of style, politics, and morality that produced a seismic cultural shift under the Augustan principate.

It is difficult to accept that such aesthetic and political uniformity ever existed, much less to believe it of an era well before the advent of mass communications. But one need not endorse Zanker's conclusion to appreciate his thesis about the high visibility of Augustus as exemplar.[28] This is especially true in the realm of religion: the "pious princeps" was consistently depicted on coins at sacrifice or in prayer. Such imagery simultaneously reflected and fostered an already established sense of mission and identity, namely, that Romans were divinely ordained to rule the world. Tracing Roman success directly to Roman *pietas*, Cicero remarks that "Spaniards had the advantage over them in point of numbers, Gauls in physical strength, Carthaginians in sharpness, Greeks in culture, native Latins and Italians in shrewd common sense; yet Rome had conquered them all and acquired her vast empire because in piety, religion, and appreciation of the omnipotence of the gods, Rome was unparalleled."[29] As J. P. V. D. Balsdon notes, Romans were "the gods' own people," and who better than they to bring to the world a "Golden Age"?[30] In a famous "messianic" passage from the *Eclogues*, Vergil prophesies the imminent birth of a godlike child, whose birth will bring about a miraculous transformation in ecology.[31] The epic *Aeneid* expressly attributes the realization of this fertile *aurea saecula*, along with the establishment of a cosmic empire, to Octavian: "This, this is he, whom you so often hear promised to you, Augustus Caesar, son of a god, who shall again set up a Golden Age . . . and shall spread his empire (*imperium*) past Garamant and India, to a land that lies beyond the stars."[32]

Vergil's epic dreams of a utopia causally linked to indefinite expansion, a project inspired by the gods to secure well-being for the peoples of the inhabited world.[33] Yet, the advance of Rome east across the Mediterranean and north into Europe was not, as some have argued, "accidental imperialism" or "defensive." If anything, Roman expansion followed a "best defense is a good offense" policy, which, as P. A. Brunt shows, stemmed from a belief that "the conquest of the world would be of benefit to all its inhabitants, and confer immortal fame on the conqueror."[34] For the pious Roman, the earth was his to rule, and there was none more religious than Augustus. He appears on the south frieze of the Ara Pacis in a priestly procession and records his sacerdotal activities in the *Res Gestae*: "I was *pontifex maximus, augur*, belonged to the colleges of the XV *viri sacris faciundis* and the VII *viri epulonum*, was an Arval Brother, *sodalis Titius*, and *fetialis*."[35] These religious duties, listed with pride in the *Res Gestae*, a marble Augustus executes on his altar of peace before an enthralled Roman audience.[36]

As *princeps*, Augustus seems to have embraced the idea of leading by example. In the *Res Gestae*, the emperor notes, "and I myself set precedents in many things for posterity to imitate."[37] The theme of "emperor as exemplar" echoed throughout the reigns of his successors: the historian Velleius Paterculus writes to the emperor Tiberius, "for the best of emperors teaches his fellow citizens to do right by doing it, and though he is greatest among us in authority, he is still greater in the examples which he sets."[38] This comment points to the process by which identity emerged from a nexus of self and viewing in Roman culture. It was not only the glory of Roman rule or the promise of the *aurea saecula* on display in the public spaces of the Roman Empire; so too conduct was constantly under surveillance. A scratch on the head could be viewed, according to the interpretive principles of physiognomy, as a sign of debauchery.[39] One kept track of one's own appearance because it was assumed that others were watching. Like Augustus in Suetonius, the Octavian of Cassius Dio discovers (a century later) that he is an actor on stage. In the *Historia Romana*, the advisor Maecenas remarks to Augustus, "For you will live as it were in a theater in which the spectators are the whole world"; in light of this passage, Richard C. Beacham suggests that "the emperor himself was part of the show, both a provider and a participant in the spectacles that figured so prominently in the early principate."[40] This context simultaneously empowered and constrained the *princeps*, whose exercise of authority was expected to embody the conventional ideals of moderation and self-mastery.[41]

The further exploration of this web of viewing will carry us beyond this brief assessment of style and substance in the Ara Pacis. Before taking leave of the monument, however, one more image from the frieze can serve to map the power relations produced by the optical dynamics of Roman society. On the south face of the frieze, the emperor is drawn not only as a priest but also as a father, chiseled in stone alongside representations of the imperial family. Augustus served simultaneously as *paterfamilias*, "the head of the household," and—in a title issued to Augustus by the Roman populace—as *pater patriae*, "the father of the fatherland." Indeed, the Roman Empire itself came to be viewed as a macrocosmic Roman *domus* under the early Roman principate. The depiction of Pax Augusta discussed above suggests a similar scene: the babies who sit upon the lap of the Roman goddess represent not only fertility but also the subjects of a paternalistic empire.[42] Disseminated by image and text, this family paradigm positioned the subjects of Roman *imperium* as children, looking upward to the emperor's example: imperial virtues thus served as objects of emulation and even veneration.[43] But the theme of imperial paternity was not a "one-way" street, as the father metaphor makes apparent: at once the emperor is the viewed and the viewer. As the consummate "family man," the emperor attracts the adoring gaze of his childlike subjects; as the household disciplinarian, the emperor's watchful, parental eye follows the work and play of his offspring. Similarly, in the urban spaces of the Roman Empire, we witness a seamless sliding from viewer to viewed and back again.

O Caesar

The importance of the emperor in the Roman Empire is suggested by a funny moment in Apuleius's farce, *The Golden Ass*. Curiosity does not "kill the cat" in this story, but it does make an ass of the lead character, Lucius. Having spied on the lady-witch of the house — Pamphile — at work in her "laboratory" of sorcery, Lucius persuades his lover (Pamphile's servant) to steal a magical ointment designed, he believes, to turn the user into a bird. The servant gives Lucius the wrong ointment, however, and the ill-fated hero is promptly changed into a donkey. Shortly thereafter, while being forced to stumble, four-legged, through a busy village as a robber's beast of burden, the ass seeks aid by calling on the emperor: "As I made my way through knots of people I tried to call out Caesar's venerable name in my native Greek tongue. I repeatedly declaimed the 'O' eloquently and loudly enough, but nothing further; the rest of the appeal, the name of Caesar, I could not articulate."[44] From this fanciful moment emerges a reality of the Roman Empire, namely, "that the beneficent image of the Roman emperor was inextricably woven into the patterns of daily life in the cities of the Roman world."[45] Merely uttering the emperor's name, the *Golden Ass* indicates, afforded some protection from the vicissitudes of the cosmos.

This episode may also hint at another development during the period: the display of imperial statuary in the Roman provinces.[46] Lucius-turned-ass neglects to mention whether or not a sculpture of the emperor in the village square inspires his cry for help, but ancient readers probably assumed that the donkey grunted his plaintive "O" before such a statue.[47] Under the emperors, the imperial semblance was a site of refuge for desperate people (or donkeys) in desperate circumstances. The younger Pliny relates that a slave fled to a statue of Trajan in order to escape punishment.[48] Like pagan temples, imperial statues provided a safe haven for fugitives and also marked a space for the manumission of slaves.[49] The widespread association of asylum, freedom, and beneficence with the imperial visage, Mary T. Boatwright observes, was just one of many ways that the esteemed figure of the emperor and "not temples to Jupiter Optimus Maximus, amphitheaters, the use of Latin, or even the diffusion of Roman citizenship" served as a principal catalyst for the crystallization of Roman identity in the ancient Mediterranean world.[50]

In Roman Asia Minor, provincials most often encountered representations of the emperor in the sanctuaries of the imperial cult.[51] The public veneration of the emperor and members of the imperial family struck a chord with the people of first-century Asia Minor: by the mid-first century C.E. at least eighty cities in Asia Minor possessed priesthoods of "emperors past and present," the Sebastoi.[52] Temples, statues, and reliefs devoted to the worship of Roman emperors (and select relatives) played a vital role in civic life. Such cultic buildings and images conveyed "above all, the charisma of the central power . . . diffused, transformed, and incorporated into the Greek world."[53] And the emphasis on "transformed" and "incorporated" is crucial here: Rome did not force emperor worship on its provinces, nor did the provinces simply adopt Roman religious practices.[54] Unlike earlier scholarship, which often took for granted that the imperial cult, among the educated classes at least, was transparent propaganda and essentially meaningless, recent studies suggest that the emperor worship was part of a more complex cultural interaction between the Roman seat of power and provincial elites.[55] Seneca's satire, *Apocolocyntosis*, which ridicules the divine aspirations of Claudius, and the dying remark attributed by Suetonius to Vespasian, "Oh my, I think I'm becoming a god!," have been cited as proof that the imperial cult was considered "a huge joke."[56] Yet even if the idea of emperor worship seemed laughable in Rome, the provincial cult mattered a great deal to those living in Roman Asia Minor.

The provincial imperial cult offered an apparatus for maintaining and negotiating relationships with the distant principate. Civic efforts established emperor worship in Asia Minor, and the cult acted both as a symbol of Roman hegemony and as a figure in civic rivalries.[57] Emperor worship quickly gained a foothold in the urban spaces of Asia Minor after the establishment of the first cults to Julius Caesar, Augustus, and Roma in 29 B.C.E., and the ensuing temple structures greatly affected the visual landscape of the region's cities. As the cult spread to places such as Pergamum and Nicomedia, "monumental sanctuaries came to dominate the city centres."[58] The ubiquitous presence of imperial temples, however, did not stem from a systematic imperial program. Rather, imperial sanctuaries were founded in Asia Minor at the instigation of provincial cities, which sent delegations to Rome to compete for the honor.[59] Only fragmentary evidence of these shrines remain today in southwest Turkey, but Steven Friesen's analysis of the Sebasteion at Ephesus—a temple to the *gens Flavia*, including Titus and Domitian—indicates how imperial temples generally organized their imagery. In Ephesus, the worshiper would enter the structure and immediately confront two sets of statues: on one level rested a series of forty engaged deities from across the Mediterranean world and above these stood colossal statues of Titus, Vespasian, Domitian, and Domitia. Such an arrangement sent a clear, palpable message, according to Friesen: "the gods and goddesses of the people supported the emperors: and, conversely, the cult of the emperors united the cultic systems and the peoples of the empire."[60] The imperial cult brought together local and imperial symbolism to project a stable Roman order.

The imperial cult, part of the "faith of fifty million," played a significant role in locating provinces in an encompassing imperial framework.[61] The history of Asia Minor has suggested to some that emperor worship naturally appealed to this region because of a pre-existing ritualistic model: the ruler cults of Hellenistic kings.[62] But this evolutionary thesis has been modified. Even if it did not effect a radical innovation in religious practice, the imperial cult, according to Simon Price, forged a "new nexus of power" for the inhabitants of Asia Minor, placing worshipers in a two-tiered sacred relationship with local authorities and a distant emperor.[63] A first-century C.E. inscription from Asia Minor illustrates this "doubled" connection: here a certain Cleanax, during a stint as a local magistrate, offered sacrifices on behalf of Cyme's inhabitants "first of all to Caesar Augustus, his sons and to the remaining gods" (τοῖς λοίποισι θέοισι).[64] The magistrate accrued prestige in a typically public manner: his gift to the gods secured protection from the vicissitudes of the cosmos, that is, the *pax deorum*, before the eyes of a provincial audience, cementing the bond between a member of the local elite and the people he serves. At the same time, the imperial cult transformed the local economy of benefaction or "euergetism," in which the wealthy acquired glory by contributing to the collective good, into a translocal euergetism.[65] In this new system of exchange, Caesar Augustus received honor for protecting the subjects of the Roman Empire.

Sacrifice to the emperor suggests more than mere "civic" recognition.[66] The Asia Minor celebrants performed cult, Friesen has argued, because the emperor acted like one of the gods in relation to them. Aelieus Aristides implies just such an arrangement in his encomium to Rome and praise of Antoninus Pius: "And it seems that the gods, watching from above, in their benevolence join with you in making your empire successful and that they confirm your possession of it."[67] The imperial cult depicted a Roman ruler imbued with sacred authority; but it also provided a place for populations in Asia Minor to view this ruling figure and to enter into a relationship with him. The provincial Sebasteion, then, was a site of religious suasion at which worshipers could approach the imperial will in the same way they confronted the divine will at temples of Zeus or Artemis.

The 1979 discovery of an imperial cult complex at Aphrodisias has further provided scholars with rich evidence of the visual imagery encountered by imperial cult participants.[68] Constructed between the reigns of Tiberius and Nero, the temple's dedicatory inscription to Aphrodite, the divine emperors, and the Demos illustrates the integration of local authority with the distant rule of Rome. Throughout the complex are physical representations of myths, such as Ajax and Cassandra; and in the upper story of the south portico stand reliefs of Julio-Claudian emperors: some next to deities, Augustus with Nike, for example, others caught in the act of conquest, such as Claudius vanquishing the personified Britannia.[69] Here we focus on just one aspect of the temple's sculptured remains: the series of reliefs in the north portico dedicated to the display of "barbarian" peoples conquered by Augustus. Less than ten of the images survive, but inscriptions on the remaining twenty to twenty-five bases convey much about what the ancient viewer saw in this part of the Sebasteion. On these pedestals stood personifications of foreign nations along the borders of the Roman Empire ranging from places east, such as Egypt and Judaea, to peoples west, such as the Trumpilini and the Piroustae. While all of these peoples and places were prominent enough to be mentioned by the geographer Strabo, there is little doubt, as R. R. R. Smith observes, that "Aphrodisians had probably never heard of *ethne* like the Piroustae or Trumpilini."[70] The meanings generated by this elaborate display, then, must have been related to its overall visual effect rather than to the significance of each individual relief.

Artistic representation of geographical and political entities was a commonplace in the Hellenistic world, but the use of such representations in victory art, "art showing conquest and war," was, according to Smith, a Roman development.[71] In the case of the Aphrodisiac Sebasteion, the temple complex appears to appropriate a Roman model exemplified by the display of fourteen *nationes* in Pompey's theater and by the *Porticus ad Nationes* constructed by Augustus, which put on display images of "all the peoples" (*simulacra omnium gentium*).[72] In Aphrodisias, the "ecumenical" range of subjects would have overwhelmed the viewer. As Smith observes: "It seems clear that the selection of *outlandish* peoples was meant to stand as a visual account of the extent of the Augustan empire, and by the sheer numbers and impressive unfamiliarity of the names, to suggest that it is coterminous with the ends of the earth."[73] Like the *Res Gestae*'s list of peoples among whom Augustus exercised diplomacy and force to bring into the Roman world, the *simulacra* used the boundaries of civilization to impress upon its audience, subjects of the Roman Empire, a sense of themselves.[74] That many of these peoples would have been unknown to an audience in Asia Minor returns us to the question of identity: the imperial shrine produces knowledge of the unknown for the audience, trading on the compelling strangeness of "outlandish" peoples.

In the Sebasteion at Aphrodisias, the process of self-definition worked visually: identity was forged in the presence of images of the imperial family and of the iconography of the *ethne*. Both sets of reliefs represented a distant other: the first, Rome, was to be esteemed, while the next, the barbarian, once dangerous but now impotent, remained on the fringes of the Roman world. Here the imperial cult shows peripheral provincials constructing a visible language of power with the aid of a triumphal model developed by the center, Rome. Following a concept suggested by Mary Louise Pratt, we might helpfully view the complex in Aphrodisias and temples of the Asia Minor imperial cult generally as "autoethnographic" productions: "instances in which colonized subjects undertake to represent themselves in ways that *engage with* the colonizer's own terms."[75] The cosmic proportions and divine approval of Roman rule may have been most apparent in Vergil's poetry and the Ara Pacis in Rome, but populations in places such as Ephesus, Pergamum, and Aphrodisias also saw this theme expressed in the inscriptions and in the images stored in their imperial cult temples. So while the Roman principate doubtless benefited from the symbolic unity and sacred authority implied by the cult, the festivals and buildings of emperor worship were also, as Keith Hopkins notes, "symbolic forms by which the local elite and local populace of free men and slaves, townsmen and peasants, reaffirmed their relative positions . . . to their distant emperor."[76] The imperial cult temple, in short, was a civic space for individual worshipers and entire communities simultaneously to construct and to place themselves within a network of authority.

With this observation, we return to the figure of the emperor to which Lucius-turned-ass turned in his time of need, not only a figure in relation to whom subjects of the Roman Empire defined themselves but also a figure they defined to an appreciable degree. The ass's failed invocation of the emperor's name is not so much a plea for sanctuary as an effort to make known his true identity: by connecting himself audibly to the emperor he hopes to prove himself a full participant in Roman society. Similarly, by gazing on the diverse, physical symbols of Roman victory of the kind found in the Sebasteion at Aphrodisias, the inhabitants of Asia Minor regularly used their eyes to ground themselves in the Roman world. There is no doubt that the depiction of Claudius as conqueror had the effect of reminding populations in Asia Minor of their status as actors under the vigilant, commanding gaze of Rome. At the same time, the viewing that took place in shrines like the Sebasteion at Aphrodisias established *relations* of power, placing constraints on the behavior of the Roman emperor towards his provincial subjects. This is not meant to suggest that imperial shrines erased the asymmetry of the power relations at work. Rather, I contend, images of ruthless victory over uncivilized "barbarians" threw into high relief the very different relationship that Rome was supposed to cultivate with the civilized subjects who lived in Aphrodisias. Both spectator and spectacle in the statues and shrines of Asia Minor, the emperor had to play his part "creditably."

Making Light of Death

From the Decian persecution of Christians in the third century C.E. comes an account, the *Martyrdom of Pionius*, which conveys a government official's sense of ennui about "mortal entertainments" in the Roman province of Asia Minor. In this tale of torture and death in Smyrna, the bishop Pionius refuses to sacrifice to the gods and for this is led into the amphitheater to be burned alive. Quintillian the proconsul urges Pionius to reconsider, pointing out that many of Pionius's companions have changed their minds, sacrificed, and "they are now alive and of sound mind."[77] The soon-to-be martyr replies that death will bring him life, inspiring this exasperated response from the proconsul: "You accomplish very little hastening towards your death. For those who enlist to fight the beasts for a trifling bit of money despise death. You are merely one of those." Quintillian's remark suggests how some pagans viewed such Christian martyrs, a sentiment similar to the well-known disapproval of Christian disobedience and stubbornness recorded by Marcus Aurelius.[78] On this episode Peter Brown observes, "as the notables of Smyrna told a later bishop: they were too used to professional stars of violence—to gladiators and beast hunters—to be impressed by those who made a performance of making light of death."[79] But Quintillian's response must be the exception that proves the rule; for even in Augustine's day, spectacles possessed great appeal, attracting even those who felt superior to the "masses" that clamored for this base entertainment. The notable's insouciance, one suspects, is feigned, evidence less of the waning appeal of spectacles in the third century than of Quintillian's efforts to present himself as a self-mastered man, superior to Pionius.[80]

This section will examine the attitudes and meanings associated with the violent spectacles of ancient Rome, which were a featured component of civic ceremonies (*ludi*) under the emperors. According to Erik Gunderson, "every major theme of the Roman power structure was deployed in spectacles: social stratification; political theater; crime and punishment; representations of civilization and the empire; repression of women and exaltation of bellicose masculinity."[81] While many of these themes will emerge in this brief survey of gladiatorial contests (*munera*), animal hunts (*venationes*), and executions, I shall also describe the destabilizing effects that the spectacles had on the "Roman power structure." While other institutions of leisure, such as the theater and the circus, have relevance for the analysis of viewing in the Roman Empire, the spectacle of mortal danger brings us closest, we shall see, to the book of Revelation's own narrative shows.

We begin, nevertheless, with a famous reference to the Roman circus. Juvenal's mockery of the people's myopic desire for "bread and circuses," if we take "circus" here to stand for all spectacles, sheds light on the significance of the shows in the Roman world.[82] Under the principate, spectators flocked to the Roman arena, and the violent spectacle became a regular element of imperial euergetism during this period. In the Roman Republic, gladiatorial duels were sponsored by aristocrats for funerals and the commemoration of the dead; from Augustus forward, shows in Rome were a regulated benefaction of the emperor. Fronto sees the growing number of arenas in his day as part of an autocratic design: "Control is secured as much by amusements as by serious things."[83] But scholars have not allowed Fronto's cynicism to serve as the final word on the subject. Katherine Welch, for example, associates the increase in the construction of amphitheaters with rising prestige: Martial's *Spectacula* "elevates the Roman games to the status of high culture; the emperor's games are now a suitable subject for high literature (poetry)."[84]

High culture or no, there is little doubt that the amphitheater became, under the emperors, one of the premier sites for watching others and for putting oneself on display. The shows, as Apuleius confirms, were a reflection of the *editor*: the aristocrat Demochares, "fabulously wealthy and outstandingly generous," provides for entertainment "matching the splendour of his fortune."[85] Spectacles were evidence of the sponsor's character. In our period a trend toward segregating seating in public shows is an extension, it would seem, of the Roman Empire's status-conscious ethos. Enforcing a tradition that reached back to 194 B.C.E., Augustus, through a decree of the senate, made special seating mandatory for senators at all spectacles in Rome; and *equites*, according to Cassius Dio had fourteen rows reserved for them at the theater.[86] The entrances for such privileged seating were richly decorated, and the podium inside the arena, where the most honored seats were located, was similarly ornate.[87] Such visualized stratification suggests an analogy with Sabine MacCormack's description of the highly ritualized imperial *adventus*, in which crowds of Roman subjects beheld not only the glory of Rome in its distinguished representative, but also their place in the social system as they lined up to view the procession according to a hierarchy of age and status.[88]

In the provinces, local elites, not the Roman emperor, sponsored the spectacles, fulfilling thus part of the euergetic obligations that rich and powerful individuals possessed. In Asia Minor, Roman-style entertainment arrived in the province as an extension of the imperial cult.[89] It is no longer possible to imagine a pristine Greek East, free of violent entertainment, thanks to the pioneering work of Louis Robert, whose studies have demonstrated the widespread presence of gladiator contests and animal hunts throughout the region. For Robert, this evidence indicates that populations in the Greek East embraced the Roman shows; they were not simply about making Roman colonists living abroad feel at home.[90]

It is important to note, however, that scholars no longer view such evidence as resulting from a systematic "Romanization" of the region. The gladiatorial duels, like the shrines of the imperial cult with which they were often associated, were sponsored by local, Greek elites who delivered these performances against the background of an entrenched Hellenistic aesthetic. The physical settings that housed Roman spectacles in this region, for example, betray little Roman or Italian architectural influence; and the Roman amphitheater, while represented occasionally, did not replace the Greek theater in Asia Minor; rather, existing Greek-style theaters were modified to hold the spectacles: a high wall around the orchestra pit, for example, was built in Ephesus to protect spectators from the wild beasts on display.[91]

That Greeks welcomed this Roman form of entertainment but not, by and large, the architecture of the amphitheater itself points yet again to the complexity of cultural appropriation and identity at play between the audiences of Asia Minor and representations of Rome. Citing the lack of amphitheaters as evidence, Greg Woolf has argued that "material culture" occupied a far more important place in the operations of Roman identity when compared to Greek self-formation. "Greeks spoke Greek," Woolf notes, "worshipped the same gods, had certain customs and had a common descent that could be traced back to mythical times"; Romans, on the other hand, and those western peoples that had been absorbed by empire, valued none of these things so highly as "togas, *fora* and amphitheatres [all] loaded with moral significance."[92] Because the games of the amphitheater held no potential for dislodging those elements that mattered most to audiences in Asia Minor, spectators there "could discover the pleasure of . . . *spectacula* without feeling any the less Greek." No less Greek, perhaps, for having had a close encounter with gladiators; then again, they were not much different, I would maintain, in an important way from their counterparts in Rome who did the same. Both sets of spectators participated in the production of knowledge through spectacle: knowledge of empire and knowledge of themselves as subjects of empire. To explore further the meanings generated by the shows, we turn now to a brief discussion of the kinds of spectacles audiences in Rome *and* Aphrodisias would have witnessed.

Animal Hunts

The staged hunts of wild beasts (*venationes*), which often included exotic creatures brought to Rome from lands near the border of the empire, symbolized Roman domination of the natural world. The poet Martial associated the submission of powerful animals with imperial power: "Devoted and suppliant the elephant adores you, Caesar, he who but lately was so formidable to the bull."[93] Here wild animals were set loose on each other; in other cases, wild animals performed with trainers and against fighters (*bestiarii*) or hunters (*venatores*). The earliest examples of these hunts appear in the first Carthaginian War, in which captured African animals were killed in a symbolic gesture of triumph.[94] In the early principate, the *venationes* were a common feature of the arena: massive numbers of animals were killed. According to Cassius Dio, the dedication of the

Colosseum under Titus included the destruction of over five thousand animals in a single day; in the *Res Gestae*, Augustus records that over three thousand animals had been killed in the twenty-six *venationes* he had sponsored.[95]

Conspicuous consumption was also expressed in the acquisition and destruction of exotic and unusual animals. Indeed, the elder Pliny's classification of animal species often refers to elaborate shows, such as that of M. Aemilius Scaurus, who put on display Rome's first hippopotamus in 58 B.C.E., and that of Pompey in 55 B.C.E., which included a lynx and a rhinoceros.[96] These animals at first were simply showcased; later, from the time of Augustus forward, many exotic creatures were simply destroyed, to the delight of audiences. This, according to Pliny, is what occurred when an *orca* wandered into the harbor at Ostia: Claudius commanded nets to be placed across the mouth of the harbor so that the beast would be unable to escape; then he ordered a hunt from ships. For Kathleen Coleman, this anecdote demonstrates "that aspect of imperialism and autocracy that drives the emperor to take under his control whatever is out of the ordinary."[97] In the next chapter, we will encounter a narrative example of this imperialist impulse in Phlegon's *Book of Marvels*. First we look at another arena display that has often been construed as a technique of social control: the public execution of criminals.

PUBLIC EXECUTIONS

Aside from gladiators, *venatores*, and *bestiarii*, a different category of "performer" often supplied entertainment for the masses: criminals and prisoners of war. Such *noxii*, not gladiators, comprised the majority of dead victims in the Roman spectacles.[98] These unfortunates had no hope of survival, not even the chance to be admitted into gladiator training. The execution of *noxii* demonstrated the power of the state; the punishments were intended to humiliate — the evangelists' accounts of the passion of Jesus are of course famous descriptions of systematic degradation — to deter, but, most importantly, to reassert the Roman social order over the dead bodies of those who, inside the Roman Empire or outside of it, had seemingly attempted to undermine it. Christian *noxii*, martyrs such as Polycarp in Smyrna, also participated in this civics lesson.

Yet, there were dimensions of public execution that could lead to quite different conclusions. An intriguing aspect of these public punishments was their elaborate staging. Kathleen Coleman's essay on the "fatal charades" of Roman capital punishment suggests that Roman executions were often dressed in mythological garb.[99] While there existed a variety of ways for convicts to die, by the sword (*damnatio ad gladium*), for example, or being tossed to the beasts (*damnatio ad bestias*), the most striking accounts drew on Greek or Roman myths. To cite one example: following Tertullian's observation that pagans provided "plots and themes" for their capital punishments, Coleman sought out the reality behind Martial's line, "When you are being torn apart like this, Daedalus, by a Lucanian bear, how would you wish you had your wings now!" Coleman argues that Martial and his fellow spectators observed an actual execution in which a criminal, "Daedalus," was hung in the arena by a crane and then released, only to be mauled by a bear.[100]

On one hand, the Coleman's catalogue of examples seems to be evidence of the absolute power of the state under the emperors. On the other, the elaborate staging of these executions blurred the line between theater and reality, just as Nero's theatrical escapades did in a different context, and made the person responsible for the charade—typically the emperor, in the sources that Coleman investigates—part of the spectacle. These elements suggest a relational, not absolute, model of power. Bartsch, following Coleman's lead, observed that it was the presentation of death in mythological terms that made such executions palatable to the assembled spectators: the "audience in the second half of the first century found the idea of theater and death could merge in the amphitheater a singularly congenial topic and chose to conceive of what took place on these occasions in those terms."[101] Furthermore, in Rome, at least, this merging of representation and reality forced the emperor himself into the spectacle: as *editor*, the emperor was the dramatist behind the charade, and he was expected to compose the successful transformation of the body of the condemned into the reenactment of a communal myth.

GLADIATORS

The figure of the gladiator is connected inextricably to the Roman world. As David Potter and David Mattingly have observed: "Few images are as evocative of Roman culture as those of the gladiator standing amid a pile of bodies, waiting for a crowd to pass a death sentence on his defeated foe."[102] The production and execution of such a show was a complex affair: duels were widely advertised, and the combatants themselves usually had to be procured through "middle-men." Gladiators, some members of a troop owned by the sponsor of a show, but most arranged by contractors who managed troops for these sponsors, were recruited from across the empire.[103] The night before they fought, gladiators dined at a lavish banquet (*cena libera*), to which the public, too, was sometimes invited.[104] After lunch, the morning being reserved for animal hunts and executions, the gladiators would "take the stage," according to whatever style of fighting had been determined. The *retiarius*, for example, used a trident and a net; some duels took place on foot, other gladiators squared off on horseback or driving chariots.[105] Not all duels were to the death, nor, in those that were, was it the case that the crowd alone determined the fate of the loser with the *pollice verso*. Rather, the sponsor of the show decided whether or not to destroy this commodity, weighing this consideration against the advice of the clamoring crowds. The victor received rewards ranging from the crown to palms, or, far more valuable, the *rudis*, a staff of wood that indicated the gladiator's performance had earned him manumission.[106]

Such was the course of a gladiatorial duel. And while moderns tend to describe the contests and their participants in negative terms, ancient views on gladiators reveal a complex assessment.[107] For a few, the valor and skill of the gladiator made him an exemplar of "manliness" (*virtus*), a key Roman virtue. Martial writes of a well-matched contest that resulted in a draw: "to both men Caesar sent palms; thus *virtus* and skill had their reward."[108] A number of Roman writers, however, regard gladiators — often slaves or criminals — with disdain or, at best, with ambivalence; for them, like the proconsul Quintillian who derides Pionius, status seems to have precluded the possibility of favorable remarks from their mouths and pens.[109] The historian Tacitus offers perhaps the harshest status-driven condemnation of gladiators, labeling them "worthless blood" whose shame was passed down to their children.[110]

Still there were some, like Martial, who found an educational value in gladiator contests. The valiant gladiator could serve as a model of Roman manliness, and putting such a figure on display was one of the ways that the spectacles could inculcate this in the audience. The younger Pliny, in a panegyric to Trajan, observes that exhibits of death in the arena inspire "neither weakness nor softness but a manly spirit" (*animos virorum*) in the crowd.[111] Similarly Cicero urged his audience to watch closely the struggle of gladiators, who suffer blows in order to satisfy *editor* and people: such uncompromising devotion, J. P. Toner observes, transformed "the most desperate criminal into a model of Romanness."[112] The battle on the arena floor, if discharged properly, could simultaneously instruct and entertain spectators. Gladiatorial contests seem to have carried implicit meanings about Roman valor, even if most elites found the participants beneath contempt.

The recurring theme of the relationship between manliness and the gladiator in the ancient sources has been a central subject of Carlin Barton's work. For Barton, the rise to prominence of the gladiator in the early empire signals a tectonic shift in Roman culture; with the arrival of autocracy in the form of the principate, traditional, agonistic interactions had been disrupted: "The Roman aristocrat had been able to compete for honor, glory, and *dignitas* while there had existed the possibility of a relative equality of means and power between himself and the other members of his class."[113] The constituent elements of Roman *virtus*, in other words, used to be acquired in a contest between equals. But under the crushing weight of Augustus's achievement, Barton observes, "one was compelled to elevate oneself by prostration, by kissing feet and other extremeties." If securing manliness, honor, and glory had once been a matter of open battle, now, under the principate, it was reduced to strategic acts of dissimulation and sycophancy.

How did the gladiator respond to the exigencies of this new world? In a plethora of ways, Barton suggests; here I will stress one in particular. Calling special attention to the frequency with which privileged Romans not only attended the games but actually served as fighters, Barton highlights "voluntarism."[114] But where Barton casts the gladiatorial duel as a reenactment of "a lost set of sorely lamented values" that enveloped aristocratic gladiators and audience alike in a nostalgia for the ancient republic, I wish to focus on a different framework of volition, which in turn throws into relief a one-on-one struggle. Whatever the status of the gladiator in view, and regardless of whether the combatant had entered the arena voluntarily or under compulsion, the contest always introduced a kind of freedom: either a willingness to die or the desperation of the alternative would be expressed in the faces and gestures of the gladiators. A battle for self-control, for one's very self, this was a contest between equals, the positive result of which would be self-vindication and the acquisition of *virtus* the "old-fashioned" way.[115]

But, when death drew near, so too did danger, especially that the gladiator would succumb finally to fear and weakness. In a famous passage

Seneca described what seems to modern eyes a perverse thirst for blood that the scene of the unwilling gladiator aroused in the audience: "Kill him! Lash him! Burn him! Why does he meet the sword in so cowardly a way?"[116] The gladiator in view here was a condemned criminal; yet even he had an opportunity to "redeem" himself. Risk was part of the structure of the combat: the possibility of achieving manhood was counterbalanced by the possibility of failure. It was risk that authenticated the action of the arena, lending to this space, so carefully scripted in other ways, "the excitement of an uncertain and dramatic outcome."[117] This is why the Roman arena held so much authority as a site of the real, an institution that produced knowledge for all of its participants. Animal hunts, public executions, gladiatorial contests: each in its own way contributed to the definition of boundaries — between familiar and strange, civilized and barbarian, self and other. At the same time, these shows also engaged viewers in the transgression of boundaries, none more significant than the line, repeatedly erased in the spectacles, between viewer and viewed.

Seeing and Being Seen

In the first book of his poetic guide to seduction and lovemaking, the *Arts of Love*, Ovid describes the value of public sites of entertainment for erotic adventure. The crowded benches at the Circus, for example, make a plausible excuse for the lover who wished to sit close to the object of his affection. At the same time, the contest itself provides plenty of items for "wooing" conversation: " 'Whose team is that?' enquire with earnest air, and back her fancy, be it whatsoe'er."[118] And, as Ovid indicates elsewhere in a different love poem, there is also a show in the stands: "You watch the course, and I watch you; together let's both watch what we want and feast our eyes."[119] In the *Arts of Love* the poet observes that a fan, innocently buying a program one moment, could be suddenly struck by love's dart the next, so that he "himself becomes an item in the show."[120] Moreover, at shows of all kinds both the erotic "hunter" and the "prey" arrive ready for action:

> So to the play the well-dressed bevies throng
> Such wealth of choice as keeps one doubting long
> They come to look and to be looked at too.
> Ah! Virtue, it's a fatal spot for you.[121]

Ovid's verse supports Jaś Elsner's conclusion that the public rituals of the Roman Empire "were intensely visual: the audience or congregation went both to watch and to be seen."[122] The boundary between viewed and viewer was constantly crossed, turning the spectator into the spectacle in a fluid movement that characterized especially the activities of the emperor, the most visible personage in the Roman Empire. Depictions of the *princeps* and his relatives were found in all corners of his realm: reliefs in temples devoted to the Sebastoi made the imperial family present for provincials who might never travel to Rome to see the emperor at the games. His statue was associated with benevolence, and his name synonymous with Roman civilization. Even the gods, looking down, could not help but be impressed with the emperor: "He [Mars] gazes upon the temple [of Mars Ultor] and reads the name Augustus. Then the monument seems to him even greater."[123] In the theater and at the games, rulers continued to be objects of attention, as Bartsch's treatment of Nero and Suetonius's depiction of the "brain-sick" Gaius, who played at gladiator in the amphitheater, indicate.[124]

More conventional forms of interaction between emperor and his subjects pressed both parties into a performance of imperial administration, visible to all: Titus promised to grant any petition made to him at the circus, and Tiberius eventually quit attending the shows because he had been deluged there with requests.[125] Based on such evidence, Alan Cameron has observed that "it was at the circus and theatre above all that the Roman emperor was answerable to the voice of the people": "answerable" not only to their voice, but to their eyes as well.[126] This sentiment was captured well by the younger Pliny, who praised Trajan for abandoning the couch reserved for emperors at the games and joining the crowd: "Caesar as spectator shares the public seats as he does the spectacle. Thus your subjects will be able to look on you in their turn; they will be permitted to see not just the emperor's box, but their emperor himself, seated among his people."[127] Pliny's remark parallels the image of the paternalistic emperor, both empowered and constrained by the expectant faces of his children. But the emperor was also bearer of the disciplinary gaze, and the arena was the context for frightening episodes in which spectators at the *ludi* were compelled to entertain the assembled crowd. During a gladiatorial duel sponsored by Domitian, Suetonius records that a fan was tossed from the stands to the dogs for an indecorous remark. Dio tells a similar story of Gaius, who responded to a paucity of criminals by ordering that spectators be given to the beasts.[128] Being a spectator could be a dangerous business.

Yet, it could not be avoided, as long as one joined in the public life of the Roman Empire. As Averil Cameron comments, "Roman imperial culture, especially in the cities of the Greek East, in the second century, a crucial time for the incipient Christian faith, had become in political terms a spectator culture. . . . Showing, performance, and affirmation became as important as argument."[129] And while the culture of elites provides the context for this observation, I suggest that it can be extended to describe the behavior of all members of the empire, whatever their background or pretensions, to the degree that they participated in regimes of public viewing. In a world of elaborate pageantry, the subject of Rome was, in Florence Dupont's words, *homo spectator*.[130]

A curious detail from Suetonius's biography of Domitian brings to the surface the volatile character of viewing relations, drawing together the themes of this chapter and providing a fitting transition to the next. Suetonius observed: "Throughout every gladiatorial show Domitian would chat, sometimes in very serious tones, with a little boy who had a grotesquely small head and always stood at his knee dressed in red."[131] The historical veracity of this story is not as important as its cultural meaning, which, at first glance, seems to reflect a set of normative values in the Roman Empire: the familiar and the strange, the strong and the weak, seated side by side in the same booth. As Suetonius's account unfolds, however, it becomes increasingly difficult to keep categories distinct. Domitian here is a lustful, gluttonous monster who nearly destroys Rome: the emperor himself interprets a recurring dream of a golden hump sprouting from his back to indicate that "the Empire would be far richer and happier when he had gone."[132] Rather than seeing Domitian and the dwarf as expressing "normal" and "abnormal" for Roman audiences, I wish to emphasize here the proximity of the nearby dwarf, an anticipation of the "grotesque" tendencies in Domitian that Suetonius will later expose: in the context of spectacle the difference between emperor and dwarf is not as great as it first appears. Watching the gladiators, absorbed in conversation with the "grotesque" boy, the emperor Domitian remains unaware that he has himself been transformed into a monstrous figure under the unflinching gaze of Suetonius.

The next two chapters of this book will continue to explore viewing and identity in Roman culture. As the imagery of the imperial cult and the contests of the arena led subjects of Rome to define themselves visually in relation to the other, so too the other described in the literature of the empire — including Revelation — enabled self-fashioning. Chapter 3 examines images associated with imperial viewing under the Roman Empire, which, like the reliefs of *ethne* and the hunts of wild animals in the arena, made the "outside" world, the world of the other, into an exhibition. Chapter 4 looks to moments of sexual viewing and gender construction in Revelation, focusing on the Lamb and the problem of masculinity. What reverberates throughout these chapters, and what will remain a central concern of the final chapter, is the theme of the spectator's vulnerability in a society "where vulnerability could be turned to an advantage."[133]

3

A Vast Spectacle

IN HIS SINGULAR BIOGRAPHY OF ABRAHAM THE "sage," the Jewish philosopher Philo embarks on a digression about the physical senses. Invoking a
traditional, Aristotelian hierarchy of the senses, he explains that "a special
precedence must be given to sight, for God has made it the queen
(βασιλίδα) of the other senses."[1] Not all members of the sensorium are
created equal. In support, Philo draws on the link between the eyes and
the soul. The eyes reflect the "phases" (τροπαῖς) of the ψυχή, so that
"when the soul feels grief, the eyes are full of anxiety and depression; but
when it feels joy, they smile and rejoice." The sense of hearing, more
"womanish" (θηλυτέρα) than sight and thus subordinate to it, nevertheless remains worthy of philosophical examination. But beneath contempt
are taste, smell, and touch, "the most animal and servile [senses] . . .
which cause particular excitation in the cattle and wild beasts most given
to gluttony and sexual passion." "An image of the soul," the faculty of
sight holds nothing in common with those senses that rouse base, "animal" instincts. Three centuries later, Augustine in his *Confessions* also assigns a chief importance to sight: "the eyes are paramount among the
senses in acquiring information."[2] But famously the church father remains
deeply suspicious of vision: sight ignites curiosity, "the concupiscence of
the eyes," leading the viewer into temptation.

Like Philo and Augustine, the book of Revelation privileges sight.[3]
To be sure, a blessing is pronounced upon "those hearing the words of
this prophecy" (Rev. 1:2), but the book associates its own composition
with the eyes. "Now write what you have seen" (εἶδες), commands "the
Son of Man" to the trembling John (Rev. 1:19). This foregrounding of vision and writing, Catherine Keller contends, represents a "qualitative
break from the rest of the Bible," in which the *hearing* of the *voice* of God
establishes the authority of the message and messenger.[4] John "sees voices"
(Rev. 1:12), Keller further argues, because Revelation, like other ancient

Jewish and Christian apocalypses, "straddles the distinction between scribe and prophet."

Thus sight surfaces in the genre as the "queen of the senses."[5] The great "bowl judgment" (Rev. 15–16), for example, which leaves no organ of the sensorium wanting for stimulation, demonstrates this point. The description evokes a wide range of sounds and smells, but the experience remains principally visual. Accompanied by harps, the faithful perform the "song of Moses and the Lamb" (Rev. 15:2–4), and the sun, touched by the contents of the fourth bowl, scorches the unfaithful with a fierce heat (Rev. 16:8–9). The smell of smoke rises out of the heavenly temple (Rev. 15:8), and the thirsty taste blood not water after the third angel pours his bowl into the rivers and springs (16:3). Still, it is to the seer's gaze that this episode first calls attention: "Then I saw another portent in heaven, great and amazing (μέγα καὶ θαυμαστόν): seven angels with seven plagues" (Rev. 15:1). Before he hears, feels, smells, or tastes the judgment of God, John sees it.

John is not alone while watching the end of the world. Indeed, the Apocalypse pays special attention to the eyes of its main characters: the Son of Man has eyes "like a flame of fire" (Rev. 1:14), and the "four living creatures" that surround the heavenly throne are "full of eyes in front and behind" (Rev. 4:6).[6] More significant for the present study are the countless spectators that take in the apocalyptic events. In the account of the "bowls of wrath," a righteous chorus, "those who had conquered the beast and its image and the number of its name," stands on one side of the glass sea, observing the unfolding drama (Rev. 15:2–4). Like the crowds of the arena, these spectators acclaim the "great and amazing" works and "just and true" ways of their ruler. Textual viewers appear throughout Revelation, watching and reacting to the apocalyptic "shows." When Rome, depicted as a beast and a prostitute, is finally destroyed (Rev. 17–18), narrative spectators gaze upon, and thereby participate in, the gruesome tableaux.

Harry O. Maier has called attention to the spectacle and "theatricality" of ancient Jewish and Christian apocalypses.[7] Like other commentators, he focuses on Revelation's "paraenetic" or exhortative function, but takes issue with the argument that the book is aimed primarily at encouraging a persecuted community. Revelation, in Maier's view, does not formulate a "theology of hope"; rather, it challenges the audience to give the performance of a lifetime. The audience is thrust into a textual theater, an apocalyptic spectacle: invited to identify with characters in the narrative, they become "actors" playing roles under the direction of a panoptic divinity. As actors, the members of the audience must choose between desirable and undesirable parts played by the book's heroes and John's sectarian opponents, such as Jezebel, whose sexual immorality is first exposed in Rev. 2:20–23 and later "writ large" in the prostitute Babylon. "Scripting" the audience, Maier insists, constitutes the fundamental rhetorical goal of the apocalyptic genre, which "seeks ideally to persuade audiences to sympathize with faithful characters and to condemn those who suffer judgment."[8] Further, Maier contends, the book's vituperative language and grotesque imagery chiefly reflect the anxieties of intra-Christian rivalry.[9] John folds his competition into the monsters that symbolize Rome, positioning both as cosmic enemies. In sum, the book's ever-watchful deity, who discloses the secrets of heaven to John, reveals the seer's Christian opponents to be wolves in sheep's clothing. These wolves will eventually meet their maker; until then, John invites his readers to anticipate their downfall.

Two aspects of Maier's treatment will continue to surface in the remainder of this book. First is his view that Revelation draws the audience into a world of sectarian rivalry.[10] Of particular relevance is Maier's suggestion that the depiction of Rome is coextensive with the portrayal of John's opponents, to which we return in Chapter 5. Second is the connection Maier makes between narrative spectacle and audience "self-fashioning": he contends that the book regulates its readers with the threatening presence of God's unblinking eye. This conclusion is based on the application of a spectacle (or theatrical) paradigm to the book: "Unmasking and remasking, positioning and displacing the hearers [i.e., the book's audience], all of these scenes reveal mimetically the audience to itself as playing out idealized, carnivalesque scenes during which the plot of tribulation and reward unfolds. Through them, John hopes to win allegiance to his own point of view and to persuade his audience of the danger in the views of his opponents."[11] Proceeding from Maier's insights, the present chapter will examine moments of narrative spectacle in the Apocalypse. Revelation tells a story not only about beasts but also about spectators—some righteous, some unrighteous—who witness the end of the world. The chapter will also reflect upon the dynamic that Maier explores between narrative characters and the ancient Christian audience of Revelation's "shows." As will become clear, the book's strange and vio-

lent images, like beast-hunts and public executions, would have appealed
to first-century readers. They were members of a society that appreciated
such displays.

Here, then, we continue the investigation of the "culture of viewing"
in the early Roman Empire, taking the grotesque visions of the Apocalypse as an expression of this culture.[12] As Chapter 2 explained, institutions such as the imperial cult and the amphitheater collaboratively
formed a viewing self in Roman culture. This same subjectivity—a model
for performing the self in the world—was also produced by the literature
of the period, including Revelation. Further, by representing Rome in
monstrous and foreign terms, I will argue, the Apocalypse engages the audience in *imperial* viewing: reversing the relation in the reliefs of the imperial cult, Revelation seeks to establish authority by putting Rome on
display as other. Revelation presents the Roman Empire as "a vast spectacle."[13]

At the same time, the unstable nature of viewing itself, so evident in
the public spectacles of the empire, is also apparent in Revelation, threatening to undermine the mastery of the viewing self. No less than in
Roman society generally, viewing poses a problem in Revelation. Where
Maier focuses on the constellation of immoral behaviors associated with
Revelation's villains, this chapter will describe specifically the viewing
habits of characters in the narrative and will examine the vulnerability that
inheres in being a spectator at the end of the world. The relationship between the characters in the text and the audience outside the text is established through viewing. Revelation, I will show, offers a "lesson" in
viewing practices, conveyed by a series of narrative spectators who gaze
upon the rise and fall of the Roman monster. Further, I will suggest that
this lesson was absorbed mimetically by Revelation's ancient audience,
who themselves "watch" as these textual viewers encounter the end of the
world. We will chart both the book's representations of the other and the
formation of a viewing self, the witness that gazes on these images, sometimes at great peril. Before pursuing this agenda, I establish a literary context for the analysis of imperial viewing in Revelation. In Roman Asia
Minor, as an ancient "book of marvels" indicates, unusual sights were certain to attract attention.

A Book of Marvels

The *Book of Marvels*, a record of thirty-five "wonders" by Phlegon of Tralles, gives scholars a glimpse of the popular imagination of Roman Asia Minor, the provenance of another "book of marvels," the book of Revelation. An example of the ancient paradoxography genre, Phlegon's second-century C.E. composition anticipates modern-day *Ripley's Believe It or Not* books and supermarket tabloids.[14] Under the rubric "Discoveries of Live Centaurs," for example, Phlegon explains that "a hippocentaur was found . . . [whose] face was fiercer than a human face, its arms and fingers were hairy and its ribs were connected with its front legs and its stomach."[15] Under "Monstrous Births," the author notes that "a child was brought to Nero that had four heads and a proportionate number of limbs."[16] As if these "amazing facts" were not sufficiently titillating, most of these prodigies surface in exotic settings, far away from Phlegon's Asia Minor. A woman gives birth to twenty children ("in the course of four deliveries") in Alexandria, while hippocentaurs roam the streets of Saune, a village in Arabia that shares its name with a deadly drug found in the region.[17] Like the *Wonders Beyond Thule* of Antonius Diogenes, Phlegon's paradoxography removes the audience from its everyday surroundings and transports it to a distant landscape filled with fabulous creatures. There, near the "edges of the earth," freakish figures thrive.[18]

A striking feature of Phlegon's account is the catalogue's matter-of-fact tone, even as it lists marvel after marvel, prodigy after prodigy. The city of Rome contributes to the "facticity" of the paradoxography, serving as an immovable point of reference and grounding the curiosities in time and space. Snake-children, for example, are born "when the consuls in Rome were Domitian Caesar for the ninth time and Petilius Rufus for the second time," and Roman officials show a four-headed child to Nero when "the consuls in Rome were Publius Petronius Turpilianus and Caesennius Paetus."[19] Furthermore, even though Rome is typically not home to these marvels—they are usually born elsewhere—in one revealing case, Phlegon's report cites the purported display of a marvel in the city to buttress the claim.[20] The unfortunate hippocentaur, stuffed and preserved in honey, eventually finds its way to Rome, where Pliny the Elder observed the creature.[21] "Anyone who is skeptical," writes Phlegon indignantly, "can examine it for himself, since as I said above it has been embalmed and is kept in the emperor's storehouse." Presumably, one could journey to Arabia to see a *live* hippocentaur, for "there were also said to have been other hippocentaurs in the city of Saune."[22] But such a trip is not countenanced: instead when Phlegon wishes to cloak the hippocentaur and Saune with the veneer of reality—to make this marvel and, by implication, its native setting a "fact"—he directs the audience to an exhibition of the beast in Rome.

The *Book of Marvels* is not especially novel in the depiction of Rome as a "consumer" of curiosities. The prodigy was a traditional feature of Roman religion.[23] Some, of course, found dubious the reports of prodigies and other monsters. The philosopher Lucretius writes, "However, it must not be thought that all members can be conjoined in all manners: for then you would commonly see monstrosities (*portenta*) come into being." Similarly, Vitrivius, an architect under Augustus, lashes out at artists who "prefer to paint monstrosities (*monstra*) on plaster rather than faithful copies of natural objects . . . Such a thing has never existed and never will."[24] But while the voices of a few skeptics have survived in the literature of the period, and while the official reporting of prodigies seems to have disappeared under the emperors, it seems that "belief in the significance of signs and portents was a permanent feature of Roman religion."[25] According to Livy, prodigies attend most significant moments in Roman history. Before a great loss to the Carthiginians at the battle of Traismene, for example, sweat was seen on the statue of Mars. Prodigies both signaled a disruption in the relationship between gods and humans and confirmed that the "gods were not only an audience of watchers, eternal, impassive, but moved now and then to care for a human's predicament."[26] To make the most of these periodic intrusions of the "invisible" into the visible world, specific Roman priests—the *haruspices* or the *quindecimviri*, who kept the books of Sybilline oracles—devoted themselves to the divination and expiation of portents. And since the *pax Romana* was coextensive with the *pax deorum*, the protocol for dealing with these disturbances in human-divine relations was closely followed.[27] Phlegon himself includes an example: when a two-headed baby is born in Rome, shortly thereafter it is thrown into the Tiber on the advice of priests.[28] Inside the city's sacred precincts, prodigies were met with the swift discipline of Roman authority.

Yet, in the *Book of Marvels*, this result is exceptional; Phlegon's account, like other stories about the unusual in the Roman Empire, places a greater emphasis on encountering marvels than on exterminating them. Suetonius remarks that "whenever a strange or remarkable animal was brought to the city, he [Augustus] used to exhibit it in some convenient place for days when no public shows were being given." According to Pausanias, statues from Greek sanctuaries were transferred to Rome under the emperors; and Josephus reports that sacred vessels from the plundered Jerusalem Temple were put on display in Vespasian's "Temple of Peace."[29] The "trophies" from the Judean conflict, like the Greek statues and the unusual animals displayed by Augustus, announced the continuing dominance of Rome in the Mediterranean world. A useful comparison may be drawn here with the link, examined by Timothy Mitchell, between "the construction of otherness" and "the manufacture of national identity and imperial purpose" in the nineteenth-century, European "world exhibition."[30] In other words, the knowledge of the world "out there" that visitors acquired was not disinterested but was driven both by an imperialist agenda and by the exigencies of European self-definition. Similarly, the display of marvels from exotic locales in Rome created an "interested" knowledge. When curiosities arrived in the Roman Empire, they were made into spectacles, and thus into "facts" about the world for a captivated public. This is imperial viewing: making the world, especially the world as "foreign and fantastic," into an exhibition.

By casting the encounter with marvels and prodigies as a production of knowledge, I do not mean to diminish the anxiety that such phenomena triggered in Romans. For them, the deliberate consideration of fascinating sights of any form could lead to disaster. To us it seems far safer to join the inquiring public in Rome and gaze there on the dead hippocentaur than to travel to an Arabian village crawling with the monsters. We shall see, however, that viewing marvels, dead or alive, posed a great threat to the self-possession of the ancient viewer.

And danger lurked everywhere for the spectators of the Roman world, because strange images were everywhere. Processing to the imperial altar in Aphrodisias, worshippers of Aphrodite at the Sebasteion passed by reliefs of foreign tribes conquered by Augustus. This merging of religious piety and the otherness of distant societies declared the divine ordination of Roman dominance over alien peoples. The same message about Roman supremacy emerged in certain amphitheater events. Unusual animals roamed the arena floor as part of the *venationes*, and their submission was taken as a sign of Rome's dominion over the natural world. By comparison, Phlegon's account, with its straightforward record of marvels, seems quite disinterested in broadcasting Roman superiority. Yet, it provides a revealing example of imperial viewing: the *Book of Marvels* equipped an audience in Asia Minor with "imperial eyes" with which to gaze upon monsters and distant lands. At the same time, audiences in Rome, peering at Saune's hippocentaur "in the flesh," joined the production of imperial knowledge.[31] The paradoxography also indicates that there was a market for marvels in Phlegon's corner of the Roman Empire, a corner occupied at about the same time by the writer of Revelation. So too there were other writers in Roman Asia Minor who employed spectacle in their work. The next section will prepare the way for an analysis of Revelation's marvels by investigating some examples of narrative viewing in the Greek romance.

Word Pictures

Phlegon's book was composed during the "Second Sophistic," a period that witnessed a dramatic rise in the importance of rhetoric and the teachers of rhetoric in Mediterranean society. The flow of this cultural current was carried throughout the eastern Roman Empire by both the magisterial performances of orators and the texts that focused on the tactics of persuasion—especially "word pictures"—that were part and parcel of these rhetorical shows. If the audience "saw" the object described by the narrative or rhetorician, then the author or orator could more effectively train, educate, or move the listener.[32] In the second-century C.E., this renewed interest in the skills of the sophist inspired serious reflection about the relationship between viewed and viewer, aesthetic object and audience.

Indeed, a highly technical approach to representation and explication is evident in the sophistic literature that survives. The third-century *Imagines* of Philostratus (Lemnius) the Elder—the son-in-law of the man who coined the phrase "Second Sophistic"—relates an encounter between artwork and critic. In this set of essays, the narrator describes and "interprets" (ἑρμηνεύειν) the mythic figures and events painted on panels set in the walls of his host's house. Here Philostratus engages in ecphrasis (ἔκφρασις)—the art of detailed description—as he analyzes subjects ranging from "the birth of Hermes" to "the burial of Abderus," one of the twelve labors of Hercules.[33] A technique used to support epideictic rhetoric, ecphrasis receives attention in the educational handbooks (*progymnasmata*) from the period. The *progymnasmata* outline precise methods for the ecphrasis of artwork, dreams, and spectacles; there is a repeated insistence on the power of narrative description over the visual imagination of the audience. "Ecphrasis undertakes to fashion spectators (θεατάς) out of auditors (ἀκούοντας)," concludes the third-century rhetorician Nicolaus; it also fashioned interpreters out of spectators.[34] While the *progymnasmata* and Philostratus's *Imagines* exemplify an education—a παιδεία—available only to a select few, these exercises linking visuality and meaning represented the tip of a cultural iceberg.[35] The public spaces of temples and arenas, designed and maintained by elites, reached a cross section of society in Roman Asia Minor, enabling all patrons of such venues to participate in the visual values of the period.

Visual training, then, was not the exclusive domain of art connoisseurs and rhetoricians such as Philostratus. Neither was ecphrasis: even though the term itself was not employed regularly until the Second Sophistic, the technique has its prototypical example in the famous description of the shield of Achilles in book 18 of the *Illiad*, and is employed by the dramatist Euripides.[36] Under the Roman Empire, ecphrasis was popularized by a different genre, the ancient Greek romance, whose tales of love and adventure commonly include lengthy, florid descriptions. Indeed, this collection of literature has often been denigrated for its "irrelevant," discursive passages, ranging from an account of peacock mating habits to the "festival of the Nile." Shadi Bartsch has suggested that this "purple prose"—the detailed description of persons, animals, events, and even dreams—is "bound to elicit the interpretive activity . . . of the audience at which it is directed" and is likely to provoke this audience to reflect on its capacity for reading and interpretation.[37]

This call for audience participation highlights the active character of spectatorship, something that ancient narrative spectacles shared with Roman institutions of public viewing. The second-century C.E. novel of Achilles Tatius, *Leukippe and Kleitophon*, furnishes a useful example. When Pantheia—the mother of the heroine Leukippe—dreams that her daughter is sliced open at the groin by a brigand's sword, the suspicious mother takes it to signal that her daughter has consummated an illicit relationship with the hero, Kleitophon. The reader, Bartsch observes, having been drawn into the narrative through the ecphrasis of Pantheia's dream, is expected to draw the same conclusion. Later, however, Leukippe—in a ruse to escape her kidnappers—appears to be cut open by a bandit. Hence the "enactment" of the dream later in the romance surprises the audience.[38] The "dual call to interpretation" to both a narrative character and the audience, Bartsch observes, creates a complex dynamic in which the audience observes closely not just the plot but the interpretive activity of the characters themselves.[39]

Two modes of ecphrasis in the romance that require further elaboration involve travel and narrative spectators.[40] Like Phlegon's paradoxography, extant novels invite the audience repeatedly to gaze on the fauna and flora of faraway places.[41] Adventure is central to the genre, and the hero and heroine typically find themselves in distant lands, harassed by strange people with strange customs, and desperate to find their way home to "civilized society" so that they might enjoy their love. Longus's *Daphnis and Chloe* remains the only exception: the setting throughout is the island of Lesbos. But even this novel, as Kate Cooper rightly observes, expresses "displacement" though its story about two adolescents who undertake a *quest*, beset by many obstacles, to acquire the knowledge and maturity that leads eventually to consummation. David Konstan has suggested that the genre's travel motif reflects the gradual absorption of the πόλις into the οἰκουμένη of the ancient Mediterranean world.[42] Whatever the impetus, these references to foreign places and things serve a function analogous to Phlegon's description of Saune and its hippocentaur. Greek romances, even though their stories are set in the distant past, provided "facts" about the world for the audiences of Roman Asia Minor.[43] Just as Phlegon's account prompted them to "view" the hippocentaur, so too the novel made members of the Asian city into spectators: they follow the trials of hero and heroine, learning, from this novelistic exhibition, about the strange world "out there."[44]

Does the Greek romance, then, provide further examples of imperial viewing? After all, strange beasts and strange places are a regular feature of most extant examples of the romance, as when Kleitophon relates an encounter with a "crocodile": "And I saw another creature of the Nile, a beast celebrated as being more ferocious than the river horse. Their name for it is a crocodile."[45] Like a *National Geographic* correspondent, Kleitophon brings the unfamiliar world "home" to the audience of *Leukippe and Kleitophon*. Nevertheless, this episode, and others like it in the Greek romance, represents a different mode of imperial viewing than Phlegon's description of the hippocentaur. Phlegon creates a sense of authenticity for his curiosities by placing them in relation to the Roman Empire: recall that the beast from Saune languishes in the "emperor's storehouse." In the romance, the transformation of the Nile's crocodile into fact depends entirely on the reports of the leading characters themselves, usually young, urban elites, who also serve as representatives of the classical Greek past. The Roman Empire is conspicuously absent from the Greek novels; not missing, however, is the production of knowledge through imperial viewing. In contrast to Phlegon's *Book of Marvels*, imperial viewing in the Greek romance circumvents the authority of Rome.

Because distant lands so frequently provide the setting for the action of the romance, spectacle in the romance is deeply intertwined with the travel motif. As Bartsh defines it, narrative spectacle in the Greek romance includes one or more narrative spectators, characters that are part of the overall description. When confronted by textual spectacle, Bartsch notes, "we actualize ourselves [i.e., the readers] as a second and extratextual audience."[46] The "extratextual" audience, in other words, looks over the shoulders of another interested party. To convey the emotion of the scene, ecphrasis often calls attention to a textual spectator's *actio*. This is a technical term that Bartsch borrows from classical rhetoric, denoting "a speaker's communication with his body, his hands, his expression, the tone of his voice."[47] At the beginning of *An Ethiopian Story*, for example, the heroine Charikleia communicates her wish to be taken captive with her beloved, not with words, but with gestures and tears. In *Leukippe and Kleitophon*, Pantheia expresses disgust with her daughter's apparent fornication by slapping Leukippe and pulling her hair.[48] Watching the bandit's attack on Leukippe in her dream, Pantheia is transformed into a spectator, and her emotional but misguided *actio* plays a role in the extratextual audience's interpretive response.

Achilles Tatius, Philostratus, Phlegon: not the authors a reader usually meets in treatments of Revelation. Still, I suggest that their compositions share with Revelation a sustained dynamic between extratextual audience, narrative spectator, and narrative spectacle. Cooper, making reference to the Greek romance, has described the "peculiar power of romance to create complicity" between the reader and the main characters; I point to narrative spectacle as a particularly effective technique for "creating complicity" in romance and Revelation.[49] Further, I suggest that unfamiliar places and things surface in similar ways in these texts. Should we put down this common set of concerns to παιδεία, to a shared cultural knowledge? Even were there to exist evidence of John's rhetorical training, focusing on the educational background of the author, in this case, risks missing the forest for the trees.[50]

Rather than emphasizing the formal παιδεία of Greek elites, this chapter continues to explore the remarkably pervasive use of spectacle, across diverse texts and institutions in the Roman Empire, as a technique for shaping identity. Subjects of the Roman Empire, no matter their socioeconomic background, were repeatedly engaged as spectators, and it is from this vantage point that they played a part in the ongoing creation of their world. Revelation is no less given over to spectacular moments than the Greek romance, and such moments, especially when they put on display the "foreign and fantastic," invite the audience to participate in the story. Now that we have encountered the work of spectacle in other texts from John's neighborhood, as it were, we return to Revelation to explore spectacle and self-fashioning there. In so doing, we will also return to the dangers of spectatorship, a problem recognized by Plutarch, Apuleius, Augustine, and, yes, by the seer of Patmos, too.

Amazement and Ambivalence

An exchange between John the seer and an angelic guide, or *angelus interpres*, and a distressing ecphrasis mark the beginning of the end of the world in the Apocalypse.[51] John's interpreter carries him into the wilderness to gaze upon the prostitute Babylon, a courtesan dressed in purple who rides a scarlet beast with seven heads and ten horns. This sight inspires powerful, even overwhelming, emotions in the narrator, who reports: "When I saw her, I was greatly amazed" (καὶ ἐθαύμασα ἰδὼν αὐτὴν θαῦμα μέγα; Rev. 17:6b). The angel immediately detects the seer's visceral response to the vision, as the question in verse 7 makes apparent: "Why are you so amazed?" inquires the angel. But before John can answer, the guide promptly launches into a lengthy explication of the scene (Rev. 17:8–18).[52] For the moment, we will not concern ourselves with the components of the angel's interpretation but will focus instead on the tension that surfaces here regarding the seer's "amazement." In view of the many strange visions John encounters, the reaction of θαῦμα seems unsurprising; indeed, of these visions, the figure of Babylon is particularly troubling: "And I saw that the woman was drunk with the blood of the saints and the blood of the witnesses to Jesus" (Rev. 17:6a). Amazement is to be expected: θαῦμα, as the title of Phlegon's περὶ θαυμασίων indicates, was, for ancient viewers, the standard by-product of seeing strange things.

Why, then, does the angel note John's wonder, his amazement? One interpretation finds that the angel's question implies censure: "The reaction is given an immediate negative response by the angel," avers Timothy Dwyer, a view confirmed by the angel's subsequent association of "amazement" with those "whose names have not been written in the book of life" (Rev. 17:8).[53] But Dwyer's conclusion that "amazement" is given a "negative cast" in Revelation disregards some important counter examples. The angel's interrogative is balanced by moments in which θαῦμα is a proper reaction to the book's visions: John reports that "the song of Moses and the song of the Lamb" intoned by the faithful in heaven includes the verse "Great and amazing (θαυμαστὰ) are your deeds, Lord God the Almighty!" (Rev. 15:3). Two verses before John himself describes the scene as "great and amazing (θαυμαστόν): seven angels with seven plagues, which are the last, for with them the wrath of God is ended" (Rev. 15:1).[54] Given these passages, which place θαῦμα in a positive context, is the angelic reproach of John a rejection of wonder *qua* wonder or is it, rather, an intervention? The angel's remark disrupts the moment, shifting the focus from John's reaction to the image of Babylon, which gives rise to the seer's response in the first place.

Revelation is not the only text from the Roman Empire to pose the viewing of strange sights as a problem. "Thaumastic" viewing in Revelation conforms to a broad pattern of thought about the effects of spectacle on spectators in the Roman world.[55] As we have already seen, Philo, following a long philosophical tradition, valorizes sight as the sense closest to the soul. For others, such as Quintilian and the authors of the *progymnasmata*, ecphrasis and "word pictures" buttress the orator's skills of persuasion.[56] The first-century C.E. dialogue *On the Sublime*, attributed to Longinus, estimates the capacity of these strategies for moving an audience: "Weight, grandeur, and urgency in writing are very largely produced, dear young friend, by the use of 'visualizations' (φαντασίαι) . . . In all such cases the stronger element seems naturally to catch our ears, so that our attention is drawn from the reasoning to the enthralling effect of the imagination, and the reality is concealed in a halo of brilliance."[57] Skillfully-drawn "fantasies," according to this advice, will usually distract readers from the dull facts. More than a rhetorical flourish, visualizations, according to Longinus, provoked a tremendous change in the audience, moving it from "reason" to "enthrallment."

But it is precisely the enthralling power of spectacle that other Greek and Roman writers distrust. In a society that featured shows, it should come as no surprise to find Greek and Roman writers commenting on the effects of viewing on viewers. Too much visual stimulation, as in the paradigmatic Narcissus myth, led to glazed eyes and a wasting away. As Car-

lin Barton shows, Greek and Roman writers maintained a traditional condemnation of curiosity, a vice connected to excessive viewing; for them,
the dynamic between object and viewer could produce a problematic
"transfixion."[58] This was especially true for those too easily drawn to unusual items. Plutarch, for example, laments the crowds "who take no account . . . of the beauty of the boys and women for sale, but they haunt
the monster-market (τὴν τῶν τεράτων ἀγορὰν), examining those who have
no calves, or are weasel-armed, or have three eyes, or ostrich-heads, and
searching to learn whether there has been born some commingled shape
and misinformed prodigy." "Curiosity" (ἡ πολυπραγμοσύνη), according
to Plutarch, is not a benign impulse, for it leads to a confusion of values;
it must therefore be kept in check: we must begin "early to train and teach
ourselves to acquire this self control" (τὴν ἐγκράτειαν).[59] This is a lesson,
of course, learned too late by Apuleius's Lucius, whose curiosity makes
him an ass.[60] Viewing makes the viewer vulnerable to passions better left
alone, as the famous story of Augustine's friend Alypius confirms. In this
chilling account, Alypius falls victim to a "fascination of bloodshed" in the
arena.[61] Before attending the shows, Alypius is disinterested in gore, but
during the show, the North African bishop notes, he mutates into "one of
the crowd which he had joined." Alypius exemplifies the point that Augustine makes later in the *Confessions*: of the sensory organs, the eyes are
the most dangerous, for through them passes the world, and with it,
temptation.

The cumulative effect of this testimony is to suggest a deep ambivalence about the viewing of strange sights under the Roman Empire. There
is no question that this form of spectatorship was widely practiced: from
the "monster-market" to the bloodshed of the arena, strange displays
were alluring to ancient viewers, and John's Revelation, like Phlegon's
περὶ θαυμασίων, exploits this attraction. At the same time, ambivalence is
also apparent in the viewing of strange sights in the Apocalypse, as John's
amazement at the sight of Babylon indicates: angelic sanction or no, the
seer is drawn to wonder at the grotesque figure.

Even when Revelation fails to invoke explicitly the term θαῦμα, the
book calls attention to the strong emotions its monsters provoke in textual spectators. To explore the convergence of amazement and ambivalence in Revelation, I focus on the narrative spectators, including John,
that inhabit three episodes: the death and resurrection of the two witnesses in Rev. 11:1–13, the rise of the beasts from sea and land in Rev.
13:1–18, and the scene of Babylon's demise in Rev. 17:1–18:24, parts of

which I have already briefly discussed. These episodes, I shall argue, build toward a dramatic performance of imperial viewing as the Roman Empire, figured as Babylon and the beast, is made into an exhibition. This will lead to a concluding consideration of the "multitude in heaven" that watches the apocalyptic unfolding of events (Rev. 19:1). From the vantage point of Revelation's righteous spectators—a perspective shared, bear in mind, by the *extratexual* audience of Revelation—the fall of Babylon is a "great and amazing" deed of God.[62] Others, however, will view the events differently: watching Babylon burn, the kings, merchants, and shipmasters of the earth discover that being a spectator is dangerous.

THE TWO WITNESSES

The death and resurrection of the two witnesses (Rev. 11:1–13) begins with the promise of destruction and ends with a natural catastrophe.[63] Following a measurement of the "temple of God" and a prediction about a Gentile conquest of Jerusalem (Rev. 11:1–2), a voice relates to John that "two witnesses" (τοῖς δυσὶν μάρτυσιν) with divine authority will prophesy for three and a half years (Rev. 11:3). A strange scene ensues. The main characters, evidently the olive branches and the lampstand of Zech. 4:3, at first appear to be invincible: "and if anyone wishes to harm them, fire pours out of their mouths and consumes their enemies; anyone who wants to harm them must be killed in this manner" (Rev. 11:5).[64] For the people of the earth, the arrival of the witnesses, a portent in and of itself, is not auspicious, since "they have authority . . . to strike the earth with every kind of plague, as often as they desire" (Rev. 11:6). They desire often, the narrator later confirms (Rev. 11:10). These prophets provoke opposition not by a condemnatory proclamation but by bringing plagues upon the people of the earth, by making the rain cease and the waters to turn into blood (Rev. 11:6).[65]

Contrary to initial impressions, however, the fire-breathing witnesses are not omnipotent: the unvanquished prophets soon encounter an overpowering opposition. In a reversal of the Roman *venationes*, an exotic animal, the beast "from the bottomless pit," emerges to "conquer" (νικήσει) them (Rev. 11:7). For the careful reader, the book presents here a paradox: the beast has performed the action—"conquer"—that the book's seven epistles repeatedly insist will earn salvation, mimicking successfully the behavior prescribed for the righteous.[66] When the people of

the earth notice that the witnesses are dead, they leave the bodies unburied and celebrate, exchanging gifts (Rev. 11:10).[67] Their response is not
unreasonable: after all, "the two prophets had been a torment to the inhabitants of the earth" (Rev. 11:10). But the party is premature: after three
and a half days, a time period that refers both to the death and resurrection of Jesus and to verse 3, the witnesses rise again and ascend to heaven,
leaving behind the once joyous crowd (Rev. 11:11). God issues judgment
"in that hour" (Rev. 11:13), when an earthquake kills seven thousand of the
spectators.[68] "The second woe has passed," understates the narrator, "the
third woe is coming soon" (Rev. 11:14).

The shocking series of events, which culminates in an earthquake,
takes place in a strange, unnamed, and unfixed location. Like the hippocentaurs of Saune, the beast is framed by an unusual geography. This
city is a cosmopolitan πόλις, the "great city" where "members of the peoples and tribes and languages and nations" live (Rev. 11:8–9). The place
might be Rome: Revelation, as we shall see, later transforms the capital
city into the beast's lair and "a dwelling place of demons" (Rev. 18:2). Or
"the great city" might refer back to "the holy city" and temple that marks
the beginning of the passage: Jerusalem, "where even their lord was crucified" (Rev. 11:8).[69] Rather than decide the identification, the allusions to
both cities overdetermine the meaning of the narrative setting. The story
slips between two geographical points of reference, Rome and Jerusalem,
both of which lie a great distance from Revelation's audience in Asia
Minor.

To this spatial distance the seer adds "in spiritual terms" (πνευ-
ματικῶς) the mythic garb of Sodom and Egypt (Rev. 11:8), an appellation
that explodes any attempt to ground the story in time and space.[70] The
"great city," as Greg Carey observes, is "Sodom, plus Egypt, plus Babylon, all the great bad cities rolled up into one."[71] Sodom and Egypt cloak
the πόλις in a "biblicized" past that is preserved only in narrative, a wholly
"textualized" other. Edward Said's description of "Orientalism" provides
an instructive analogy: "The Orient . . . existed as a set of values attached,
not to its modern realities, but to a series of valorized contacts it had with
a distant European past."[72] We shall encounter this technique of representation again, when the "great city" of Rome, depicted as Babylon, is
dislodged from its foundations in the contemporary world of John and his
audience. As "Babylon the Great" (Rev. 18:2), the Roman Empire is transformed from the *present* observer of curiosities in Phlegon to a curious
object of the biblical *past*.

With mundane boundaries erased, the city becomes an arena. The entire cosmos has been absorbed by the city, and thus the entire cosmos bears witness to a universal, "amazing" spectacle.[73] The bodies of the martyrs lie in view of "members of the peoples and tribes and languages and nations" (Rev. 11:9). The public murder, like the mysterious appearance of the martyrs, is a sign for the crowd of onlookers to interpret. But in this task the spectators fail miserably; like Pantheia in Achilles Tatius's novel, they misunderstand the sign. Rather than repent (Rev. 16:9), these observers "rejoice" (χαίρουσιν) over the beast's victory and the death of the witnesses. For the moment, at least, the *actio* of the narrative spectators aligns them with the beast.

Another sign reverses this state of affairs: "And after three and a half days, the spirit of life from God came into them, and they stood up on their feet, and a great fear fell upon those watching them" (Rev. 11:11). The resurrection of the witnesses divides the gazing crowd into two groups. The first group, the "enemies" (οἱ ἐχθροὶ αὐτῶν) of the two witnesses, recover from their initial shock and "stare" (ἐθεώρησαν) intently as the martyrs ascend to heaven (Rev. 11:12; cf. Rev. 1:7). Still, these spectators do not understand. After the earthquake, however, a second group of observers forms, comprised of the survivors who "become afraid and give glory to the God of heaven" (Rev. 11:13). The second group grasps the meaning of the death and resurrection of the witnesses, and their proper *actio*—a fearful response—precedes comprehension, a lesson reiterated by a subsequent angelic pronouncement: "Fear God and give him glory" (Rev. 14:7).[74] For the extratextual audience, the story shifts attention from the beast's conquest of the two witnesses to the divine spectacle of their resurrection. The "great and amazing deeds" of God surpasses the short-lived victory of the beast.

THE BEASTS FROM THE SEA AND THE LAND

Two chapters later, the figure of the beast again emerges as a figure of spectacular might. When the beast from the sea slouches onto the scene, it immediately catches John's eye (Rev. 13:1–18).[75] This seven-headed, ten-horned creature is a monstrous hybrid: "And the beast I saw was like a leopard, its feet were like a bear's, and its mouth was like a lion's" (Rev. 13:2). Just as the fourth beast of Daniel's nightmare frustrates the prophet's descriptive powers (Dan. 7:7), so commentators have observed

that "the figure . . . is wholly fantastic and not plastically conceivable."[76]
While the creature's appearance remains "inconceivable," its behavior
plainly imitates the book's righteous exemplar: the Lamb "that stands as
if it had been slaughtered" (Rev. 5:6). Like the Lamb, who sits on the divine throne (Rev. 22:1), the beast possesses symbols of royalty: ten crowns
rest on its ten horns, and blasphemous names are inscribed there, too
(Rev. 13:1). And like the Lamb, the beast has several horns. The beast suffers a "death-blow" (ἐσφαγμένην εἰς θάνατον; Rev. 13:3), calling to mind
the image of the slaughtered lamb, the author of "the book of life," a
heavenly volume that is mentioned in this very chapter (Rev. 13:8). Finally,
the beast here, as in chapter 11, emulates the Lamb's behavior: it "conquers" (Rev. 13.7). But other features and actions clearly mark the beast as
unrighteous: blasphemous names are inscribed on its horns, and like
Daniel's little horn, it utters blasphemies against God and "his dwelling."
But the beast's resemblance to the Lamb provides, as Carey notes, an example of "internal parody, in which one aspect of the Apocalypse plays
against another."[77]

The dramatic recovery from a "mortal wound" is perhaps the beast's
most remarkable feat. Commentators often note that this miracle seems
to allude to a Near Eastern Nero *redivivus* myth.[78] According to the anti-
Roman *Sibylline Oracles*, a "blazing matricidal exile" will return, backed
by ten Parthian kings, to capture Rome's wealth and then redistribute it
to the cities of Asia.[79] But it is not the promise of a reversal of wealth or
an imposing military might that captures the attention of "the whole
earth" (Rev. 13:3). Rather, it is the sight of the beast's "resurrection" that
engenders a specific series of reactions from the textual spectators. The
narrator observes, "In amazement (ἐθαυμάσθη) the whole earth followed
the beast" (Rev. 13:3). Gaping in wonder, the crowds—comprised of no
less than "all the inhabitants of the earth" (Rev. 13:8)—pledge their
allegiance to the godlike monster, asking, "Who is like the beast, and who
can fight against it?" (Rev. 13:4). Their mesmerized response, an *actio* of
amazement, leads to destruction. Like the spectators killed in the earthquake, those who follow and "worship" (προσεκύνησαν) the beast will
soon face divine wrath (Rev. 13:4, 8). Their names will not appear in the
"the book of life of the Lamb" (Rev. 13:8), and they will be cast into the
lake of fire (Rev. 20:15). The beastly spectacle condemns the spectators.

The progression from spectacle to perdition repeats itself in the mis-
leading signs performed by the beast from the earth (Rev. 13:11–18). Here
the appearance of a second beast, a false prophet (see Rev. 16:13), serves as

the catalyst for spectacle and response. This monster rising from the earth, like its sea-borne predecessor, is an amalgam of imagery found elsewhere in the book: "it had two horns like a lamb and it spoke like a dragon" (Rev. 13:11). But the beast from the land is a wolf in lamb's clothing, since it "makes the earth and its inhabitants worship the first beast" (Rev. 13:12).[80] For spectators already fascinated by the first beast's miraculous recovery, the second beast's deceptive guise and its signs prove overwhelmingly seductive. "Who is like the beast, and who can fight against it?" is the cry of the deceived; in the same way, the land-beast's pyrotechnic display enthralls the credulous audience (Rev. 13:14).[81]

For viewers "on the ground," the beastly display remains a source of endless fascination. And as viewers of and then as participants in a beastly conspiracy to defeat the forces of heaven, the earthly spectators seal their own fate. Still under the spell of the portents produced by the second beast, the inhabitants of the earth are persuaded to make an "image" of the first beast (εἰκόνα τῷ θηρίῳ; Rev. 13:14). To assure compliance with the demand of worship, the second creature adds "breath" (πνεῦμα) to the image (Rev. 13:15), threatens death for those who refuse, and causes all—at least those who wish to remain alive (Rev. 11:16)—to receive the infamous "mark of the beast" (Rev. 13:18). The tattoo, which the entranced spectators accept, places them in opposition to those sealed by God (see Rev. 7:2), an act that decides their eternal fate: "Those who worship the beast and its image, and receive a mark on their foreheads or on their hands . . . will be tormented with fire and sulfur" (Rev. 14:9–10). Further, spectacle surfaces even in the afterlife: the never-ending torture of the condemned will take place "in the presence" (ἐνώπιον) of the holy angels and of the Lamb (Rev. 14:9–10).

But some of the spectators oppose the false prophet and refuse to worship the image of the beast (Rev. 13:15), and they are executed for their obstinacy. By resisting fascination, the viewers are granted entrance to a heavenly gallery, and from there they will watch as the Roman beast is destroyed. Revelation 13 recapitulates the lesson of chapter 11: the "great and amazing" deeds of God ought to remain the focus of attention, because the spectacles of the beast lead to destruction. Unlike the amazed followers of the beast who will have "no rest day or night" from the punishment meted out by the Lamb, the blessed believers "who from now on die in the Lord . . . will rest from their labors" (Rev. 14:13). In sum, earthly spectators in the narrative demonstrate one of two emotional reactions to the portents they view. Those who express φόβος at the sight of the resurrection of the two martyrs acquire lucidity and ultimately salvation (Rev. 11:13; see also Rev. 14:7). Those who succumb to θαῦμα at the sight of this beastly spectacle (Rev. 13:4), on the other hand, remain unable to perceive clearly the danger of accepting the mark: bedazzled, these viewers stumble into eternal suffering.

THE CONFLAGRATION OF BABYLON

The last apocalyptic spectacle I will consider returns us to the scene that opened this section: the judgment of Babylon, "the great prostitute seated on many waters" (Rev. 17:1–18:24). Babylon's conflagration weaves together elements of the previous scenes. The matrix of beastly spectacle and amazement resurfaces along with a "biblicizing" motif even more pronounced than the one found in the Sodom and Egypt setting for the spectacle of the two martyrs.[82] The narrative prepares the extratextual spectator for this exotic vision in advance: an angel announces, "Fallen, fallen is Babylon the great!" three chapters prior to the account of the city's fiery demise (see also Rev. 16:19). In the proleptic passage, the book borrows Isaiah's prophetic cry (Isa. 21:9) to transform the object of divine wrath, the city of Rome (see Rev. 17:9), into the historical enemy of Israel's past. John's book demands that his audience forget the Rome they "know" from the cult shrines and monuments of Asia Minor. The book instead cloaks the Roman Empire in an ancient costume, creating thus a writhing, drunken version of the great πόλις (Rev. 18:2, 6). The "makeup" that this portrayal applies to Rome calls to mind the "mythological enactments" and "fatal charades" of capital punishment in the Roman arena. There, as we have seen, mythological themes were evoked in the execution of criminals. Here Revelation has transformed the "myth-maker," into a "myth" of its own: Babylon, the ancient enemy of Israel, is summoned from the biblical past and called into service.

John is not alone in this strategy: 4 Ezra, 2 Baruch, and 1 Peter employ the same code language for Rome.[83] The great prostitute who sits on the seven-headed scarlet beast is the current manifestation of Babylon, a manifestation that remains both more potent, in its capacity for evil, and more impotent, in its battle against heaven, than the ancient captor of Judah. As Royalty maintains: "John's Babylon overshadows all precursors."[84] The book again shifts perspective: no longer the place where curiosities are put on display, the Roman Empire has been made into an ex-hibition. Now a scarlet θηρίον, Rome is a sign of divine displeasure, and like the two-headed toddler tossed into the Tiber, the prostitute and the multiheaded monster appear to be bound for destruction.

By substituting a foreign monster for the Roman Empire, the book transports the members of its audience into an expansive cosmos, en-abling them to surround this display of Babylon, just as crowds in Rome and Phlegon's audience gathered around the embalmed hippocentaur. At the same time, the seer himself is transported "into the wilderness" (εἰς ἔρημον)—a striking contrast to Rome's own urban environment—to be-hold this episode of divine judgment (Rev. 17:3).[85] Prior to delivery of the verdict, though, the angel grants John an opportunity to witness directly Babylon's malevolence, leading us back to the amazement of John with which we began this section. In the wilderness, John sees "Babylon the great, mother of prostitutes and of earth's abominations" riding a great beast, "drunk on the blood of the saints and on the blood of the witnesses (τῶν μαρτύρων) of Jesus" (Rev. 17:6). Unable to make sense of the sign, he yields to the interpreting angel.

A similar moment of interpretive uncertainty occurs earlier in the nar-rative: John is asked to identify the white-robed figures encircling the heavenly throne. Twice in Revelation the seer is thrust into an authorita-tive interpretive position, and twice he passes the hermeneutical reins to others (Rev. 7:13–14). A gap opens up between ecphrasis and explication, allowing the extratextual audience to ponder the meaning of these por-tents, and in both cases a supernatural character articulates the proper in-terpretation. In the throne vision, the elder answers the questions he first posed to John, and in the Babylon vision, the *angelus interpres* gives the authorized reading of the sign: "The woman you saw is the great city that rules over the kings of the earth" (Rev. 17:18). The prostitute is none other than the Roman beast, a monster bound for destruction. Only those who can view the strange creatures of Revelation in the context of the "great and amazing deeds" of God will be saved. Those unable to do so are en-thralled by the prostitute and "marvel" at the beast; these deceived spec-tators are "the dwellers on the earth whose names have not been written in the book of life from the foundation of the world" (Rev. 17:9). To be seduced by Babylon is to be amazed by the beast (Rev. 17:18).

The remainder of the scene is devoted to judgment of Babylon-Rome, a spectacle managed not by the beasts but by God. Significantly,

Babylon is not alone on the narrative stage, for Revelation 18 also describes a set of narrative spectators that perform acts of mourning. The text calls attention to the posture and to the emotional response of each group of spectators: kings, merchants, and mariners stand "far off" (ἀπὸ μακρόθεν) to watch with profound sorrow as the flames consume Babylon (Rev. 18:10, 15, 17).[86] But the repetitive dirge makes clear that, unlike the textual observers, the extratextual audience is not supposed to sympathize with the suffering of Babylon. "The parallelism between the kings and the merchants," Collins concludes, "makes it unlikely that the author sympathized with their mourning or regretted the loss of their great wealth."[87] First appear the kings of the earth, who "weep and wail over her when they see the smoke of her burning" (Rev. 18:9). The next group, the merchants of the earth, also "weep and mourn for her, since no one buys their cargo anymore" (Rev. 18:11). The third group, the shipmasters and seafarers, cry out with dust on their heads: "What city was like the great city?" (Rev. 18:17), a rhetorical question that bears an eerie resemblance to the one posed earlier by a different set of bedazzled observers: "Who is like the beast, and who can fight against it?" (Rev. 13:4). The grieving of the kings, merchants, and seafarers not only reveals them to be allies of Babylon and the beast but also makes them "actors in the audience," to adapt Bartsch. These spectators have unwittingly become part of the spectacle of Babylon's demise: their sorrowful *actio* condemns them as a heavenly gallery looks on.

A Multitude in Heaven

After the destruction of Babylon, Revelation focuses on spectators in heaven. This crowd of viewers—"a great multitude in heaven" (Rev. 19:1)—performs an *actio* far different from the distraught reactions of the doomed kings. Rather than weeping at the sight, this audience rejoices: "Hallelujah! The smoke goes up from forever and ever" (19:3).[88] Commentators have largely associated this group with the "great multitude" that John glimpses earlier but is unable to name, a congregation of "they who have come out of the great tribulation" (Rev. 7:14). Further, the white-robed crowd, it seems, should be identified with the martyrs who cry out from under the heavenly altar in Rev. 6:9–11.[89] First and foremost, though, the crowd in heaven is a crowd of viewers, who gaze with approval at Babylon's destruction.

The view from the ground, then, contrasts sharply with the view from heaven, a perspective that Revelation affords its extratextual audience. Phlegon locates the display of the hippocentaur in Rome, but Revelation makes Rome into a display. The careful presentation of the Roman Empire, layered with exotic and monstrous details, is only part of John's labors. To make this depiction of Rome into "fact," to turn Rome into Babylon, it must also be made into an exhibition. Hence, the Apocalypse locates Babylon and the beasts in relation to viewers of the Empire of Heaven, which context serves to infuse the description with authenticity, just as the emperor's storehouse vouches for the claims of Phlegon. Like a set of concentric circles, the beastly spectacles and the fall of Babylon are finally enclosed within an encompassing arena, cosmic and imperial.

Imperial viewing occurs in a different mode in Revelation as well, one akin to that found in the Greek romance. There, rather than relating strange figures and places to a specific locus of authority, Rome, the production of knowledge hinges on the character of characters, such as Kleitophon, whose elite background represents a classical Greek ideal. Turning again to the "portent in heaven" in which the "great and amazing deeds" of God are honored in song, we find that the choir, standing beside the sea of glass, is composed of "those who had conquered the beast and its image and the number of its name" (Rev. 15:1–3). Here Revelation connects righteous viewing with the capacity for resisting the spectacles of the beast. While others were transfixed in amazement at the beast, these martyrs, witnesses to God's awe-inspiring performance, firmly refused to be seduced by its miracles. The character of these witnesses derives not, as in the Greek romance, from the raw materials of privilege and tradition, but from having withstood the menacing force of θαῦμα: they came face to face with the potent spectacles of the beast and emerged from the encounter unscathed by monstrous amazement. If, as has already been suggested, the spectators in heaven are to be identified with "they who have come out of the great tribulation" (Rev. 7:14), then the cosmic kingdom of God, according to Revelation, is full of viewers who have similarly stared into the abyss of wonder but have not succumbed to it. It comes as no surprise, then, that when the thrones of judgment appear, the judges who sit upon them are "they who had not worshiped the beast or its image and had not received its mark on their foreheads or their hands" (Rev. 20:4). Seeing the beast, they were not amazed.

Such Sights

Around the year 180 C.E., a Jew or Christian predicted for Rome a fate similar to that described in Revelation: "No longer will Syrian, Greek, or foreigner, or any other nation place their neck under your yoke of slavery," prophesied the Sibyl. "You will be a 'triumph' spectacle to the world and a reproach of all."[90] Not only will the authority of Rome come to an end but a parade will mark the occasion, as the empire's former vassals line the route and cheer. About the same time, Tertullian records his own fantasy of Rome's destruction. In his essay *De spectaculis*, the apologist criticizes the pagan shows and concludes with a "Christianized" show of his own. In rousing prose, Tertullian lists the pleasing components of this vision:

How vast the spectacle that day, and how wide! What sight shall wake my wonder, what my laughter, my joy and exultation? As I see all those kings, those great kings, welcomed (we are told) in heaven, along with Jove, along with those who told of their ascent, groaning in the depths of darkness! And the magistrates who persecuted the name of Jesus, liquefying in fiercer flames than they kindled in their rage against the Christians![91]

In a treatise aimed against the shows of the arena, Tertullian substitutes a violent Christian spectacle for the pagan shows. A second palpable irony surfaces in the description of a divine judge who, according to Tertullian, "looks at cheating, adultery, fraud, idolatry, yes, and the spectacles, too": not even God can turn aside from the allure of the amphitheater.[92] Here the divinity becomes a kind of *deus spectator*, making, as Maier has argued, this criticism of the theater "paradoxical, for while Christians are to steer clear of the theater or the arena, in the ongoing eschatological drama God has a front-row seat."[93] So does Tertullian.

The thrill of spectacle brings Tertullian (and God) into a matrix of self-fashioning. Simon Goldhill contends that the essay "lapses into violent self-contradiction," revealing "the complex dialectic of conflict and appropriation in such writing against the Empire."[94] While not denying the relevance of Goldhill's conclusion for the topic at hand, I wish to press the issue of "violent self-contradiction" further by putting Tertullian's fantasy alongside John's own disquieting brush with the paralysis of amazement. Spectacle in the Apocalypse, I have argued, is a site for testing the limits of self-control against the force of amazement, and, as writers from Plutarch to Augustine to Tertullian attest, diverse forms of this kind of testing pervaded the society of ancient Rome. If John fails, it is only for a moment: the angel's intervention allows John to regain his composure, his self-possession, so that the work of viewing can continue. John's momentary faltering, I suggest, buttresses, even constructs, the authority he commands as a spectator. He has survived the ordeal that others in the narrative could not.

In this reading, *De spectaculis* evinces less a "violent self-contradiction" than a tour de force of viewing. Like God, Tertullian gazes intently at "a vast spectacle"; but unlike the spectators at the Roman shows, the North African apologist looks at "things of greater joy than circus, theater, or amphitheater."[95] The Roman patrons are soon lost in "madness, anger, discord" (*furias et animos et discordias*), achieving nothing, and losing their self-control.[96] Tertullian, in contrast, remains in command of his faculties, fixing his gaze on the glory of the saints and the future "reign of the righteous," and challenging his audience to do likewise: "Such sights, such exultation . . . all these, in some sort, are ours, pictured through faith in the imagination of the spirit."[97] Transfixion is not apparent here, neither is the inconsolable grief of the kings and merchants who become part of the scene of Babylon's fall. Tertullian instead rejoices at the roasting of his enemies, like the heavenly spectators of Revelation who shout, "Hallelujah! The smoke goes from her forever and ever" (Rev. 19:3).[98]

John, in the same way, seems mindful of the slippage from viewer to viewed, conscious that, at any moment, he could become an "actor in the audience." Maier, I noted, has argued that the power of apocalypse lies in the genre's depiction of a panoptic deity, which forces the extratextual audience to see itself not only as viewers but also as players who must give the performance of a lifetime. But this kind of "panoptic consciousness" was already embedded in the Roman culture of viewing: in the spectacles of empire, all participants, including the audience, were on stage. To attend the shows was to take a risk, and because viewing was dangerous, it held great potential for the fashioning and presentation of the self. The following chapters will place the risk of being a viewer in relation to the most important performance of all in the Roman world: masculinity.

4

As If Slain

THE CRITICAL AND COMMERCIAL SUCCESS OF THE 2000 film *Gladiator* indicates that the ancient Roman combatants continue to intrigue modern Americans. Appealing to this interest seems to have been the goal of a recent United States Marine Corps television advertisement, which features a kind of gladiatorial contest. Fast and furious, the ad tells its tale in less than thirty seconds. At first, a gigantic arena, filled with cheering spectators, looms on the horizon. Then we see a young man in a t-shirt and jeans against a dark, animated background of thunderclouds and whirring machinery, a scene from some science-fictional, post-apocalyptic wasteland. He negotiates treacherous obstacles to enter the stadium, then, suddenly, he is joined in battle with an immense but amorphous gray-black beast with yellow eyes. In a flash, the contest is over: our gladiator in blue jeans grabs a glistening sword, slices the beast wide open, and metamorphoses into a Marine in a shiny new uniform.

The visual effects are stunning, but the narration also deserves comment. As the hero swings for his opponent, a baritone voice intones: "If you can master your fear, outsmart your enemy, and never yield, even to yourself—then you will be changed forever. The few, the proud, the Marines." This message assigns the monster a double identity. On one level, the beast represents an external threat to the hero: the ideal Marine will "outsmart" and defeat this villain. On another, the shadowy behemoth symbolizes the internal fear that must be mastered, the inner chaos to which the soldier must not yield. This is a story about the (trans)formation and mastery of the self, a story that reflects an axiom formulated by Stephen Greenblatt in his now classic study of Renaissance subjectivity: "Self-fashioning is achieved in relation to something perceived as alien, strange, or hostile."[1] The spectators in this gloomy arena view two contests: one between the hero and the monster and another between the hero and himself. Triumph over these opponents turns a civilian into a soldier and a boy into a man.

I have described this television advertisement to add the theme of masculinity to our consideration of viewing in the texts of the Roman Empire. Furthermore, its emphasis on self-mastery bears a striking resemblance to the moral prescriptions of philosophers under the early principate. Brent Shaw has argued that, for Roman Greeks such as Plutarch and Epictetus, Stoicism addressed the problems of identity that were created by the shifting political landscape. "[I]n the great changes," he contends, "that marked the shift from the *polis* community to the world of the Hellenistic kingdoms, from that milieu to the Roman empire. . . . Stoicism was the integrative idea to which political elites had access, the mental anchor to which they could relate their whole world view."[2] With the transformation of the *polis* in the Hellenistic and Roman periods, Stoicism reassured aristocratic Greeks that identity remained, in some measure, a matter of their own control and was now to be forged within the setting of the grand, cosmic order of things.[3]

The problem that the arrival of the Roman Empire introduced to traditional notions of self-control was articulated in a different, yet complementary, fashion in the work of Michel Foucault: following a suggestive essay of Paul Veyne, Foucault took this theme as an object of study, observing that the relation between morality and self-control "intensified" during the Roman period and coalesced into a technology that he labeled the "cultivation of the self."[4] By contrast with the setting of the *polis*, where sense of self was linked to the exercise of authority over others, the imposition of imperial Roman structures "made it more difficult to define the relations between what one was, what one could do, and what one was expected to accomplish."[5] The household, not the city, came into service as the proving grounds for a new ethics of the self, and the domination of others became a practice of the past, while increasing attention was paid to the internal passions, sexual desire in particular, as "a dangerous site of possible disruption . . . that must be controlled."[6] The violent submission of household members — slaves, wives, and children — said the moralists, played no part in the virtuous life of the head of the household. Rather, as Plutarch advised a pair of newlyweds, "marriage and the household shall be well attuned through reason, concord, and philosophy."[7] The loss of the *polis* as an effective context for interaction and self-formation resulted in the "privatization," the domestication, of self-mastery.

Foucault's work has been subjected to criticism on several fronts.[8] In his quest to uncover the power relations masked by the rubric "sexuality," Kate Cooper argues, Foucault neglected to consider the tactical aspect of ancient moralizing, presenting instead the writings of ancient philosophers as "bound in an unproblematic manner to social reality": "The rhetoric of conjugal unity in antiquity served primarily as a means by which aristocratic families could broadcast the moral character of their menfolk, a point of much significance which has been missed by the much-discussed attempts of Paul Veyne and Michel Foucault to explicate the Roman rhetoric of affection between the spouses."[9] Further, as much scholarship since *The History of Sexuality* has pointed out, Foucault failed to consider the significance of gender.[10] These problems in Foucault's analysis led Cooper to an important reassessment of the rhetoric of conjugal unity in the Roman Empire. The emphasis on marital harmony, according to Cooper, is evidence that the disclosure of details about a man's private life, especially as it involved relations with women, had implications for the public self-presentation of *men*.[11] The man who had reportedly mastered sexual desire in his bedroom — that is, had demonstrated self-control — could be trusted to do so in other contexts. In this way, men were able to "shore up" their reputations, to construct a facade of masculine self-control for themselves, not through direct competition with other men, but indirectly, through "insinuations" about self-mastery that "womanly influence" put to the test. In other words, women, figured as "wife," were absorbed into an economy of masculinity under the sign of conjugal harmony.

Bearing in mind the insights of Cooper and Foucault, I shall attempt, in this chapter and the next, to explore representations of masculinity in the book of Revelation. In so doing, these chapters will point up the complexity of gender fashioning under the emperors, using the framework of viewing relations to elaborate the ways that cultural products of the Roman Empire such as the Apocalypse were able, as Virginia Burrus has phrased it, "to turn vulnerability — frequently figured as a capacity for feminization — to advantage."[12] The television advertisement, an electronic spectacle, grants a preview of this work: viewing, penetration, and the exhibition of the other converge in the portrayal of masculinity, but not in an unproblematic fashion. The "other" is both external and internal to the hero, who is at once spectator and spectacle: for this is a contest that pits the hero against his own fearful self. At the same moment that the hero pierces his foe with a sword, he is himself "penetrated" by narration that discloses the monstrous enemy crouching inside the soon-to-be Marine.

This chapter continues our exploration of spectacle in Revelation, which is, I shall argue, similarly ambivalent in its presentation of viewing and penetration as modes of masculinity. Where the previous chapter emphasized the imperial viewing that "orientalizes" the other—representing it as foreign, beastly, and inferior—the present chapter will call attention to "sexual viewing," which has the potential to make an exhibition of both the desired body and the desirous viewer. I begin with a discussion of gender and Roman sexuality, taking the Greek novel *Daphnis and Chloe* as the point of departure. Guided by the sure hand of John Winkler, we explore the ways this story serves as a window for the observation of gender and sexuality in the Roman Empire. Then, turning to the Apocalypse, I shall contend that the book's central character, the "Lamb standing as if slain" (Rev. 5:6, 5:12, 13:8), undergoes a kind of transformation: at first "feminized," a commanding performance of viewing "masculinizes" the Lamb. But this transformation, I suggest, remains partial. As this chapter and the next chapter will illustrate, the Lamb, like other figures under the Roman Empire, vacillates between subject positions, destabilizing the categories of penetrator and penetrated, masculine and feminine, viewer and viewed.

Educating Daphnis

We begin our investigation of ancient sexuality with one of the five extant Greek erotic novels. *Daphnis and Chloe*, a romance written by Longus in the second century C.E., relates an account of love deferred, consummation interrupted. The plot is typical of the genre: boy meets girl; boy and girl fall madly in love; boy and girl's every attempt to act on their mutual lust meets with frustration. Despite the "simple" structure and conventional subject matter of these stories, they were not mere pulp fiction for the masses. Rather, as Simon Goldhill has demonstrated, the Greek romance provides ironic versions of classical and Hellenistic philosophical discussions about nature, knowledge, and desire.[13] By engaging and parodying lofty discussions of epistemology, the genre contributes to the formation of an ancient discursive field of gender and sexuality. The ancient romance, as much as the Roman philosophical and medical texts explored by Foucault, simultaneously reflected and inscribed sexual relations and gender construction in imperial Roman culture. More than anyone else, Winkler, in his chapter on "The Education of Chloe," has been able to articulate the serious dimensions of *Daphnis and Chloe*'s erotic play.[14]

Serious dimensions, however, are difficult to detect at first blush. Central to the plot of Longus's novel is a running joke about the sexual naivete of children: Daphnis, the young goatherd, and Chloe, a shepherd and Daphnis's beloved, simply do not know how to "do it." The pair's ardent quest to consummate their relationship—dressed, undressed, lying down, standing up—makes for slapstick humor, furnishing the fiction with a "country bumpkin" atmosphere. From first to last, the novel presents itself as a tale untouched by metropolitan sophistication: the setting is rural, the names of the characters are pastoral, and the action—from goatherding to bungled lovemaking "in the woods," on the outskirts of society—remains unhurried and innocent.[15]

While the story might have brought smiles to the faces of its ancient audience, the romance also teaches the gentle reader a lesson in the "big city" sexual values and gender roles of Mediterranean society, over which Rome cast its long shadow. Indeed, the novel combines comic and didactic elements in a memorable scene that pairs sex and violence. Here Daphnis catches the eye of the urban and urbane Lycaenion, a seductress whose motives for bedding the boy are simultaneously altruistic and self-centered.[16] Lycaenion knows that the couple's intimate moments have left both Chloe and Daphnis dissatisfied, and, according to the narrator, "she sympathized with their trials and saw a twofold opportunity—for rescuing them and satisfying her desire."[17] Surprisingly (or perhaps not), Daphnis, who had earlier pledged his unflagging devotion to Chloe, quickly assents to the elder woman's plan to teach him how to make love. So the lesson commences: first Lycaenion leads Daphnis into the forest, away from prying eyes, for the purpose of sexual congress. Afterward, to make certain there are no ambiguities, she carefully explains to Daphnis what just happened between them. The goatherd, for his part, is impatient to find Chloe and practice what he has learned. But Lycaenion stops him short with a speech, drawing a sharp distinction between herself and Chloe as a sexual partner/object:

You've still got this to learn, Daphnis. Because I happen to be an experienced woman, I didn't suffer any harm just now (long ago another man gave me this lesson, and took my virginity as his reward). But if Chloe has this sort of wrestling match with you, she will cry out and weep and will lie there, bleeding heavily as if slain (καθάπερ πεφονευμένη) . . . remember—I made you a man (ἐγὼ ἄνδρα . . . πεποίηκα) before Chloe did.[18]

"As if slain": Lycaenion's chilling admonition puts Chloe on display. Like the Lamb of Revelation, she appears wounded, penetrated, murdered. This is not the image of reciprocity, of household harmony and conjugal unity, that one expects to encounter in the society imagined by Foucault's philosophers; it seems instead to reflect the "protocols" of patriarchal violence.

Daphnis's initial hesitation to fulfill this manly role, his reluctance to "educate Chloe," is one of the narrative elements that leads Winkler to wonder whether Longus's text supports patriarchal force or challenges it.[19] Daphnis's reservations remain only until the novel's conclusion, which describes the lavish marriage of the pair, a ceremony the entire city attends. The chamber door closes behind the newlyweds, but the wedding guests stand immediately on the other side, singing "with harsh, rough voices, as though they were breaking up the earth with forks, not singing a wedding hymn."[20] Then, concludes the narrator with a wink and a nod, "Daphnis and Chloe lay down naked together, embraced and kissed, and had even less sleep that night than the owls. Daphnis did some of the things Lycaenion taught him; and then, for the first time, Chloe found out that what they had done in the woods had been nothing but 'children's games' (παιδίων παίγνια)."[21] "May we presume," asks Winkler, "that Daphnis and the reader have not forgotten . . . [Lykaenion's] careful description of defloration as trauma—the screams, the tears, the pool of blood?"[22] By invoking Lycaenion precisely at this moment, Winkler observes, Longus does not allow the reader to forget the earlier episode.

It would seem that the moral of the romance surfaces in the final paragraph. Among other things, we learn that sex is not a private act "in the woods" but a public performance authorized by the civic gaze. More important, the novel suggests that not only Chloe but Daphnis too has received an "education"—first from Lycaenion, then from the community. The nuptial sanctuary, a symbol of societal approbation, mitigates the apprehension of Daphnis about "inflicting" intercourse upon his beloved. Daphnis has become a man: he possesses the knowledge that, as a man, he could hurt Chloe; as a woman, she is "vulnerable to sexual wounding." But, "like Abraham and Isaac journeying up the mountain," to quote Winkler's vivid description, Daphnis must instead protect her, above all by keeping hidden from her the knowledge of his own potential violence.[23] Daphnis has become a man, and this is what men do.

Yet, as Winkler further observes, Longus's conclusion, rather than sanctioning these "erotic protocols and prior violence," calls them into question precisely by exposing them as the product of education—that is, nuture—that nonetheless was counted as the result of "nature" in Chloe's society.[24] Neither Lycaenion's words have been forgotten, nor the role she played in making Daphnis a man. Further, the "elliptical quality" of the conclusion reveals little about what happened between Daphnis and Chloe on their wedding night, except "that it was *not* childish and that it was *not* play"; the harshness implied here is matched by the wedding song, which, it turns out, is delivered "not as a wedding song," casting the whole episode in ambiguous tones.[25] Winkler's reading hammers notes of discord, making *Daphnis and Chloe* less a clear statement about what constitutes manliness than a novel that explores the performance of manhood as a cultural problem.[26]

Not Far from the Intercourse of Bodies

In this section, I wish to extend Winkler's point about the cultural problems posed by *Daphnis and Chloe*, examining briefly viewing practices as depicted in ancient novels. To comprehend the ways that narrative viewing could disrupt conventional notions of sexuality and gender, we must first sketch out the symbolic realm that weighed upon Roman-era society. "Roman sexuality was a structuralist's dream"; or so one scholar of ancient gender and sexuality has determined.[27] As is widely accepted by now, a traditional grid informed Roman imperial society, dividing sexual roles according to "active" and "passive" positions. Gender—the behaviors and appearances constitutive of both "masculinity" and "femininity"—was linked inextricably to this system, ordering for Romans the details of their culture. As Bernadette J. Brooten remarks: "Active and passive constitute foundational categories for Roman-period culture; they are gender coded as masculine and feminine respectively . . . for this reason they [Romans] described passive men as effeminate and active women as masculine."[28] According to this scheme, "masculinity" corresponded to "activity" and could be demonstrated by penetrating the orifices of the body.[29] The genitalia of this object-body had little, if any bearing on the gender coding of the "active" partner: a male penetrator was "manly" no matter the physiology of his mate. Indeed, as Amy Richlin discusses, ancient poetry based on invective sometimes defends the fortress of Roman masculinity with the threat of male on male sexual assault.[30] Likewise, a woman who sexually penetrated another (but this is rarely reported) was also "manly."[31] And, as one might expect in a structuralist's dream, the reverse held true: the breached body, male or female, was "feminine" or "effeminate."

In the penetration grid, the body of the mature Roman male was presented as inviolable. As Jonathan Walters observes, "the impenetrable boundaries of the social body are being drawn around those of the [adult male] physical body."[32] The right to protect the body against physical assault corresponded directly to social standing. Penetration, for elite Romans, at least, equaled domination, making sexuality and gender expressions of mastery.[33] Aristocratic women and free youths were thus afforded some legal protection; slaves, on the other hand, were treated in terms of property: the rape of a slave represented the invasion of the master's *domus*, not of the slave's body. The second-century dream interpretation manual of Artemidorus, as both Winkler and Foucault have described, blatantly articulates this social pattern—a "structuralist's dream," indeed—placing status on an axis of penetration.[34] A dream depicting the dreamer (assumed here, it would seem, to be a free adult male) being penetrated by his slave, for example, is "inauspicious," but "having sexual intercourse with one's servant, whether male or female is good; for slaves are possessions of the dreamer, so that they signify, quite naturally, that the dreamer will derive pleasure from his possessions, which will grow greater and more valuable."[35] Sex is only "active" or "passive" in Artemidorus's guide: one either penetrates or is penetrated. And the pervasive status shading of this opposition illustrates the close alignment of the body and society, making the *Oneirocritica* a "dream" text indeed for both Claude Lévi-Strauss and Mary Douglas. Indeed, *dreaming* of passivity is not always "inauspicious," not if the penetrator ranks higher on the social scale than the dreamer: "For a man to be penetrated by a richer, older man is good," writes Artemidorus, "for the custom is to receive things from such men." The penetration grid, superimposed over both fantasies and reality, expressed a basic principle of Roman hierarchy: at the top of the social ladder stood the impenetrable penetrator.

Preoccupied with the rudimentary elements of this logic of invasion, ancient writers both well before and under the reign of the Roman emperors raised and answered, in a variegated and often ribald fashion, the

question, "who's penetrating whom?"[36] As we have seen, providing a socially acceptable response to a question like this forms part of the impetus
for "educating Daphnis." The goatherd learns to penetrate, how to be
manly, while Chloe learns to distinguish between playful embraces and
being penetrated, a dyad of gender and sexuality expressed even at the
linguistic level for Greeks. Dale B. Martin describes succinctly the cultural
underpinnings of this instruction: "Greek language seems almost always
to have constructed sexual intercourse as a one-way street; the pleasure
was assumed to belong naturally to the penetrator, and the penetrated was
expected to submit without enjoyment. Whoever enjoyed being penetrated was considered weak, unnatural, or at least suspect—or (to sum up
all three terms into one body) a woman."[37] Against this background, the
warning of Lycaenion seems concerned less with Chloe's "enjoyment"
than with the desires of Daphnis. Chloe's body is painted in bloody hues,
like the bodies of classical Greek tragedy examined by Nicole Loraux. In
this theater, the female body is a spectacle of death, and the heroines of
Euripides are brought into view most clearly at the moment they embrace
the sword.[38]

　　Yet, under the Roman Empire, there are signs that this erotic trian-
gle of metaphors—sex, sword, and death—became an unstable geome-
try, enabling writers and their audiences to imagine sexuality and gender
in terms different than the penetration grid—the "structuralist's
dream"—would have it. The sexual escapades of Photis and Lucius in the
Golden Ass illuminate this development. Before he turns into an ass, Lucius is eager to take part in "Venus's gladiatorial games" (*gladiatoriae
Veneris*) with the comely Photis. After noticing his aroused state, Photis
exhorts Lucius: "Engage . . . and do so bravely. I shall not yield before
you, nor turn my back on you. Direct your aim frontally, if you are a man
(*si vir es*), and at close quarters. Let your onslaught be fierce; kill before
you die (*et occide moriturus*). Our battle this day allows no respite."[39]
Later in the story, during a different night of debauchery, Lucius recounts: "When I was finished with her feminine generosity, Photis offered
me a boy's pleasure as a gift."[40] The sexualized Photis, the object of Lucius's desire, is a collection of orifices made available for the pleasure of
penetration. But this is not to say that Lucius embodies an ideal of "hy-
permasculinity": as Winkler observed, the hapless hero is "at once armed
yet vulnerable" in these encounters with Photis, presenting himself as a
"victim" to Cupid's arrow.[41] Lacking self-mastery, both Photis and Lucius
repeatedly succumb to their mutual passions. On the one hand, Photis

serves the wants of Lucius, changing from "woman" to "boy" to provide pleasure for him. On the other, Photis is depicted as the sexual aggressor, fully in command of the situation, urging Lucius to "kill before you die." If Chloe had had no idea what would happen on her wedding night, Photis, it seems, is well-informed and ready for the contest.

The portrayals of Chloe and Photis hold more in common than the association of sex with violent penetration: they both anticipate aspects of contemporary theorizing about the gaze.[42] Chloe and Photis seem to connote, in the phrase coined by Laura Mulvey, "to-be-looked-at-ness."[43] Physicality emerges in the eyes of the penetrator: Lucius becomes a "phallus with eyes," describing the "supple movements" of Photis's back and her adroit sexual positioning. Where the "gaze carries with it the power of action and of possession," E. Ann Kaplan notes, gender-fashioning is in play, generating both a "feminized," objectified body and a "masculine" gaze.[44] Neither is meant to represent an essentialized expression of gender, but to point instead to the structure of domination and submission erected by the viewing relation. In short, the bearer or subject of the gaze occupies a position superior to the one inhabited by the object of the gaze.

Still, in the texts of the Roman Empire, we encounter more complexity than we might expect, a complexity that derives from an ancient emphasis on the materiality of viewing relations. Tracing the "tactile gaze" back to Platonic theories of vision, in which "a fire within the eye flows outward to create a visual ray of such force that it 'collides' with its object," Georgia Frank provides a survey of the close association of sight and touch in the Hellenistic and Roman periods. Not all philosophers simply adopted this "extramission" theory of the gaze. Some, like Aristotle, spoke of images being stamped upon the eye, and others, like the Epicureans, devised an "intramission" system of "images flowing off objects" and striking the eye. Regardless of their particular configuration, all of these theories "retained the idea of vision occurring through contacts."[45] When we turn to accounts of the "desiring eye" in ancient literature, examples of tactile viewing are not difficult to find. For some, sight triggered arousal. As Aline Rousselle notes, there exists a widespread assumption in ancient medical texts that "the presence of women or young boys generally aroused male desire and that erotic pictures or stories aroused desire in the normal woman."[46] But the erotic look is not simply the prelude to intercourse: in some texts, it is intercourse. As Kleinias explains to Kleitophon, viewing and being viewed by one's

beloved is better than sex: "This pleasure is greater than that of consummation, for the eyes receive each others' reflections, and they form there
from small images as in mirrors. Such outpouring of beauty flowing down
through them into the soul is a kind of copulation at a distance. This is
not far removed from the intercourse of bodies."[47] Here there is little ac-
knowledgment of a "masculine" gaze. The "intercourse of bodies" of
viewing suspends the penetration grid, allowing both parties simultaneously to penetrate and be penetrated.

The desirous Kleitophon acts on Kleinias's advice a few passages later,
and, at first, the passage seems to narrate the masculine gaze, until
Leukippe returns Kleitophon's stare. Kleitophon discloses how he con-
spired to look at Leukippe while she, distracted, looked elsewhere in a
"grove of very pleasant aspect," surrounded on all sides by erotically
charged flowers, fruits, and birds. Taking the plumes of a nearby peacock
as his starting point, Kleitophon tells a slave about mating practices in nature, engrossing Leukippe, who stands within earshot. The "erotic lesson" allows Kleitophon to stare with impunity on the object of his
affection. Mission accomplished, Kleitophon paints a vivid picture of his
beloved:

I was looking at the young lady to see how she reacted to my erotic lesson. She
discreetly indicated that she had not been displeased by my discourse. The radiant
beauty of the peacock struck me less forcefully than that glance from Leukippe.
The beauty of her body challenged the flowers of the field: her face was the
essence of pale jonquil; roses arose on her cheeks; her glance was a revelation of
violet; her hair had more natural curls than spiral ivy. Such was the meadow of
Leukippe's face.[48]

The seemingly innocent ruse turns Kleitophon into the bearer of the gaze
and objectifies Leukippe. But before he is able to describe the sublime
beauty of the object of his affection, she looks back, and Kleitophon is
"forcefully struck," penetrated by the touch, as it were, of Leukippe's
eyes. Kleitophon, a second Lucius in this respect, presents himself as a victim, casting doubt upon what might otherwise have been a virtuoso performance of the masculine gaze. In the remaining sections of this chapter
we shall see that Revelation similarly explores representations of gender
through the mode of sexual viewing. Less decorously perhaps, but no less
potently than "that glance" of Leukippe, the book was able both to sum-
mon the penetration grid and to mitigate its effects.

The Feminized Lamb

In view of the vehemently anti-Roman stance taken by Revelation, it can be surprising to discover parallels in this text with tenets of Augustan morality. After all, this same book repeatedly attacks Rome—"the great city that rules over the kings of the earth"—and its empire (Rev. 17:18), and depicts the city as the prostitute Babylon, a "haunt of demons" fated to drown in a lake of fire. Yet, the book's stirring, final vision of the "promised land," the utopian New Jerusalem that descends from the heavens, holds much in common with the moralizing propaganda of Augustus. Granted, evidence in the Apocalypse for such a parallel is cast in negative terms: the persons barred entrance to the New Jerusalem, those who remain outside its walls, include "cowards, the faithless, the polluted, the murderers, promiscuous persons, sorcerers, idolaters, and all liars" (Rev. 21:8).[49] We should also note that the book denies paradise to at least one courtesan, Babylon, with her serpentine consort.

Likewise, Augustan Rome sought to proscribe immoral behavior within the sacred boundaries of the city. Augustus, like emperors after him, was deeply interested in establishing a pattern of morality and piety for imperial subjects to emulate. Augustus further reinforced his moral example with legislation aimed at forcing members of aristocratic families to marry; the emperor felt no apprehension, it seems, about "legislating morality." In Augustan Rome, adulterers were subject to legal action and capital punishment under the *lex Iulia de adulteriis* of 18 B.C.E., while the activities of the "infamous," including prostitutes and actors, who "lied for a living," were repeatedly restricted.[50] Magicians and sorcerers, as Ramsay MacMullen discusses, were perennially numbered among the "enemies of the Roman order."[51]

In this context, "cowards" are the most detestable moral failures on Revelation's list. Such persons were viewed to be hopeless degenerates, unable to control their fears, lacking in *virtus*. Cowardice, then, symbolized the "un-Roman," smacking of softness, passivity, and effeminacy, all obstacles to hurdle in the tireless pursuit of masculine self-mastery. An opposition commonly invoked during this period pitted Roman bravery against Greek *mollitia* ("softness") in everything from warfare to literary style.[52] Martial mocks a Corinthian's "effeminate" appearance, while Cicero highlights Roman moral superiority over Greeks.[53] To separate out "morality" from "manliness" in this context is unhelpful. Revelation glorifies the art of war and employs a vocabulary of manly achievement: it counts among the blessed a potent army of 144,000 and promises "to everyone who conquers (τῷ νικῶντι), I will give permission to eat from the tree of life that is in the paradise of God" (Rev. 2:7). Revelation, like Rome, seems to be enamored of virility.[54]

But this is only part of the apocalyptic story, and, as we have seen, only part of the story of masculinity under the emperors. Like Barton's gladiator, the "Lamb standing as if slain" (ἀρνίον ἐστηκὸς ὡς ἐσφαγμένον; Rev. 5:6) seems to contradict an ideal of manliness based on domination.[55] For some scholars, the symbol of the slain Lamb is evidence that nascent Christianity was "able to sublimate and highly differentiate itself from the socio-cultural world outside."[56] Even were we to grant this claim, it would not be able to explain the conflict internal to the text: not between "sublimated Christianity" and the "Roman Hellenistic world," but between the meek Lamb and, say, the destruction of Babylon, where seeds of aggression flower. Against this textual backdrop, the Lamb seems out of place. The Lamb seems weak and compromised when it first appears in the heavenly throne room, its posture bearing witness to the death of the crucified Christ. Parts of the animal's anatomy counter its apparent impotence: the horns of the slaughtered Lamb represent authority and might, the kind of power symbolized by another member of the animal kingdom, the lion.[57] The association of might is also made by the narrative dialogue, in which a heavenly elder identifies the creature as the conquering "Lion of the tribe of Judah" (Rev. 5:5). But the honor and authority it is assigned—it alone has the strength to open the scroll (Rev. 5:5)—stand at odds with its physical bearing.[58]

If we relate the Lamb to the penetration grid, it applies great pressure to this structure, for the authority that Revelation invests in the Lamb is linked here at least to the portrayal of a pierced body. Indeed, following the elder's introduction, the chapter accents the passivity of the Lamb, effectively feminizing the character. The Lamb's open wounds inspire song in the diverse members of the heavenly court: "You were slaughtered (ἐσφάγης) and by your blood you ransomed God's saints," they sing, "worthy is the lamb that was slaughtered" (Rev. 5:9, 12).[59] The participles are different—πεφονευμένη in the romance, ἐσφαγμένον in Revelation—but Lycaenion's speech to Daphnis includes the same imagery. As Lycaenion's violated Chloe lies in a pool of blood, so too the violence inflicted upon the Lamb leaves broken skin.[60] This is not to suggest that Revelation portrays the Lamb's sufferings as rape; rather, I intend to highlight the similar manner in which passivity and femininity are connoted and aligned in these passages: through the display of a bloody body. Yet, as Lycaenion's description does not, Revelation's account of the Lamb's appearance frames the passive body of the Lamb with expressions of mastery and self-control. Even as the narrator is overcome with emotion, "weeping bitterly," the Lamb hobbles forth to take the scroll, receive worship, and open the seals (Rev. 5:4–6:1).

This is not the only chapter in Revelation to dwell on the Lamb's bleeding body. Indications of fleshly fissures precede and follow this appearance of the Lamb: the book's first chapter, for example, follows a reference to "Jesus Christ, the faithful witness . . . [who] freed us from our sins by his blood" with an allusion to Daniel 7:13: "Look! He is coming with the clouds; every eye will see him; even those who pierced (ἐξεκέντησαν) him" (Rev. 1:7). And, after a brief account of a war in heaven between the angel Michael and the "ancient serpent," John hears a heavenly voice announce, "But they have conquered him by the blood of the Lamb" (Rev. 12:11). But Revelation 5 provides the fullest description of the creature: the penetrated Lamb, its bleeding body, comes into focus most clearly at this moment. On one hand, the repeated attention the text calls to the Lamb's open wounds seems to reproduce the scheme we have already encountered in the narrations of Chloe and Photis, a mode of representation that reveals far more about masculine desire than about "women." At the same time, the various depictions of Chloe and Photis, in different ways, called into question the stability of the invasive, "masculine gaze." Likewise, the passive body of the powerful Lamb disrupts the penetration grid.

That the Lamb of Revelation suggests a significant reworking of traditional concepts has been noted before: "Precisely by juxtaposing these contrasting images [i.e., of the passover Lamb and the Lion of Judah], John forges a symbol of conquest by sacrificial death, which is essentially a new symbol."[61] What I would emphasize, by contrast, is that John's "symbol" parallels in striking ways other figures of masculinity to be found in the texts and institutions of the Roman Empire, which all traded on the capacity of viewing relations to problematize masculinity. In this context, as the figure of the gladiator suggests, the penetrated body could serve as a site of self-mastery and, hence, as a model of masculinity. At the same time, the display of passive flesh, in all of its forms, remained, first and foremost, seductive and could guide the viewer away from masculinity, leaving one's clothing of self-control in tatters. By indulging himself with Photis, Lucius takes his first step toward becoming an ass; the spectator at the arena, taking in the shows, becomes part of the spectacle.

Was the Lamb, also, dangerously seductive for the audience of Revelation? Answering this question in full is part of the agenda of the next chapter. Now I wish to turn to a second moment in Revelation that catches the Lamb in a set of viewing relations. By contrast with its first appearance, the Lamb is later presented exclusively as the bearer of the gaze. Nevertheless, the body of the Lamb, as presented in Revelation 5, is not entirely erased from view, but lingers in the narrative as a sign of its eternally fragmented masculinity.

Arrested Masculinity

Unlike scholars who have attempted to find in Revelation a manifesto of societal change, with the Lamb serving as the chief dissident, Stephen Moore's recent consideration of masculinity in Revelation makes a sustained attempt to ground the text in the Roman Empire. For Moore, Revelation modifies or, more precisely, reformulates Roman conceptions of masculinity: the book defends "passive resistance as a legitimate masculine stance."[62] Yet, I wonder if this nuanced proposal about masculinity in the Apocalypse remains part of a long line of scholarship that separates the book from the culture of the Roman Empire. To summarize this view: if the book at all mimes aspects of this culture, it is only "window dressing"; Revelation's ambitions and objectives ought to be understood as subversive, even revolutionary.[63] Such evaluations naturally alight on the Lamb as a symbolic rejection of societal values: in a world that idealizes domination, the broken Lamb portends a reversal of the status quo.

Rather than crystallizing a "legitimate masculine stance" over against an ideal of virility, Revelation, in my reading, raises questions about what counts as masculinity under the Roman Empire. To support this contention, I wish to turn now to an episode that portrays the Lamb as a supremely active figure. In a disquieting angelic decree, the Lamb is described as presiding over the eternal agonies of the doomed: "Those who worship the beast and its image, and receive a mark on their foreheads or on their hands . . . will be tormented with fire and sulfur in the presence of the holy angels and in the presence of the Lamb" (ἐνώπιον τοῦ ἀρνίου; Rev. 14:9–10).[64] This episode has caused commentators no little consternation: is it possible that this book celebrates, revels in, the woes of the wicked? Some have argued vehemently against an affirmative response to this question, despite evidence to the contrary gathered from contemporary apocalypses.[65] 4 Ezra's account of judgment day, for example, includes this prediction:

> Then the pit of torment shall appear, and opposite it shall be the place of rest; and the furnace of Hell shall be disclosed and opposite it the Paradise of delight. Then the Most High will say to the nations that have been raised from the dead, "Look now, and understand whom you have denied, whom you have not served, whose commandments you have despised! Look on this side and on that; here are delight and rest, and there are fire and torments!" (4 Ezra 7:36)[66]

Later Christian writers, too, indulge in the apocalyptic gaze: the previous chapter noted Tertullian and the rapture that filled his heart when he imagines the suffering of Roman governors on judgment day.[67] In Moore's words, these texts picture "a spectacle calculated to fill [the onlookers] with grim satisfaction, or outright delight, since it manifests the Divine Sovereign's impartial justice and implacable hatred of sin."[68]

The remainder of chapter 14 supports Moore's interpretation: "And the smoke of their torment goes up forever and ever. There is no rest day or night for those beast-worshippers and for anyone who receives the mark of its name" (Rev. 14:11). A punishment of Foucauldian proportions awaits the beast's followers: the condemned announce their guilt in the number pressed into their flesh; and their bodies, tossed about in the flames, testify to the truth of the divine judgment found against them.[69] The episode concludes by describing the scene "as a call for the endurance of the saints, those who keep the commandments of God and hold fast to the faith of Jesus" (Rev. 14:12). The followers of God and the Lamb are expected to find comfort in this graphic display: it is a promise that the wicked will indeed be held accountable for rejecting the powers of heaven.

As I noted earlier, this kind of disciplinary moment, which exposes to view the sufferings inflicted upon the condemned body, was central to the Roman arena, and recognized to be integral to the development of manliness. Thomas Wiedemann has observed, "it was meant to be part of the Roman character to be able to watch the bloodshed of the arena."[70] The younger Pliny, in an encomium to Trajan, praises the production of the imperial *editor*: "Then there was seen a spectacle neither feeble nor dissolute nor likely to soften and break the manly spirit (*nec quod animos virorum molliret et frangeret*), but one to rouse them to beautiful wounds and scorn for death (*ad pulchra vulnera contempumque mortis accenderet*), when even in the bodies of slaves and criminals the love of praise and the desire for victory was visible."[71] Pliny here seems to draw a distinction between the audience and the "entertainment." The observers might find inspiration to "beautiful wounds"—the trophies collected by the Roman soldier in the field of battle—by watching slaves and criminals die. A "manly spirit" of domination was also on display in other forms of spectacle. An infamous episode in *The Golden Ass* tells how Lucius-turned-ass was to be a participant in the infliction of bestiality upon a woman accused of murder. Before the show could be held, however, the ass, suspecting that he likewise would meet with death after the event, runs away.[72] Community-sanctioned violence often included various forms of sexual assault, against men as well as women. In Lucian's satire *The Passing of Peregrinus*, an anonymous witness at the immolation of Peregrinus stands up to testify against the character of the self-styled "Proteus": "as soon as he came of age, was taken in adultery in Armenia and got a sound thrashing (πολλὰς πληγὰς ἔλαβεν) . . . with a radish stopping up his vent" (ῥαφανῖδι τὴν πυγὴν βεβυσμένος).[73] For his adulterous indiscretion, Peregrinus is systematically emasculated: his accusers twice penetrate his body, first with beatings and then with a vegetable.

Against this backdrop, the episode of divine punishment in Rev. 14:9–10 reveals more than a mere vengeful streak in the Lamb. Like Peregrinus, the followers of the beast, "those who receive a mark (χάραγμα) on their foreheads or on their hands," are penetrated. No radishes exist in Revelation; instead, before the torment begins the followers of the beast bear the signs of penetration, their flesh stamped by the mark of the beast.[74] The sulfur inflicted on these bodies also suggests puncture: as David E. Aune observes, sulfur was widely viewed as an effective weapon in battle "because it stuck to the body," melting away the skin.[75] Later the narrative again details compromised corporeality in the vision of the seven bowls: "So the first angel went and poured his bowl on the earth, and a foul and painful sore came on those who had the mark of the beast and who worshiped its image" (Rev. 16:2). The cumulative effect of this imagery, reflecting the grid of a dominating masculinity, is to present the bodies of the condemned as perforated. "Here is a call for the endurance of the saints" (Rev. 14:12; cf. 13:10), states John, after relating what he glimpsed in the Lamb's arena of torture. Having watched the horror that follows, it is clear that the audience of saints has been asked to endure multiple scenes of abject violence against flesh.

But it is not only fleshly torments or tattoos that bring these bodies into submission; after all, others in the book are marked. In close proximity to the account of the Lamb's torture chamber, the book describes the armies of God: 144,000 strong led by the Lamb who receive a "seal" (σφραγίς) on their foreheads that bears the names of the Lamb and of the Lamb's father (Rev. 14:1–2; see also 7:3–8). Both "brand" and "seal" suggest sympathy, support, and even ownership in this book: those branded by the beast belong to the beast, those sealed by the Lamb follow the Lamb. This initial relation of power, though, is superseded by a different one that takes shape under the watchful, commanding gaze of the Lamb. The number "666" signals not only allegiance to the Lamb's enemies, but also the defeat and submission of the beast, a constellation of meanings written deep in the skin of these docile bodies.

The most significant change in this scene, however, lies not in the shifting connotations of bodily impressions but in the figure of the Lamb. To state the obvious: the "tables have turned." The Lamb presides over the punishment delivered to these prisoners, a scene that transforms the creature from passive victim to active "victimizer," a gendered mutation, under the penetration grid, from effeminacy to masculinity. Here the penetrated Lamb is an agent of discipline, issuing divine retribution to its former persecutors, "even those who pierced him" on the cross (Rev. 1:7). The structure of power remains stable, the hierarchy of domination and submission intact, but the actors have changed positions: those bound to suffer have learned too late that the Lamb does not play "children's games." In chapter 5, authority is ascribed to the Lamb through symbol or acclamation; in chapters 6–8, the Lamb breaks the seals of the divine scroll. Here, however, the Lamb dominates, controlling and executing the demise of the enemies of God. As if to confirm the truth of the Lamb's manly bearing, the creature's posture goes unmentioned in this episode; and the gash in the Lamb's body, so apparent earlier, disappears from view.

The Lamb's active character stems largely from its position as bearer (and no longer as object) of the gaze. In chapter 5, the Lamb manifests, partially, at least, "to-be-looked-at-ness," its presence reduced seemingly to a collection of wounds. Here the shape of the Lamb's body receives no narrative attention, while the tortured bodies writhe unobstructed before the audience. Viewing in the book is a relation of power, and visual activity constructs diverse subject positions for the characters. The followers of the beast are made vulnerable by looking at the creature's amazing appearance and deeds; others, like the heavenly spectators that cheer on the

destruction of Babylon, participate in an exercise of domination. In Rev.
14:9–10, the Lamb shows no signs of succumbing to the θαῦμα that overwhelms other viewers; rather, the Lamb's gaze, like the fire and sulfur
bubbling in the background, serves as an instrument of torture.

The Lamb, we should recall, possesses not a pair of but seven eyes, a
grotesque exaggeration that calls attention to the creature's ocular capa-
bilities. Optical power, especially when associated with the judgment of
God, typically implies invasion in the Apocalypse. Much of the biblical literature portrays an "all-seeing God": the book of Psalms, for example,
states simply, "His eyes behold, his gaze examines humankind" (Ps.
11:4b). The Letter to the Hebrews suggests further the penetrative force
of the divine: "The word of God is living and active, sharper than any two-
edged sword, piercing (διϊκνούμενος) until it divides soul from spirit,
joints from marrow; it is able to judge the thoughts and intentions of the
heart. And before him no creature is hidden, but all are naked and laid
bare to the eyes of the one to whom we must render an account (Heb.
4:12–13)." So too Revelation explicitly acknowledges the sharp gaze of divine and semi-divine figures: not in the Lamb, but in a different member
of the heavenly retinue, "one like a son of man" who possesses "eyes of
fire." Alluding to Jer. 17:10a, this figure announces: "I am the one who
searches mind and hearts (ἐγώ εἰμι ὁ ἐραυνῶν νεφροὺς καὶ καρδίας), and
I will give to each of you as your works deserve" (Rev. 2:23).[76] Like the
Fourth Gospel's Jesus, who reveals to the Samaritan woman her past, the
deputies of God in Revelation possess a piercing, "second sight."

A close connection exists, then, between vision and penetration in
Revelation, making the scene of punishment in Rev. 14:9–10 a site of *sexual* and *gender* significance. Two examples, drawn from the world of early
Christian female martyrs, illuminate the play of gender in a public setting
and bring into clear focus the potency of the Lamb's masculine gaze.[77] In
the first case, the *Acts of Paul and Thecla*, Paul's young female disciple
finds herself in deep trouble for rejecting a marriage proposition. To punish this nonconformity, the governor sentences Thecla to expire in the
arena. And while the account never diminishes the threat posed by the
wild beasts she faces there, a different danger rivals the mere prospect of
death. After throwing herself into a pool containing fierce seals, the narrator notes, "and there was round her a cloud of fire so that the beasts
could neither touch her nor could she be seen naked."[78] The fiery cloud
deflects the beasts that seek to devour her; it also keeps her safe from ex-

posure to the eyes of her captors. Here a miraculous barrier deflects the penetrative gaze of the narrative characters and the extratextual audience, obstructing the view until the governor relents, calls off the execution, and provides Thecla with clothes to wear.

That the narrative seeks to thwart the gaze of the spectators indicates the connections forged in the arena between sexuality, penetration, and viewing. The second case, the *Martyrdom of Perpetua and Felicitas*, by contrast, shows little or no interest in protecting the martyr's body from death or desire, even though the account makes explicit the same associations implied by Thecla's fiery cloud.[79] Like Thecla, Perpetua and Felicitas are thrown into an arena, and like Thecla, they are stripped of clothing. Their nakedness is momentary, however, for the sight of Felicitas, "fresh from childbirth with the milk still dripping from her breasts," horrifies the crowd and both women are dressed again in tunics.[80] Then the restless spectators—having already watched bears and other beasts maul the women's male companions—request that the execution of the Christians proceed in front of them. "But the mob asked for their bodies [of the martyrs] be brought out into the open," says the narrator, "so that their eyes could share (*comites*) the killing as the sword entered (*penetranti*) their flesh." Perpetua is thus executed, and though she dies a noble death, it is the corporeality of the martyr that lingers: "she screamed as she was struck on the bone."[81] What is implied by Pliny's comments on the masculine inspiration of Trajan's games rises forcefully to the surface in this ghastly episode: the gaze of the crowd becomes a murderous weapon, effortlessly penetrating the body of the female martyr.[82]

Body, punishment, and the spectator: these three elements combine to unveil Rev. 14:9–10 as a crucible for masculinity. The Lamb here realizes manhood by exacting divine vengeance upon the bodies of the condemned. This is not the erotic "intercourse of bodies" described in *Leukippe and Kleitophon*, but it is, nevertheless, sexual viewing, forcing the viewer and the viewed into a hierarchical structure of domination and submission, into the masculine gaze. The Lamb may not directly pierce its enemies, but the creature's set of seven eyes here invades the bodies of the damned even as the sulfur melts their skin.[83] Concomitantly, the Lamb seems to acquire bodily integrity: after this point, no mention is made of the Lamb "standing as if slain." By defeating and dominating the followers of the beast, the Lamb has transcended the threat of penetration. The flesh of the unrighteous remains exposed: "you are wretched, pitiable, poor, blind, and naked" (γυμνός), the "one like a son of man" warns the "lukewarm" Laodiceans (Rev. 3:17–18; cf. 16:5). But the flesh of the Lamb seems hidden from view: only the bodies of its foes burn ceaselessly before the audience. More Daphnis than Chloe now, the Lamb has applied an education in manly domination against the enemies of heaven.

In the wake of the Lamb's transformation, the imagery employed in the remainder of chapter 14 buttresses the creature's newly achieved masculinity, locating the Lamb in a setting of violent penetration. A pastiche of blood, death, and farm implements, the chapter continues to articulate the theme of God's wrath, "poured unmixed into the cup of his anger" (Rev. 14:10), introduced by the Lamb's torment of the ungodly followers of the beast.[84] First, "one like a son of man," he of the fiery, intrusive gaze, appears "with a golden crown on his head, and a sharp sickle (δρέπανον ὀξύ) in his hand!" (Rev. 14:14). On his heels follows a different character, an angel, "and he too had a sharp sickle" (Rev. 14:17). Both figures "reap the earth" with their sickles, but the grapes they toss into "the great wine press of the wrath of God" produce a great flow of blood, "high as a horse's bride, for a distance of about two hundred miles" (Rev. 14:20). Against a narrative background that valorizes the manly pursuit of domination in diverse forms—the book rails against cowards, urges conquest, idealizes war—it is difficult not to view these sickles and the deeds they accomplish in phallic terms.[85] The agents of God in Revelation conquer the world with piercing, agricultural instruments, like the "forked" voices outside the chamber of Daphnis and Chloe.

But no sooner have the brandishing sickles called attention to the Lamb's manhood than they begin to detract from it. While there is no doubt that the Lamb occupies a position of authority in the Apocalypse, the creature seems to exercise this authority as domination, to perform it as violent subjugation, only for a moment. By contrast, other righteous figures that execute the will of God are constantly engaged in waging war, in domination, in conquest. The two most prominent envoys of God in Revelation, "one like the son of humanity," and the "rider on the white horse," both "lead the charge," as it were, while the Lamb fades into the background, preserved from conflict. The "one like a son of man" has already been mentioned in this discussion. He first appears in all his splendor immediately following John's salutation, a seeming conflation of two figures in Daniel: the "Ancient of Days" (Dan. 7:9) and "the one like a son of man" (Dan. 7:13–14; 10). Revelation describes the physical attributes of the "one like a son of man" in lavish detail:

and in the midst of the lampstands I saw one like a Son of Man, clothed with a long robe and with a golden sash across his chest. His head and his hair were white as white wool, white as snow; his eyes were like a flame of fire, his feet were like burnished bronze, refined as in a furnace, and his voice was like the sound of many waters. (Rev. 1:13–15)

Rather than an objectified, passive body, this character embodies active destruction: "and from his mouth came a sharp, two-edged sword" (ῥομφαία δίστομος ὀξεῖα; Rev. 1:16).[86] The body of the "one like the son of man" evokes not submission but domination. Further, the figure "walks like a man" in the remainder of the narrative: he possesses a penetrating gaze, he reaps the earth with a sickle, and, in a highly disturbing scene, he throws "that woman Jezebel" onto a bed (Rev. 2:22).

The "rider on the white horse" similarly performs masculine deeds.[87] The audience encounters this figure in Revelation 19; he wears "a robe dipped in blood" and his body is marked—"he has a name inscribed that no one knows but himself" (Rev. 19:12)—and his thigh is revealed (Rev. 19:16).[88] In this scene, which most scholars agree is meant to depict the second coming of Christ, the messianic "parousia," the enemies of God fall before the sealed armies gathered earlier in the narrative (Rev. 7:3–8; 14:1–3). The war is over before it begins; the rider and his army utterly destroy their opponents. The details of the gruesome aftermath remain difficult to stomach: the two beasts of chapter 13 are captured and cast into "the lake of fire that burns with sulfur," while the beastly infantry, "those who had received the mark of the beast," are killed by the "white horseman," by "the sword that came from his mouth; and all the birds were gorged with their flesh" (Rev. 19:20–21).[89]

Two aspects of this passage deserve comment. First, this story plays out before the eyes of its audience the troubling saying found earlier: "If anyone is for captivity, to captivity he will go; if anyone with the sword is to be slain, he with the sword will be slain" (Rev. 13:10). While this passage is sometimes taken both as an indictment of warfare in the book and as a warning to the faithful about the suffering they must endure, the events of chapter 19 suggest that a proleptic purpose, too, lurks within this saying: the beasts become prisoners, and their followers are massacred by the sword.[90] Second, and more important for the present discussion, the masculinity of "the rider on the white horse" is palpably evident here. The armies that follow the rider stand far behind their leader, watching as he engages the hosts of hell with his "sharp sword" (ῥομπαία ὀξεῖα), striking them down; then, the rider who has vanquished the nations "will shepherd them with an iron rod" (ποιμανεῖ αὐτοὺς ἐν ῥάβδῳ σιδηρᾷ; Rev. 19:15). In commenting on this description, Moore makes a playful but salutary allusion to Freud: "sometimes a rod is just a rod."[91] In the penetration grid, however, a sword is never "just" a sword: penetration calls into existence the opposition between conqueror and conquered, domination and submission, masculine and feminine. When the audience peers at the rider's thigh, they see not the vulnerability of Perpetua's nakedness nor the open wounds of the Lamb, but a sharp, "double-edged" instrument that belongs to the "King of kings and Lord of lords" (Rev. 19:16).

Revelation's trilogy of messianic figures—the "one like a son of man," the "rider on the white horse," and the Lamb "standing as if slain"—share in the victory over the enemies of God and, to varying degrees, participate in the subjugation of heaven's opponents. At the same time, next to its more aggressive colleagues, the Lamb is a shrinking violet. Revelation 14:9–10 depicts the creature in a moment of visual domination, only then to *replace* the Lamb in successive chapters with its colleagues. Even before chapter 14 ends, it is the "son of humanity," wielding a sharp sickle, who reaps the earth and sheds blood. Later, in Revelation 19, the rider performs deeds initially associated with the Lamb. The Lamb stands on Mount Zion as the leader of a chaste army of 144,000 (Rev. 14:1–5). Further, the *angelus interpres* tells John that the allies of the beast will make war on the Lamb, "and the Lamb will conquer them, for he is Lord of lords and King of kings" (Rev. 17:14); and earlier, in the heavenly throne room, the Lamb, an elder tells John, will be a "shepherd" (Rev. 7:17). Yet, when the battle is joined, the Lamb is nowhere to be found; rather, it is the rider, not the Lamb, who destroys the allies of the beast, and the rider, not the Lamb, who becomes a shepherd (Rev. 19:15).[92]

In relation to the penetration grid, then, the glimpse of the Lamb's manhood afforded by Revelation is fleeting; indeed, the Lamb's masculinity shows signs of arrested development. At the same time, the penetration grid is clearly not the only discourse of sexuality and gender at work in Revelation or in the Roman Empire generally. If it is unlikely that Longus's audience would have forgotten the visceral narration of Chloe's deflowering by the novel's conclusion, it is also unlikely that John's audience would have forgotten the gaping wounds of the Lamb, even though these details go unmentioned later in the book. In both texts, the penetration grid provides little help in deciphering the multiple representations of gender in play. What I have endeavored to expose, by juxtaposing the Lamb of chapter 5 with the Lamb of chapter 14, is a fault line in Revelation that was coextensive with the one running through the floors of amphitheaters throughout the ancient Mediterranean world. What counts as masculinity? What were the limits of masculinity? Rather than the firm earth of the penetration grid, unstable ground lay beneath the construction of gender in the texts and institutions of the Roman Empire.

Not a Wedding

The most telling evidence of the Lamb's "arrested masculinity" is an absence: the wedding of the Lamb is announced, but the wedding itself does not materialize, nor is the marriage consummated. As the world comes to an end in the Apocalypse, the Lamb, in an unlikely parallel to Daphnis, appears to be headed for the signal performance of manhood: "for the marriage of the Lamb has come, and his bride has made herself ready" (Rev. 19:7).[93] Like the conclusion to *Daphnis and Chloe*, Revelation makes the wedding a public occasion. The witnesses are gathered, and they sing hymns, songs chanted—it is tempting to suggest—"with harsh, rough voices, as though they were breaking up the earth with forks, not singing a wedding hymn."[94] This is, after all, the same congregation that had exulted over the systematic destruction of Babylon: "Hallelujah! The smoke goes up from her forever and ever!" (Rev. 19:30). Unlike Longus's conclusion, however, the wedding of the Lamb remains deferred, or, at least, hidden from view. A wedding feast is announced (Rev. 19:9), and the bride, "the holy city, the new Jerusalem, coming down out of heaven from God, prepared as a bride adorned for her husband" (Rev. 21:2), arrives, but this is all merely a prelude to the Lamb's royal role in the New Jerusalem, where it sits on the throne of God (Rev. 22:1). Where are the nuptials?

If Winkler is right, that Longus calls into question the erotic protocols of a phallocentric society in his romance, this critique is predicated upon the novel's allusion to sexual violence in the "not a wedding song" that frames the education of Chloe, which points up the refusal of this society to countenance "children's games." The same form of critique cannot be found in Revelation: there is no wedding. Still, like *Daphnis and Chloe*, Revelation makes use of a body, depicted "as if slain," to explore the boundaries of a masculinity based on the domination of others, even if such domination is not altogether rejected. The significance of the Lamb's "arrested masculinity" and the feminization of Rome will provide the substance of the next chapter, which seeks to bring together patterns of imperial and sexual viewing that so far have been treated separately.

Here, by way of summary, I wish to return briefly to the television advertisement for the U.S. Marine Corps that inspired the introductory meditation on penetration and spectacle, themes that, this chapter has suggested, appear in a similar fashion in the literature and institutions of the Roman Empire, Revelation included. An instructive difference surfaces if we compare the televised scene to the scenes of torment and destruction narrated by the Apocalypse. The commercial invites the television audience to participate in themes of self-mastery and masculinity, but its astounding special effects allow only a vicarious experience for the viewer. One simply does not encounter towering monsters in the streets of modern America.

The Lamb of the Apocalypse, in contrast, models a performance of masculinity—"spectatorship"—to which readers of this text have direct and immediate access. Against the background of public displays of punishment and death, Revelation's depiction of torture in chapter 14 channels the book into cultural currents that flowed throughout the Roman Empire. The audience sees the Lamb focus its gaze on those who suffer fiery torments: "and the smoke of their torment goes up forever and ever" (Rev. 14:9–10). After studying the Lamb's example, the audience is then able to view the suffering for themselves: they witness the rape of Babylon (Rev. 17–18); they watch as the armies of the beast are killed and their flesh fed to the birds (Rev. 19:20–21); and they are the spectators when the beast is "tormented day and night" (Rev. 20:10) and when the smoke of the burning Rome "goes up forever and ever" (Rev. 19:3). But, as the next chapter will explore, more than the Lamb as spectator, it is the Lamb as spectacle that takes center stage in the book, a broken body that quickened the hearts of John's audience and of later generations of ancient Christians.

5

Wherever the Lamb Goes

A REMARKABLE ECPHRASIS SURFACES IN THE middle of the Greek romance *Leukippe and Kleitophon*, one of the "purple passages" for which the genre is famous.[1] After a shipwreck, the novel's two leading characters float to shore in Pelousion, where they enter the temple of Zeus Kasios. There Leukippe and Kleitophon view a painting, evidently a diptych, in the rear of the temple.[2] It depicts the myths of Andromeda and Prometheus, which, suggests the narrator Kleitophon, contain several parallels. Both Andromeda and Prometheus are chained to rocks; both are pursued by wild beasts; and both are rescued by Argive heroes. Turning first to Andromeda, Kleitophon describes what he sees: "The girl was placed in a recess of the rock which was just her size. . . . Looking more closely at her installed in her shelter, you might surmise from her beauty that she was a new and unusual icon, but the sight of her chains and the approaching monster would rather call to mind an improvised grave." Kleitophon lingers further over the shackled body of Andromeda. He observes "a curious blend of beauty and terror" on the face of Andromeda; the painter, remarks Kleitophon, "had enhanced her beauty with this touch of lovely fear." Throughout, Andromeda remains completely passive—"her arms were spread against the rock, bound above her head by a manacle bolted in the stone"—a point that receives no little attention. Her extremities seem already to have succumbed to fate: "the color of her arms shaded from pure white to livid, and her fingers looked dead." Finally, the sheer fabric of Andromeda's garment, "delicately woven, like spiderweb more than sheep's wool, or the airy threads that Indian women draw from the trees and weave into silk," leaves little to the imagination. Fettered, quiescent, and virtually naked, Andromeda awaits destiny.

Two more figures occupy this portion of the painting, a sea monster and Perseus. Ready to strike, the sea monster appears opposite Andromeda.[3] Only the beast's head surfaces above the water, its "long and large" jaws spread wide. Opposite the creature, Perseus is poised to thwart the monster's attack. The hero hovers above the beast: in his left hand he holds the Gorgon's head; with his right hand Perseus grasps a weapon of war:

His right [hand] was armed with a twin-bladed implement, a scythe and a sword in one (εἰς δρέπανον καὶ ξίφος ἐσχισμένῳ). The single hilt contains a blade that divides halfway along its extent—one part narrows to a straight tip, the other is curved; the one element begins and ends as a sword, the other is bent into a sinister sickle, so a single maneuver can produce both a deadly lunge and a lethal slash.

The ecphrasis renders the painting in narrative form, but offers no further explication: Kleitophon says only that "This was Andromeda's drama" (τῆς Ἀνδρομέδας δρᾶμα).[4]

A scene of even greater despair appears in the other painting. Here Prometheus is bound by iron and stone, and his body is exposed to attacks from the air: "A bird is enjoying a visceral banquet. Poised at mid-incision, his beak continues to cut an already gaping wound, deeply inserted in the gastrointestinal trench, excavating for the liver, which the artist has slightly revealed through the abdominal slit. His talons grip the giant's thigh."[5] The danger and violation that only threaten Andromeda—she will, of course, be rescued by Perseus—materialize on the flesh of Prometheus. He writhes in pain and "signs of his agony are etched on his face: arching brows, lips twisted to expose the teeth." Salvation is near: Herakles, bow drawn, arrow aimed at the pecking eagle, stands ready to rescue Prometheus from further torment. Yet, Kleitophon observes, Prometheus's expression betrays conflicted emotions; he is "torn by hope and despair: he stares both at his own wound and at Herakles, wanting to concentrate on the hero but forced to focus at least half of his attention on his own agony."

Here I wish to read this ecphrasis alongside Revelation 12, a chapter that includes a "woman clothed with the sun" and an account of the cosmic battle that rages between the forces of heaven and "a great red dragon."[6] John relates that the dragon "with seven heads and ten horns" pursued the pregnant "sun woman," standing nearby, "so that he might devour her child as soon as it was born" (Rev. 12:1–4). After the boy is born, he is "snatched away to God and to his throne" before the dragon can eat him, and the woman flees to the wilderness for safety (Rev. 12:5–6).

In the midst of her escape from the dragon, a war explodes in heaven. Michael, the leader of the heavenly host, successfully expels the dragon, "that ancient serpent, who is called the Devil and Satan" (Rev. 12:9). Satan again regards the woman and attempts to drown her—"from his mouth poured water like a river after the woman"—but the earth rescues the "sun woman" from death: "it [i.e., the earth] opened its mouth and swallowed the river that the dragon had poured from his mouth" (Rev. 12:16). Child saved and his plot foiled, the dragon, "angry (ὠργίσθη) at the woman," stalks off to fight with the rest of the woman's children, "those who keep the commandments of God and hold the testimony of Jesus" (Rev. 12:17). The tale of the dragon's defeat thus at once explains why the forces of evil have aligned themselves against the faithful and gestures ahead to God's victory and to the lake of fire that awaits the ancient serpent (Rev. 20:10).

Greek mythology has been summoned before to investigate the apocalyptic vision of the war between dragon and woman. Adela Yarbro Collins, for example, famously outlines the contours of a "combat myth" in Revelation, and argues that the story of Python waiting to devour Apollo after Leto's delivery provides the most apt background to chapter 12.[7] That a mythic type underlies the conflict has been widely accepted by scholars, and I make no challenge to this consensus. I will not argue, for instance, that the myths of Andromeda and Prometheus provide a better background to Revelation than the Apollo story. Nor will I attempt to pursue the striking but isolated parallels between the ecphrasis and images elsewhere in the Apocalypse: Perseus wields a sickle (cf. Rev. 14:14, 17); a beast emerges from the sea (cf. Rev. 13:1); and birds gorge themselves on flesh (cf. Rev. 19:21). My interest here is not typological.

Rather, I suggest that these descriptive passages similarly position the viewing audience. Like Kleitophon's ecphrasis, the "sun woman" and the dragon, characters that David Aune labels "the *dramatis personae*" of chapter 12, lead us back into fields of sexuality and gender that we traversed in the previous chapter.[8] When Revelation's episode is paired with the romance's ecphrasis, we see that both texts lay open the bodies of Andromeda, Prometheus, and Revelation's sun woman to the threat of penetration. The heroes of the painting meanwhile engage the menacing beasts armed with their own sharp, piercing instruments—arrows, swords, sickles—all, evidently, weapons of conquest. For Jaś Elsner, the effect of the romance's scene is obvious: "Clearly, Andromeda is 'spread out against the rock' as an erotic vision to satisfy and excite the viewer of the picture and the reader of the text."[9] In Revelation's episode, by comparison, eroticism seems entirely absent.[10]

Still, Revelation's scene does holds something in common with diptych: both have much to tell us about ancient gender and viewing, and about the complexities of both. It should be noted, for example, that while there are three bodies under the threat of penetration, this threat is realized only upon the tortured Prometheus, a moment highly suggestive of the vulnerability of masculinity under the Roman Empire: the flesh of Prometheus is hardly impenetrable. Further, a comparison of Andromeda and the sun woman reveals important differences between the two figures. Elsner is probably right to emphasize sexual titillation in Andromeda's portrayal: as Kate Cooper has observed, "the charm of a heroine's fear" was a device employed often by ancient authors.[11] The sun woman, by contrast, is neither charming nor fearful. As Virginia Burrus has recently emphasized, she is protected by the wilderness, which "cradles her body, both feeding her and swallowing what she cannot when the dragon floods her with her vomit."[12] Further, if Elsner's defenseless Andromeda is objectified as the sublime victim, the description of the sun woman, which includes a jolting, mundane detail—her physical hunger—resists this kind of objectification.[13]

Before taking leave of these passages, I wish to comment further on spectacle and viewing in these scenes. On one hand, the passages call attention to monsters—serpentine, avian, or otherwise—all destined for destruction. Perseus will free Andromeda; Heracles will destroy the bird; and the dragon and his minions will be defeated by the angel Michael and the hosts of heaven. Like the wonders of Phlegon's catalogue, these curiosities, we can safely assume, would have captivated ancient audiences. On the other hand, the description of Prometheus's sufferings cautions against drawing too sharp a line between monster and "man": beast and bound victim merge, and the audience is directed to consider the gaping, fleshly hole cut by the eagle's jagged beak. Entwined with the ferocious bird, the compromised Prometheus is in grave danger of being mistaken for the monstrous target. This problem we have encountered before: Domitian, a monster in Suetonius's narrative, is no less grotesque than the dwarf with whom he shares the imperial booth.

But the ecphrasis is not content to leave the pain of Prometheus as the only display. Prometheus is not only part of the spectacle, he is also a spectator, meeting with his own eyes the gaze of Herakles. Kleitophon's description goes on to bring to the surface an inner conflict: the stare of Prometheus is fractured, since the agony of his own body demands "at least half of his attention."[14] Janus-like, Prometheus must look in two directions at once, at other and at self. Is the gaze of the audience likewise fractured? Kleitophon, in a revealing comment, addresses the reader: so great is the palpable anguish of Prometheus, "You would have pitied the pain in this painting." Such pity is capable of overwhelming the spectator, so the audience must be on guard against the loss of self-control even as it absorbs the spectacle of the suffering Prometheus.

This chapter continues to investigate the ways that Revelation's spectacles similarly complicate viewing relations. In previous chapters, viewing was considered under the rubrics of "imperial" and "sexual": here I allow these categories to overlap in order to make plain the pressure that this narrative applies to the audience, forcing it, like Prometheus, to scrutinize simultaneously the monstrous other and the self that threatens to come undone. The distant menace of Babylon and the beasts, the nearby danger of Jezebel and the synagogue of Satan: these figures are constituted by specific techniques of exhibition, producing knowledge about the menacing other for the audience of Revelation. At the same time, I shall contend, the Apocalypse exploits the danger of getting too close to monsters, giving the audience an opportunity to demonstrate self-control and thus "making men" out of extratextual spectators. As the principal object of desire in Revelation, the Lamb remains central to this process: problem and potential, the Lamb suspends the rules of the penetration grid, enabling the audience, paradoxically, to achieve masculinity.

First we undertake a survey of recent scholarship on the role that signs of femininity played in the maintenance of ancient masculinity, and then turn to a consideration of 4 Maccabees and the *Martyrs of Lyons*.[15] The martyrs of 4 Maccabees and of the *Martyrs of Lyons*, we shall see, throw into relief Revelation's own "martyrs," textual witnesses who chase down the monsters that roam across the pages of the book. Looking over the shoulders of these witnesses, the extratextual audience is able to conquer the enemies of heaven and to "follow the Lamb wherever he goes."[16]

Between Men

In "Why Is Diotima a Woman?" David M. Halperin addresses gender and sexuality in Plato's *Symposium*, focusing on the role of "Diotima," ostensibly a female acquaintance from the childhood past of Socrates.[17] According to Socrates, it was Diotima who taught him about sexual desire. Rather than the unidirectional pleasure of Athenian pederasty, Diotima championed a reciprocal model in which both partners experience homoerotic desire and grow philosophically. This brings us to what prompted Halperin's question: "Why did Plato select a woman to initiate Socrates into the mysteries of a male, homoerotic desire?" Some scholars have suggested that had Socrates's mentor been an older, wiser male, then his argument—that is, the argument of "Diotima"—would have been compromised by the traditional model of pederastic engagement. Others have noted that Diotima's femininity adds the weight of objectivity to the proposal of Socrates. A female mentor, Diotima has nothing to gain by training the boy Socrates in sexual desire, since the pleasure of pederasty is unavailable to her. Because of this, she seems to be an impartial judge; thus Diotima proves herself to be a peerless source of knowledge about male desire. Halperin sums up the scholarship in this way: "It takes a woman to reveal men to themselves."

Dissatisfied with these answers, Halperin presses the question further, seeking out other reasons for Diotima's presence in the *Symposium*. Female procreation is key: "She speaks of *erôs* as no male does, striking a previously unsounded 'feminine' note and drawing on a previously untapped source of 'feminine' erotic and reproductive experience."[18] Yet, in spite of the positive valuation of pregnancy and attendant images of "femininity"—menstruation and breast-feeding, for example—Halperin continues to wonder if Diotima is a "real person" or a "pure device," an instrument for fashioning masculinity in the narrative. That the latter is likely is indicated in several places: particularly revealing is the performance of Socrates himself, whose transmission of "Diotima's view of *erôs*" consistently anticipates and undercuts the views of the other participants in the *Symposium*. As Halperin observes, in these exchanges Plato appears "to expose 'Diotima' as an effect of Socratic ventriloquism."[19] That is to say, even if Diotima were a real person from Socrates's past, the philosopher has manufactured a useful vessel from which to retrieve his own knowledge of erotics for the occasion.

So we find that the answer to Halperin's initial question—"why is Diotima a woman?"—arises ultimately from male concerns about male self-representation. Rather than represent authentic female experience, the chilling assessment offered by Halperin is that "Diotima's femininity is illusory—a projection of male fantasy, a symbolic language employed by men in order to explain themselves and their desires to one another across the generations."[20] Diotima, then, is not the villified other, but an "alternative male identity whose constant accessibility to men lends men a fullness and totality that enables them to dispense (supposedly) with otherness altogether."[21] Not a figure but a figurine, Diotima generates erotic energies for a congregation of males: she is passed "between men" for the sake of masculinity.[22]

The literature of formative Judaism and ancient Christianity is replete with examples of this kind of "traffic in women." According to Howard Eilberg-Schwartz, ancient Jewish monotheism wrote into its literature strategies for mediating between a masculine God and his masculine children.[23] Traditions about Moses, for example, call attention to his feminized position as a "go-between." To hide his shining, terrifying countenance after the revelation at Sinai, Moses dons a veil (Exod. 34:29–35). The article of clothing suggests that the leader of the Israelites encountered more than just "holy ground" in congress with the deity: "It points to his transformation into the intimate of God," argues Eilberg-Schwartz. Attempts to hide God's maleness in biblical traditions indicate ambivalence: if God is male, then Israel is "unmanned" through the covenant struck with the deity.[24] A divine Father leaves nothing for his "procreating sons" to do.

There were techniques, however, for mitigating the anxiety triggered by God's masculinity and for putting masculinity back within the grasp of his sons. A common means, avers Eilberg-Schwartz, was to hide God's sex, as when God reveals only his back to Moses (Exod. 33:23). A different method resembles what Halperin discovers in the *Symposium*: Eilberg-Schwartz finds that the workings of femininity within the Jewish Scriptures derive from concerns for Israel's masculinity. Divine wisdom, for example, is represented in feminine terms.[25] While some scholars have argued that the image reflects the advisory role played by women in the household, Eilberg-Schwartz ascertains a figural dimension to the character's femininity, much like that of Socrates's Diotima. Throughout Proverbs, Wisdom is received, ingested, and used by men: "The mouth of the righteous brings forth Wisdom" (Prov. 10:31). Thus, concludes Eilberg-Schwartz, "the image of Wisdom as a female intervenes in and thereby mediates between a male God and a male Israelite whose mutual encounter may threaten to become too intimate."[26] Like Diotima, Wisdom was a male projection; unlike Diotima, Wisdom moved in a sphere in which male-female sexual imagery remained normative. Wisdom's femininity was meant to dampen (proscribed) homoerotic flashes that might otherwise spark between a male deity and his male subjects.

Wisdom also surfaced in ancient Christianity, but the tropic quality of femininity was most apparent there in the practice of "thinking with women."[27] Peter Brown develops this theme in a masterful investigation of Christian asceticism, arguing that the accounts of female heroism in the apocryphal Acts, such as that of Thecla in the *Acts of Paul and Thecla*, reveal little about the real lives of women in Christian circles but much about the "imaginative economy of the Church." Because women, it was generally believed, were not anchored to society as firmly as men, the heroine served well the purposes of Christian men. As early Christian men became more insistent on erecting boundaries between nascent Christianity and neighboring paganism, stories about women "crossing the line" from the company of pagans to the company of Christians and vice versa helped to make clear the differences between the two "societies." A male Christian hero, according to Brown, could not have been imagined passing from one to the other without at the same time compromising his "allegiance" to his Christian brothers.

Other scholars of early Christianity have responded enthusiastically to the implications of Brown's study.[28] An important treatment by Virginia Burrus considers the fourth-century versions of the martyrdom of Agnes ascribed to Ambrose and Prudentius. Burrus exploits the different accounts of "reading Agnes" to show how masculine desire projects itself onto a female body. In both cases, the episode includes a girl who is more "manly" than her opponents: she stares down the threat of sexual assault and apostasy, and dies with both her virginity and her faith intact, as it were. For Ambrose, Agnes is another Thecla; for the Spanish author Prudentius, Agnes is a second Polyxena, the Trojan heroine who escapes rape by dying sacrificially on the tomb of Achilles.[29] And it is Prudentius's account that most clearly reveals masculine desire. Here Agnes's manly courage is contained, feminized by her death; she dies, as Nicole Loraux would affirm, "like a woman."[30] Indeed, Prudentius layers Agnes's death with sexual meanings. The girl taunts her captor: "A man who pleases me at last! So I don't delay his hot desires, I shall greet his blade's full length within my breast."[31] But the sword does not enter Agnes's breast, an act that would grant her a "virile" death. The blade instead decapitates the girl, a tragic parallel to Euripides's portrayal of Polyxena, who offers both breast and throat to her slayer but is finally killed, like Agnes, by a blow to the neck. In the end, as Burrus notes, "the Christian Agnes must be wrenched back into her womanly place."[32] Her request to die a virile death denied, Agnes's body suffers a violent end by a sword rendered phallic. "Wrenching back into place" ensures "feminine" docility and enacts masculinity for the Christian audience to whom the Spanish poet speaks.

To these discussions I wish to add Maud Gleason's treatment of techniques of masculinity in the public orations of the Second Sophistic in *Making Men*. In this "entirely masculine context," an other had to be supplied, and, as modeled by the popular Favorinus, this absence of "real women" could be exploited through a calculated display of effeminacy.[33] Rather than adopting a "hyper-masculine performance style," Favorinus transgressed traditional protocols of manliness, as his rival Polemo, a skillful physiognomist, carefully and disdainfully described: "His voice was like a woman's, and likewise his extremeties and other bodily parts were uniformly soft."[34] Charges of effeminacy were common in the arena of public speaking, but what is remarkable about Favorinus was his capacity for absorbing such accusations and still "pulling it off," delighting audiences in Rome and Ephesus. We return, then, to the lure of risk in Roman society: as Gleason observes, "There was something manly, after all, about taking risks—even the risk of being called effeminate."[35] Like a gladiator, Favorinus "manfully" led his audience to the edges of masculinity and beyond, strategically entering the territory of the other for the sake of self-presentation.[36]

Different texts, different contexts, but a similarity nonetheless: ancient moments "between men" often involved femininity. Depicted as other or "pseudo-Other," the figure of "woman" (or "effeminacy") pointed away from itself and towards the production of masculinity. The demands of the patriarchal order do not automatically translate into blatant misogyny; on the contrary, figures such as Agnes were hailed as heroes. What I wish to emphasize is that this abundance of techniques for appropriating femininity, for "thinking with women," reveals the depth of the problem that masculinity presented under the Roman Empire. To bring the discussion of gender back into the framework of viewing, we now turn to 4 Maccabees and the *Martyrs of Lyons*, texts in which dwell beasts, straining bodies, and spectators.

A Most Terrible Drama

"In the summer of 177," begins W. H. C. Frend's *Martyrdom and Perse-cution in the Early Church*, "there took place at Lyons one of the most terrible dramas in the history of the early Church."[37] Terrible, indeed: ac-cording to the *Martyrs of Lyons*, angry pagan mobs called for the torture and slaughter of their Christian neighbors. The "fortunate"—Christians who could present proof of Roman citizenship—were beheaded, those less so were mauled by animals and made to roast in a hot iron seat.[38] The persecution transpired before crowds of onlookers: in the amphitheater the Christian woman Blandina was hanged on a post and exposed to wild beasts. To describe the carnage the letter adopts the idiom of the Roman shows, calling it "a spectacle to the world (θέαμα γενόμενοι τῷ κόσμῳ) to replace the varied entertainment of the gladiatorial combat."[39] And, as Frend's opening remark on the "terrible drama" illustrates, two millennia later the account continues to evoke a sense of theater. Composed in the first or second centuries C.E., 4 Maccabees, a gory "remembrance" of the deaths of Jews during the anti-Jewish persecution of the second-century B.C.E. Seleucid king, Antiochus Epiphanes, similarly incorporated ele-ments of spectacle.[40] As we shall see, among other shared elements, both accounts will call attention to the effects of bloody spectacles on the au-dience, reminding us again of the risks of viewing.[41]

The pagan citizens of Lyons, it seems, had had enough of Christian-ity. According to the letter that documents the episode, embedded in the fourth-century *Historia ecclesiastica* of Eusebius, men, women, and chil-dren associated with the new religion were rounded up and tortured.[42] Addressed to "our brothers in Asia and Phrygia," the letter records the es-calating hostilities unleashed against Gallic Christians. At first Christians face ostracism: "we were not only shut out of the baths and the public square, but they forbade any of us to be seen in any public place whatso-ever."[43] Then they suffer imprisonment and torture: a crazed horde, an "enraged mob" (ἠγριωμένῳ πλήθει), inflict upon the Christians "abuse, blows, stoning, and imprisonment." In the midst of the persecution, in-dividual Christians rise to stand in the spotlight. There is, for example, the deacon Sanctus, who receives the blows "with extraordinary, superhuman strength." But it is Blandina, a woman, whose endurance of pain makes her the star of this account: "like a noble athlete" (ὡς γενναῖος ἀθλητὴς) she arrives at a victory by outlasting the men who torture her day and night. In the end, the corpses of the Christians are incinerated, the ashes spread in the river Rhône.[44]

4 Maccabees announces itself not as an account of martyrdom but as a philosophical exercise: "Our inquiry, accordingly, is whether reason is sovereign over the emotions" (εἰ αὐτοκράτωρ ἐστιν τῶν παθῶν ὁ λογισμός; 4 Macc. 1:13). The book's account of the martyrdom of the elderly Eleazar, an anonymous mother, and her seven sons, mounts, as many scholars have observed, a Stoic argument to demonstrate that "reason rules over those emotions that hinder temperance" (σωφροσύνης), passions such as "rage, fear, and pain" (θυμοῦ τε καὶ φόβου καὶ πόνου; 4 Macc. 1:4, 6).[45] By pursuing this agenda, 4 Maccabees conforms to societal expectations: temperance, or self-mastery, as we have seen, was a cardinal virtue, while the loss of control was a sign of effeminacy. But in some ways 4 Maccabees marks a significant disruption of conventional notions, undermining the penetration grid, as Stephen Moore and Janice Capel Anderson have observed: "The irony of 4 Maccabees is that a feeble, flabby old man, a gaggle of boys, and an elderly woman—all persons who should rate low on the hierarchical continuum of (masterful) masculinity and (mastered) femininity—triumph over someone [i.e., Antiochus] who should be at the privileged end of the continuum."[46] In 4 Maccabees, the manliness of Antiochus, "an arrogant and terrible man" (4 Macc. 4:15), withers as he is defeated in a contest of wills. His victorious opponents are the Jewish martyrs whom he attempts to torture into apostasy: they resist and the king suffers humiliation before the eyes of his army, gathered to watch the "shows" (4 Macc. 5:2; see also 15:20). The same irony surfaces in the accomplishments of Blandina, "through whom Christ proved that the things that men think cheap, ugly, and contemptuous are deemed worthy of glory before God." The persecutors exhaust themselves, but Blandina continues to proclaim, " 'I am a Christian; we do nothing to be ashamed of'."[47]

If we look closer at the accounts, a representational pattern of monsters and bodies emerges. First, the monsters: a moment before the youngest of the seven sons meets his maker, the boy labels Antiochus "a most savage beast" (θηριωδέστατε), an accusation substantiated by the ghastly deaths of his brothers (4 Macc. 12:13). The *Martyrs of Lyons* has its own brutes: here the amphitheater houses animals that ravage the Christians; but the most fearsome creatures are the "wild and barbarous tribes" (ἄγρια καὶ βάρβαρα φῦλα) . . . stirred up by the wild Beast" (ἀγρίου θηρὸς).[48] While the account indicts the emperor for allowing the savagery to occur, the immediate protagonist is the throng of pagans, maddened by "bestial anger" (τὴν ὀργὴν κατάπερ θηρίου), a desperate foe that desecrates the remains of the martyrs; so too, Antiochus exhibits a "bestial anger" through the cruel torments he orders for the martyrs. Indeed, it is the pronounced emphasis on the reason and self-mastery of the Jewish martyrs that makes the deficiencies of Antiochus conspicuous. Repeatedly, the narrator and the martyrs remark on the king's unbridled tyranny. Not reason but boiling "passions"—the emotions that bubble unchecked from the cauldron of the king's soul—rule the ruler, making Antiochus impotent on more than one level: "We six boys have paralyzed (καταλελύκαμεν) your tyranny. Since you have not been able to persuade us to change our mind or to force us to eat defiling foods, is not this your downfall?" (4 Macc. 11:24–25). The king's overwhelming defeat at the hands of the martyrs, as Moore and Anderson suggest, amounts to a feminization of Antiochus.[49] The king thus falls in two contests—an external one with the martyrs, and an internal battle with the passions—and the Jewish martyrs win.

Antiochus's monstrous nature expresses itself in unmanly traits, but neither 4 Maccabees nor the *Martyrs of Lyons* associates aspects of femininity only with beastly opponents. Rather, powerful figures in both texts inhabit flesh penetrated with unparalleled violence, greater even than the pains of Prometheus. Some of the Christians in Lyons and Vienne suffer decapitation, a speedy death, but others, like Blandina, must "run the gauntlet": "After the scourges, the animals, and the hot griddle, she was at last tossed into a net and exposed to a bull."[50] The bulk of 4 Maccabees likewise records the many torments pressed upon the bodies of the tyrant's victims.[51] To Eleazar the king first expresses a respect for the man's age, but when the elderly priest refuses to eat "unlawful" meat, he is stripped, bound, flogged, and burned (4 Macc. 6). Still, Eleazar remains courageous, and construes his suffering as vicarious: "I am dying in burning torments for the sake of the law. Be merciful to your people, and let our punishment suffice for them" (4 Macc. 6:27–28).[52] Antiochus's servants employ similar devices on the flesh of the seven brothers. The king orders a display of the instruments of torture—"wheels and joint dislocators, racks and hooks and catapults and iron claws and wedges and bellows"—in front of the prisoners "so as to persuade them out of fear to eat defiling foods" (4 Macc. 6:12–13). "Be afraid, young fellows," whispers Antiochus (4 Macc. 6:14).

But were we to conclude the investigation here, we would ignore other significant configurations of gender in the two accounts. One in particular resembles not only Prometheus but also Andromeda. The final death in 4 Maccabees belongs to the mother of the seven boys, a woman "more powerful than a man" (4 Macc. 16:14), who coaches her sons throughout the contest with Antiochus.[53] She exhorts them to remember the trials faced by their forefathers—the near sacrifice of Isaac by Abraham, Daniel in the lions' den, and the fiery furnace of Hananiah, Azariah, and Mishael—and to use these examples for inspiration.[54] Like Andromeda, the mother's body is preserved from penetration in a passage that establishes her own agency: "she threw herself into the flames so that no one might touch her body" (4 Macc. 17:1). Yet, even when the account seems to have stripped the Jewish mother of the frailties of femininity, 4 Maccabees problematizes masculinity. Having lectured her sons, the unnamed mother reveals herself to be an "ideal" woman, chaste and subject to her husband in all things: "I was a pure virgin and did not go outside my father's house . . . in the time of my maturity I remained with my husband" (4 Macc. 18:7–9). As Moore and Anderson have argued, the mother's body is preserved but not before she is domesticated.[55]

The Christian body of Blandina, by contrast, does not escape the piercing tools of her enemies, and yet her tale also relates to masculinity.[56] In a famous moment of transformation, the flesh of Blandina is hidden from view. For when the pagans choose to hang Blandina on a post as bait for wild animals, her pose invites comparison to the crucifixion of Jesus: indeed, in a subtle shift, the text proceeds beyond comparison to identification: "She seemed to hang there in the form of a cross," and her compatriots, "with their physical eyes . . . saw in the person of their sister him who was crucified for them."[57] A body remains, but now it is the body of Christ that covers Blandina. Otherness is thickly layered here: Blandina's feminized and "athletic" flesh is covered with the penetrated form of Christ, and together both have become more powerful, more capable of enduring torments: "The pagans themselves admitted that no woman had ever suffered so much in their experience."[58] Blandina has transcended the penetration grid, attaining a level of suffering that places her—"no woman"—in a category by herself.

Monsters, penetration, and body are woven into the fabric of the Jewish and Christian martyr accounts, showcasing a spectrum of representation that erupts with particular force in three figures: the raging beast, the threatened but preserved body, and the penetrated body. Masculinity is not only produced and problematized in these representations: in two moments in particular, it is also part of the relation of viewing to which the texts attend. After the curtains have closed on the gory drama of 4 Maccabees, a defeated Antiochus testifies to his own submission, directing his soldiers to watch the martyrs: "For the tyrant Antiochus, when he saw the manliness (τὴν ἀνδρείαν) of their virtue and their endurance under the torturers, proclaimed them to his soldiers as an example (εἰς ὑπόδειγμα) for their own endurance, and this made them manly (ἀνδρείους) and courageous for infantry battle and seige, and he ravaged and conquered (ἐνίκησεν) all his enemies" (4 Macc. 17:23–24). On the sidelines, the vanquished beast is still able to recognize manliness when he sees it, and so do his soldiers. In the *Martyrs of Lyons*, Blandina's spectacle on the post "aroused much desire (πολλὴν προθυμίαν) in those who were undergoing their ordeal."[59] Both moments register the impact of spectacle on the viewer: in 4 Maccabees, "manliness" is the result; in the *Martyrs of Lyons*, a positive "desire," a firm resolve, is generated in the persecuted onlookers.

We have seen, though, that the products of spectacle were not always welcome, and the spectator exposed himself or herself to danger by watching the shows. "Thinking with martyrs," like any ancient spectacle, was not a dispassionate exercise, but a risky enterprise, bringing the audience to the brink of anomie. The monsters of Revelation, to which we return in the remainder of this chapter, presented ancient Christians with the same hazards.

Let the Wicked Be Wicked Still

The book of Revelation is first cited as an authoritative Christian text, as "Scripture," in the *Martyrs of Lyons*.[60] After describing the "bestial anger" of the pagan horde, the author of the letter states "that both the governor and the populace showed towards us the same undeserved hatred that the Scriptures (ἡ γραφή) might be fulfilled: 'Let the wicked be wicked still and the righteous perform righteousness'."[61] The statement the letter borrows from Revelation is a bridge that spans the distance between the supernatural and natural worlds, helping the *Martyrs of Lyons* to cast the actions of angry pagans as a tactical move in the ongoing, cosmic warfare between good and evil. As we have seen, the account employs a specific mechanism for keeping the persecutors "wicked still," representing pagans as monsters incited by the "wild Beast," Satan himself.

The Apocalypse similarly holds Satan responsible for the persecution that the "still righteous" face; at the same time, it also represents Satan in ways that denote submission, just as the leviathan opposite Andromeda surfaces to become a target for Perseus's arrow. In Revelation 12, the defeated dragon storms off to torment the children of the "sun woman" after his plans are foiled. Now that we have encountered Antiochus in 4 Maccabees, we can better appreciate the significance of the dragon's "anger" in this episode (Rev. 12:17).[62] The dragon's impotence is announced both in the defeat he suffers against external opponents and in the rage that overtakes him.[63] The dragon yields to internal passions, presenting Satan, "that ancient serpent," not only as a beast but as a creature completely "unmanned." The dragon, of course, is not the only character to fall short of manliness in Revelation: his deputies, the beasts from the sea and the land, Babylon, and a myriad affiliated characters sound effeminate tones. Below I continue the analysis of evil characters begun in Chapter 3: the dominating gaze of empire, exemplified there by Phlegon's Rome, merges here with a dominating sexual gaze. The monsters of Revelation appear as "women" who exhibit little self-control and sustain penetrative injuries, making the characters not female but feminized. Further, this section will suggest that John's sectarian rivals, who appear in the first three epistolary chapters, suffer the same fate as Rome in the Apocalypse. To "let the wicked be wicked still" in the Apocalypse is to "allow" the opponents of God—Babylon and the Beasts, Jezebel and the synagogue of Satan—to reveal their monstrous femininity. Revelation thus stages for the audience its own "terrible drama," roasting the skin of beasts and prostitutes alike in fires of divine judgment.

BABYLON AND THE BEASTS

The prostitute Babylon has long been a focus of discussion about female imagery in Revelation.[64] There is no clear scholarly consensus about the meanings conveyed through this figure.[65] For Tina Pippin, Babylon is a perverse admixture of "death and desire," of one piece with the resentment of women voiced throughout the text: "The Apocalypse is not a tale for women. The misogyny which underlies this narrative is extreme."[66]

Others insist, however, that such a reading misunderstands John's intentions, which were to exhort Christians to proper behavior, not to debase women.[67] Most recently, Barbara Rossing has maintained that the real reasons for the negative portrayal of Babylon are illuminated through an ancient "two-women *topos*," a rhetorical structure employed when the "primary subject of argument is not real women but some unrelated topic such as politics, morality, careers, or even entertainment." Rossing repeatedly disconnects the portrayal of Babylon from sexual meanings.[68]

The argument is novel, but Rossing's interpretive standpoint, which distances the figure of Babylon from "real" women, follows in the wake of similar approaches to the apocalyptic prostitute. For Adela Yarbro Collins, Babylon indicates not so much John's hatred of women but a "parody of the honor given Roma: her supporters worship a prostitute, not a goddess!"[69] This is not to say that Collins absolves John's use of violence; on the contrary, in a Jungian moment, she observes that a "critical reading" of Revelation "leads to an awareness of how the text is flawed by the darker side of the author's human nature."[70] But even this recognition is marked by an asterisk because it issues from a "critical reading," a modern approach that ultimately reveals not John's world but our own presuppositions. Likewise Elizabeth Schüssler Fiorenza contends that female stereotypes in Revelation stand out because "we have become conscious of androcentric language."[71] Self-reflexivity here seems to correspond to a mythic moment in which the "knowledge of good and evil" is first attained. John's prelapsarian images of women belong to categories other than gender and sexuality: the female in Revelation is "merely" rhetorical.[72]

Here I hold together these disparate views, seeking out not John's misogynist personality but textual effects: femininity is indeed a trope in the Apocalypse, a rhetorical device that nevertheless operates within the parameters of ancient discourses of sexuality and gender, sometimes confirming the penetration grid, sometimes disrupting it. As J. Cheryl Exum argues, rhetoric has actual consequences: "That metaphoric violence against women is not the same as real violence is true, but . . . it is nonetheless harmful to real women because it shapes perceptions of reality and of gender relations for men and for women."[73] The "metaphoric" violence visited upon Babylon—strange and exotic, a curiosity that inspires amazement in the spectators who encounter "her"—produced knowledge in imperial and sexual registers. Thrown outside the boundaries of civilization into the "wilderness" (Rev. 17:3), Babylon's rise and fall signals both the threat of disorder that lurks on the edges of the earth and the marginality of the danger it presents: under the commanding gaze of heaven lies the "orientalized" Babylon. A further expression of imperial viewing occurs in the close association the book forms between Babylon and the beast of chapter 13: "And I saw a woman sitting on a scarlet beast that was full of blasphemous names, and it had seven heads and ten horns" (Rev. 17:3).[74] The representation of Rome as a foreign, peripheral creature—like the unusual animal that dies in the arena even as barbarians fall to the armies of Rome in the marble of the Aphrodisian Sebasteion—is coupled seamlessly with the depiction of Rome as a wanton prostitute. Beast and Babylon, monsters both, must together submit to the divine will.

At the same time, the narration of Babylon riding the beast delivers to the audience figures of femininity, exposed for penetration. The two figures, for example, share a lack of self-mastery.[75] Images of excess attach themselves to the prostitute Babylon. A second Antiochus, Babylon has collected her own martyrs and reclines "drunk with the blood of the saints and the blood of the witnesses (τῶν μαρτύρων) to Jesus" (Rev. 17:6). Like Daniel's Syrian "horn" that speaks arrogantly against God (Dan. 7:20), the beast upon which Babylon sits is "full of blasphemous names," and the cup she holds is a "golden cup full of abominations" (Rev. 17:4). The jewels that Babylon wears around her neck sparkle like the torture devices of the enraged Antiochus.[76]

The wealth amassed by Babylon provides further evidence of a yielding to unmanly passions. Clothed in purple and scarlet, and adorned with gold and jewels and pearls (Rev. 17:4), Babylon has reaped the benefits of commercial profits, and those with whom she transacts business also enjoy success: "the merchants of the earth have grown rich from the power of her luxury" (Rev. 18:3, 12). Their "cargo" (Rev. 18:12) and the wealth of Babylon are prominent topics in the dirge that rings out during the great conflagration: "Alas, alas, the great city, clothed in fine linen, in purple and scarlet, adorned with gold . . . For in one hour all this wealth has been laid waste" (Rev. 18:17). While the book briefly condemns the "business practices" of imperial Rome, reporting that the merchants trade in "human bodies and souls" (Rev. 18:13), the prostitute's lust for wealth points directly to immorality and uncontrolled passions.[77] As Robert Royalty observes in his compelling study of wealth imagery in the Apocalypse: "The insatiable appetite of Babylon for wealth and luxury portrayed in Revelation 18 is a symptom of complete depravity."[78] Her business partners ascribed authority to Babylon because of her immense resources, but the same feature attests to an absence of self-control: the glory of Babylon makes her unmanly.

The beasts of chapter 13, like Babylon, possess an illusory authority, and like Babylon, the self-mastery of the beasts is in question. The hubris of the beast—who "was given a mouth uttering haughty and blasphemous words" (Rev. 13:5)—like the boasts of Antiochus (4 Macc. 4:15), is only the first indication of unmanliness. The beast possesses no authority of his own, but inherits everything from the dragon (Rev. 13:2; cf. 2 Thess. 2:9). The second beast, the beast from the land that establishes a cult to the first beast, is no more than a puppet: "it spoke like a dragon" (Rev. 13:11). The coercive force that the beasts exert is short-lived (Rev. 13:15–17): hunters for the moment, the beasts will soon become the hunted. Both beasts are thus depicted as no more than slaves to an impotent, unmanly master: recall that the angry dragon was unable to attack the object of his fury—the "sun woman"—and hence was forced to make war on others who will later watch as the dragon and his minions are "tormented day and night forever and ever" (Rev. 12:17, 20:10).

The latent unmanliness of Babylon and the femininity of the beasts is made apparent in Revelation's gruesome scenes of judgment. The eternal damnation of the beasts reflects the ceaseless, "day and night" anguish endured by their marked followers (Rev. 20:10; cf. 14:11). Prior to being tossed into the lake, the beasts and their armies are defeated by the white rider, from whose mouth "comes a sharp sword with which to strike down the nations" and in whose hand is a "rod of iron" (Rev. 19:14). Here the coarse skin of the beasts lies exposed before the weapons of the righteous. The penetration of the prostitute Babylon is more pronounced, undertaken by "the kings of the earth, who committed fornication and lived in luxury with her" (Rev. 18:9). Further, in a decidedly troubling passage, the *angelus interpres* promises John that the flesh of Babylon will be consumed by the kings who have "lived in luxury" with her and by the beast that carries her: "And the ten horns that you saw, they and the beast will hate the whore; they will make her desolate and naked; they will devour her flesh and burn her up with fire" (Rev. 17:16). Stripped and laid bare, the body of Babylon is not only foreign, exotic, and monstrous: it is also consumed. To suggest, as does Rossing, that the imagery indicates not sexual violence but the "laying waste" of a city overlooks the mapping of the landscape in imperial *and* sexual terms.[79] The conquest of Babylon remains at all times the rape of a prostitute.

This spectacle of destruction not only "unmans" Babylon and the beasts, it also, as noted earlier, overwhelms and unmans some narrative spectators. From a heavenly vantage point, the chorus of righteous viewers sings approvingly of Babylon's demise. At the same time, the sight of Babylon's smoke throws into relief the effeminacy of the audience on the ground in three overlapping ways. First, the sexual incontinence of "the kings of the earth, who committed fornication and lived in luxury with her" (Rev. 18:9; 17:2, 18:3) unveils their lack of self-control: "illicit sex" (πορνεία) inevitably produced *mollitia* or μαλάκος.[80] Second, the kings and the merchants weep, wail, and mourn (Rev. 18:9, 11, 15). This is not just "sympathy for the devil," but the kind of emotional response associated with unmanliness in 4 Maccabees. The self-mastered Jewish mother neither cries nor turns away as she watches her sons expire: "When the firstborn breathed his last, it did not turn you aside . . . nor did you weep when you looked at the eyes of each one in his tortures gazing boldly at the same agonies" (4 Macc. 15:18–20). The royal partners of Babylon, by contrast, cannot contain themselves, giving in to their sorrow. Third, these groups of viewers "stand far off, in fear of her torment" (διὰ τὸν φόβον; Rev. 8:9, 15). While the manly Jewish mother remains steadfastly near her sons during their trials, the cowardly kings and merchants keep their distance. Blinking back tears as Babylon and the beasts enter into everlasting punishment, these viewers have come undone; watching the monster, they have become monstrous.

JEZEBEL AND THE SYNAGOGUE OF SATAN

Weak and effeminate, Babylon's royal onlookers stand in sharp contrast to the book's exemplary spectator: "Jesus Christ, the faithful witness (ὁ μάρτυς), the firstborn of the dead and the ruler of the kings of the earth" (Rev. 1:5; see also 3:14). A virile viewer, the messianic observer wields power with a "rod of iron," a sword from his mouth, and a piercing stare, a gaze he directs at Babylon and at John's opponents in the seven epistles. He is surrounded in this book by a gallery of martyrs, who have experienced defeat only to be transformed into victorious witnesses: "I also saw the souls of those who had been beheaded for their testimony to Jesus. . . . They came to life and reigned with Christ for a thousand years" (Rev. 20:4). The martyrs who cry out for vengeance (Rev. 6:9–10), the great multitude who "have come out of the great ordeal" to rejoice over Babylon's burning (Rev. 19:1–3, 6; see also Rev. 7:9, 14), all realize triumph through spectatorship. Even the army of "the rider on the horse," which engages the beastly armies, watches as the beasts "were thrown alive into the lake of fire . . . and the rest were killed by the sword of the rider on the horse" (Rev. 19:20–21). In so doing, these witnesses follow the example set out by the "one like a human son," the "faithful witness" (Rev. 3:14) of the letters to the seven churches whose "fiery" eyes both uncover and discipline the sectarian rivals of John.

Revelation 1–3, like the letters of Paul, indicates that diverse groups of Christians inhabited the towns of Asia Minor when John wrote his book. Little can be determined historically about the sects: everything about them is presented from John's perspective, a perspective that assigns to each group a name that connotes wickedness and resistance to the commandments of God.[81] The churches in Ephesus and Pergamum, for example, contend with the works of the Nicolaitans; and while the Ephesian Christians "hate the works of the Nicolaitans" (Rev. 2:6), the Pergamene Christians remain divided on the issue: "you also have some who hold to the teaching of the Nicolaitans" (Rev. 2:15). Precisely what the Nicolaitans practiced is unknown, but the book effectively "biblicizes" the group, associating them with Balaam (Num. 22–24, 31:16), a figure from the Hebrew Bible whose advice led Israel into apostasy. By the time Revelation is penned, the "error of Balaam" stands for a range of moral and religious failings, including idolatry and sexual immorality (Rev. 2:14).[82] The Ephesians also have unveiled "false" prophets, Christians seemingly unrelated to the Nicolaitans.[83] But of the labels associated with John's competition in the letters, the one that draws the deepest condemnation involves "that woman Jezebel," who is active in Thyatira (Rev. 3:20). Here I shall point out the manner in which this depiction employs the same strategies of representation found later in Revelation, as well as argue that the "synagogue of Satan" serves as the beastly counterpart to the femininity that Jezebel embodies.[84]

The threat that Jezebel poses to John and his audience is defused as soon as it materializes. Like Babylon, the figure of Jezebel is a cipher in Revelation.[85] But where Babylon stands for an external enemy, Rome and its empire, "Jezebel" stands for an internal, sectarian opponent. Her name, like the name of Babylon, denotes an infamous antagonist from Israel's biblical past: the archenemy of the prophet Elijah, Jezebel used her marriage to Ahab to persuade the king to promote the worship of Baal in the Northern Kingdom of Israel. Jezebel, for her sins, dies in a ghastly manner: thrown out of a window, her corpse is devoured by dogs in Jezreel (see 1 Kings 21:24 and 2 Kings 9:30–37). Revelation's "Jezebel," which Adela Yarbro Collins labels a biblical "antitype," "calls herself a prophet" and, like the Nicolaitans, participates in sexual immorality and eats foods offered to idols (Rev. 2:20). She has been given time "to repent," but refuses to do so; hence, she must be punished. And the book metes out a form of discipline that reinforces the femininity that Jezebel shares with Babylon: "Beware, I am throwing her on a bed (κλίνην), and those who commit adultery with her I am throwing into great distress, unless they repent of her doings; and I will strike her children dead. And all the churches will know that I am the one who searches minds and hearts" (Rev. 2:22–23). As Greg Carey has observed, "bed" held diverse connotations in antiquity: it "was a place where people slept, ate (in the sense of a dining couch), had sex, recovered from illness and died."[86] And while most scholars tend to emphasize the connotation of "sick bed," I am inclined, following Carey, to see in the passage a tapestry of humiliation. The constellation of images produces an astonishing scene of submission and penetration: the sexual immorality of Jezebel is punished on a bed by the "fiery eyes" of the "one who searches minds and hearts." Domination is on display, even if the threat of sexual assault remains veiled behind a surface suggestion of illness.

In the description of Jezebel, the book produces a powerless Andromeda. But this is not the only other to surface in the letters: a monster crawls across the chapters, too. The identification of the members of the "synagogue of Satan" has long been a contested issue for scholars. For some, the persons "who say that they are Jews and are not" must be Jews in Asia Minor who have created problems for the Christians living there.[87] For others, this label designates a Christian sect that has adopted Jewish practices to benefit from exemptions granted to Jews under the Roman Empire.[88] What has been overlooked in these debates is the beastly character that this representation assigns to these opponents, whomever they are. This group plays the "sea-monster" to Jezebel's Andromeda, gathered under the authority of "that ancient serpent, who is called the Devil and Satan" (Rev. 12:9; 20:2). The monster will soon make his presence felt among the Christians in Smyrna—"Beware, the devil is about to throw some of you into prison" (Rev. 2:9)—but, by the time the letter goes out to the church in Philadelphia, the defeat of the beast is certain: "I will make those of the synagogue of Satan who say they are Jews and are not, but are lying—I will make them come and bow down before your feet"

(Rev. 3:9). Those who follow the "faithful witness" share in his royal status, reigning high above the monsters slithering and groveling below.

SEVEN MISSILES, SEVEN MISSIVES

In the portentous year 1984 Jacques Derrida published "No Apocalypse, Not Now (Full Speed Ahead, Seven Missiles, Seven Missives)," a meditation in part on the rhetoric of "deterrence" that paradoxically buttresses the stockpiling of nuclear weapons.[89] While Derrida is disinterested in the sectarian conflicts that animated Christianity in first-century Asia Minor, the parenthetical "seven missiles, seven missives" is suggestive for understanding what is at stake in Revelation. The book's unrelenting attacks from every angle, it would seem, on the empire of Rome gives support to scholars who wish to classify the text as "resistance literature." Yet, to do so is to emphasize one agenda at the expense of another: John also takes aim at his rivals — opponents that met with success in attracting members from the seer's churches — textually taming them in short order through representations that "orientalize" and feminize.[90] The discourse of domination in chapters 17–18, which casts Babylon "into the wilderness" and then into torment, is likewise in force against Jezebel, the Nicolaitans, and the synagogue of Satan.

The seven letters, Derrida's "seven missiles," aim not only at discrediting John's opponents but at destroying them.[91] To conquer the foes of heaven, both Babylon and Jezebel, is the task given to the readers of the letters: "To the one who conquers I will give a place with me on my throne, just as I myself conquered and sat down with my Father on his throne" (Rev. 3:21). Conquest is a constant refrain in these letters (Rev. 2:7, 11, 17, 26, 3:12, 21), as the book urges its audience to stay clear of the "error of Balaam" and the "beguiling" ways of "Jezebel." And to this mix John adds a beastly menace that lurks in the "synagogues" that must also be subdued. To search for the "real" Jezebel or to decide whether the persons in Smyrna and Philadelphia are Jews or Christian sectarians is to neglect to consider the effects that *can* be measured. The Apocalypse offers its readers a choice: they can be "wretched . . . and naked (Rev. 3:17)," like Babylon in Revelation 17, or they can throw Jezebel on a bed; the members of the audience can defeat the dragon and receive obeisance from its followers, or they can become monstrous by learning "the deep things of Satan" (Rev. 2:25).

Surrounded by moments of imperial and sexual domination in the Apocalypse, the Lamb, the principal object of desire in the book, can be overlooked. This section, for the most part, has been organized around episodes in which viewing is performed aggressively by righteous characters, seemingly in accord with protocols supplied by the penetration grid. Viewing in this book, however, is relational, not unidirectional, as the shattered kings, merchants, and shipmasters remind us. In the final section of the chapter, I shall continue to highlight the risks associated with viewing, extending this theme to the relation at play between the audience and the beloved Lamb.

Thinking with the Lamb

Blandina plays a starring role in the *Martyrs of Lyons*, but a strong supporting cast shares the stage with her. The "superhuman" Sanctus has already been mentioned, but the tone of the letter is struck by the actions of Vettius Epagathus, a young man and a "distinguished person" (ἐπίσημος) who demands a hearing for the Christians.[92] The request goes ungranted and Epagathus himself comes under scrutiny: "the prefect . . . asked him if he too were a Christian. When he admitted he was in the clearest tones, he too was accepted into the ranks of the martyrs." A stirring example of "voluntary martyrdom," Epagathus contrasts sharply with other "stillborn" Christians who are "untrained, unprepared, and weak, unable to bear the strain of a great conflict." Unlike these "stillborn" Christians, Epagathus shares the unwavering attitude of the valiant martyrs who make "a full confession of their testimony with much desire" (μετὰ πάσης προθυμίας). Of the steadfast young man, the writer proclaims: "He was and is a true disciple of Christ, following the Lamb wherever he goes." Like the "desire" produced in the martyrs at the sight of Blandina, Epagathus is possessed of a strong will because he has kept his eyes on the Lamb. Gazing at the Lamb, the letter confirms, produced passions, which, when properly channeled, controlled, could lead the viewer along the path of true discipleship.

Thus we return to the figure of the Lamb in Revelation, a character whose development was mapped in the previous chapter. Other scholars have suggested different models for making sense of the figure: David J. Halperin briefly comments on the Lamb's "progress" and proposes that the Lamb embarks on an "Oedipal" journey, from standing "slain" in front of the throne of God to sharing triumphantly the throne of God. For Halperin, the Lamb's achievement expresses "the theme of the son's struggling for and finally grasping a share of his father's power."[93] I suggest that the Lamb's ascent to the throne in the New Jerusalem conveyed different meanings in the context of the Roman Empire. Not only a performance of power, the ascent also fixes the Lamb as a spectacle, making the monster a focal point of desire for the audience, as the martyrdom of Epagathus attests.

The allusion the *Martyrs of Lyons* makes to Revelation's Lamb highlights the language and imagery that link the Apocalypse to ancient literature about martyrs, and the role played by the book in early Christian self-fashioning.[94] Among the early church fathers, Revelation typically entered the conversation as evidence for the imminent, thousand-year rule of the saints (Rev. 20:1–6).[95] Both Irenaeus and Justin Martyr support their "millennial" views by adducing evidence drawn from the Apocalpyse.[96] But the *Martyrs of Lyons* puts the Apocalypse to different use. Not only does Revelation "reveal" the beastly nature of the pagan persecutors, it also provides Christians with their own monster upon which to rest their gaze. Significantly, it is not the viewing Lamb of Revelation 14— a merciless judge that presides over the ceaseless torture of his enemies— but the *viewed* Lamb that surfaces in the account of the death of Epagathus.

As we have seen, the viewed Lamb is not easily "gendered": according to the penetration grid, the body of the Lamb is feminized, yet it is able to exercise power. To begin, we consider the setting for the Lamb's appearance in the conclusion of the Apocalypse, after the end of the world. An arresting vision, the New Jerusalem descends from the heavens, "prepared as a bride adorned for her husband," and brings the throne of God to earth (Rev. 21:2).[97] The bejeweled prostitute receives scorn for the wealth she hoards, but the riches of the "holy city Jerusalem" (Rev. 21:10; cf. 3:12), as Robert Royalty observes, are "the pure, aristocratic wealth of heaven."[98] A high wall surrounds it, "built of jasper," while the city itself is "pure gold, clear as glass" (Rev. 21:18). Even the twelve foundations are composed of precious gems: sapphire, emerald, amethyst (Rev. 21:20).[99] Such wealth, as Royalty further observes, possessed for John's ancient audience a positive, ethical dimension: "The moral appeal in these passages is that 'heavenly wealth' is permanent and incorruptible whereas earthly gold and possessions are corruptible and perishable."[100] According to

Royalty, the appeal of the New Jerusalem is related to an "ideology of wealth" current in the Roman world.

But other scholars have located the appeal of the city elsewhere. For example, some have argued that the New Jerusalem presents a political and economic system that differs markedly from that imposed by imperial Rome: the city, states J. Nelson Kraybill, "will be a lavish place that gives everyone equal access to resources of the earth. Roman imperial society, with its pyramid of power and economic elites will be gone forever."[101] For Adela Yarbro Collins, the New Jerusalem is a rousing vision of "what ought to be" that balances the resentment felt by John and his community: "The violent deeds of the Roman Empire called forth a desire for vengeance." Once Babylon's oppressive reign was destroyed, all Christians would rule.[102]

Doubtless the feature that John's audience would have found most significant, if not most enticing, was that the New Jerusalem is a home to God and his people. In a poem that alludes to Ezekiel, a voice from the throne, God's voice, announces: "See, the home of God is among mortals. He will dwell with them; they will be his peoples, and God himself will be with them" (Rev. 21:3).[103] Were we to relate the New Jerusalem, a space where the presence of God inundates the people of God, to the logic of Jewish monotheism that Eilberg-Schwartz has uncovered, it would be difficult to ignore the ambivalence engendered by this vision. There is no temple in the New Jerusalem, no place that contains God's overwhelming presence. Indeed, there is no need for sun or moon to shine over the city, "for the glory of God is its light" (Rev. 21:23; 22:5). A city suffused with the "panoptic" light of God leaves its inhabitants no place to hide.[104] The most troubling aspect of this vision, then, would be precisely the prospect of "seeing God," a meeting that changed Moses' countenance and, if Eilberg-Schwartz is correct, his gender.

Yet, the New Jerusalem will facilitate just such a meeting—"they will see his face, and his name will be on their foreheads" (Rev. 22:4)—but in a fashion that significantly modifies Jewish monotheism: the Lamb is part of the relation of viewing thematized in the New Jerusalem. The Apocalypse has prepared its readers for this possibility earlier in the narrative. In the passage to which the *Martyrs of Lyons* alludes, the spectacle of the Lamb is in full view: "Then I looked, and there was the Lamb, standing on Mount Zion! And with him were one hundred and forty-four thousand who had his name and his Father's name written on their foreheads. . . . It is these who have not defiled themselves with women, for they are virgins; these follow the Lamb wherever he goes" (Rev. 14:1–5). Like the martyrs of 4 Maccabees, the Lamb has become an inspiration for the army. Further, these viewers are far different than the fornicating, unmanly kings who gaze on Babylon. While most scholars agree that the celibacy of the 144,000 derives in part from the demand of temporary sexual abstinence in preparation for a holy war, I would add that the passage's heterosexual economy—these men "have not defiled themselves with women"—also points up self-mastery and, hence, masculinity. Chaste soldiers, they have eyes only for the Lamb.[105]

The relation forged between the 144,000 gazing soldiers and the Lamb sheds light on the visual environment within the New Jerusalem: "But the throne of God and of the Lamb will be in it, and his (αὐτοῦ) servants will worship him; they will see his (αὐτοῦ) face, and his (αὐτοῦ) name will be on their foreheads" (Rev. 22:3–4).[106] The pronoun is ambiguous: does αὐτοῦ refer to God, the Lamb, or both? It is a problem difficult to resolve; we must leave the precise antecedent undetermined, or rather, overdetermined. God sits on the throne, but when the citizens of the city look up, they, like Epagathus and the sealed soldiers, see the spectacle of the Lamb.

The Apocalypse thus renders the concept of the "masculine gaze" problematic. Unlike the "one like a human son" or the "rider on the white horse," which do not pass through the gates of the New Jerusalem, the Lamb posed a challenge to the penetration grid.[107] Perched atop Mount Zion, seated on the throne of God, the Lamb rises to a position of immense power. If masculinity is to be fully within the reach of the audience in relation to this figure, it will not be through the mechanism of "the gaze," of objectification. Furthermore, even if the image of its broken, bleeding body is not explicitly invoked in these later presentations, the wounded flesh of the Lamb—like the slain body of Chloe—continues to haunt this text. Most important, as other, the spectacle of the Lamb threatens to overwhelm the self-control of the viewers.

This is not to suggest that Revelation completely eschews the penetration grid: as we have seen, episodes of penetrative violence in the service of domination permeate the book. At the same time, the book, like other cultural products we have encountered, upsets this model, enabling new configurations of gender. Keenly aware of the effects of spectacle upon spectators, John invites his audience to stand alongside the inhabitants of the New Jerusalem and to gaze upon the monstrous Lamb. To do so is to risk being consumed by the fiery passions that the images of Revelation will ineluctably ignite, transforming the audience itself into a spectacle. But this was the enticement of viewing, the reason that subjects of Rome gathered around spectacles under the empire: without the risk, without the pressure of the passions, there was nothing to master.

Despite the assurance that "the first things have passed away," the "new heaven and new earth" that the audience glimpses in the Apocalypse reconstitutes the viewing relations of the old world. The New Jerusalem invites the audience into an imperial arena: the crowds gather, the *editor* sits in attendance, and the throng, composed of worshipful servants, venerates the divine emperor (Rev. 22:3).[108] In this context, in which all are subject to the imperial will, the static masculinity of conquest gives way to the fluid masculinity of spectacle. Like the grotesque dwarf at Domitian's side, the Lamb shares the booth with an emperor; and as Suetonius transforms Domitian into a monstrous spectacle, so too John, for far different reasons, presents his own (cosmic) emperor in the guise of the Lamb—a figure no less powerful for being the viewed. We have apprehended John "thinking with the Lamb," exploiting the vulnerability built into the structure of viewing relations. Revelation's "most terrible drama" pushed the members of its audience to the very precipice of self-control, raising up the Lamb's grotesque body before their eyes, supporting their struggle to attain a righteous masculinity. Indeed, as the story of Epagathus illustrates, for many ancient Christians this finally was the great challenge of their faith: to look closely and to follow the Lamb wherever it goes.

6

Epilogue: A Well-Known Story

A Christian bishop, Polycarp of Smyrna, was executed in the year 155 C.E. in full view of an angry mob. The account of this execution, the *Martyrdom of Polycarp*, not only contains important evidence of the pagan persecution of Christians; it, like the book of Revelation, bears witness also to the workings of the early Christian imagination. But the nascent Christian mentality of Revelation seems quite dissimilar to that of the *Martyrdom of Polycarp*.[1] The *Martyrdom of Polycarp* pushes the abuse heaped upon Christians to the fore, while Revelation, as we have seen, invests its spectacular energies in the careful illustration of the horrors that await the dragon, the beasts, and Babylon. Still, the figure of the bleeding Lamb — the Lamb as spectacle — suggests that further consideration of the two writings is warranted. Here I suggest that differences between Revelation and the *Martyrdom of Polycarp* (and other Christian martyr accounts) are more apparent than real.[2]

One approach to early Christian martyr accounts has been to sift the stories for the motives behind the persecutions.[3] Christians seem to have been targeted for their impiety, that is, for their refusal to honor the gods of Rome. Ancient writers, as I noted in chapter 2, concluded that the secret to Rome's success was no secret at all: its leaders and subjects valued piety above everything else. A second martyr account illustrates the point well: in this story, a Roman governor presides over a trial of Christians who defend their religion by mocking Roman paganism. The Roman official responds curtly: "We too are religious people, and our religion is a simple one."[4] Paganism was "simple": honor the gods, and the gods would send fortune your way; dishonor the gods, and awful circumstances were in store.[5] It was an extremely tolerant religion, unless one acted impiously by refusing to pay tribute to the deities of one's neighbors. Unless, in other words, one was a Christian.

Despite the urgency of the early Christian martyr accounts, there is precious little evidence of widespread persecutions of Christians until about the year 250 C.E.[6] Fifty years later the reign of the first Christian emperor, Constantine, brought an end to the general persecutions administered by his immediate predecessors. For two centuries, then, Christianity went all but unnoticed by Roman emperors and by Roman law. One reason for this oversight may have been that the new religion, while it spread geographically at an astonishing rate, did not attract enough converts to warrant official attention. The best scholarly estimate puts the figure at less than 10 percent of the total population of the Roman Empire by the year 300 C.E.[7] This number is not statistically insignificant, but Roman emperors had more pressing issues to address.[8]

The tolerant character of Roman paganism, however, remains the leading consideration. In this climate, Christianity was never categorized as "unlawful" by the Roman legal code. On the contrary, imperial policies, such as the empire-wide sacrifice requirement of Decius in 250 C.E., were adopted principally to support the religion of the Roman state, though they appear anti-Christian in retrospect.[9] As G. E. M. de Ste. Croix has observed, "the ordinary Christian who did not insist upon openly parading his confession was most unlikely to become a victim of the persecution at all."[10] Christians were free to worship their one god in private, but they were also expected to worship the pagan deities in public, with the rest of the community. And it was this community, the neighbors of Christians, that felt endangered by the impious dereliction of public duty, as the *Martyrs of Lyons* shows.[11] With friends like Christians, pagans agreed, who needs enemies? The martyr accounts from this period repeatedly describe outraged townsfolk, motivated by fear of angry gods, dragging Christians into the courts of Roman officials. Governors such as Pliny the Younger in turn punished those discovered to be Christians, not for legal reasons but to preserve social tranquility.[12] Pagan mobs, then, not the Roman government, were culpable for the vast majority of Christian martyrdoms in the first three centuries C.E.

Such mob violence remained sporadic throughout the period: Christianity, while occasionally mocked or criticized by pagan writers, received little attention, violent or otherwise, from non-Christians. Yet, many Christians invested in the notion that their religion was a religion of the persecuted, a point that Judith Perkins emphasizes in her treatment of early Christian martyr accounts, *The Suffering Self*. Martyr accounts made for very popular reading among Christian groups across the Mediterranean region. A religious disposition was born: Christians believed that the vast resources of the Roman Empire had been mobilized against them. They believed, in short, that the entire world hated them, a conviction expressed through the stories that Christians circulated. Martyr accounts not only encouraged Christians who faced oppression, they also promoted a particular representation of Christianity, a religious identity that took shape especially in the tales about persecution. By encountering these narratives, the audience came to identify the ideal Christian with the mangled flesh of martyrs.

Here I wish to highlight two aspects of the argument that Perkins mounts in *The Suffering Self*. First, she contends that "The triumph of Christianity was, in part at least, a triumph of a particular representation of the self."[13] In other words, representations possess the power not only to mold identity but also to change whole societies. Second, Perkins argues that the "suffering self" of Christianity proceeded from "a particular preoccupation in the discursive climate of the early Roman empire." Perkins frames her analysis of Christian texts with a survey of Greek and Roman literature, ranging from medical texts to philosophical treatises to Greek romances, to show that "From a number of different locations, narratives were projecting a particular representation of the human self as a body liable to pain and suffering."[14] Christian martyr accounts joined with non-Christian texts to create the "suffering self," a self-representation not invented by Christians but enhanced by them. The depiction of individuated physical agony in the *Martyrdom of Polycarp*, for example, bears a striking resemblance to the way that Aristides recounts his afflictions in the *Sacred Tales*.

By focusing on representational strategies, Perkins does not mean to deny the reality of pagan persecution of Christians. Rather, she wants to show that the effects "in front of" the text hold as much significance as the reality "behind" the text. What is perhaps obscured in Perkins's emphasis on the suffering self is that the vast majority of Christians in the ancient world did not experience persecution. At the same time, it is clear that many Christians in the ancient world heard about martyrdom through texts such as the *Martyrdom of Polycarp*, and equally apparent that Christian audiences wanted to hear such accounts. A modern analogy throws the situation into relief: there are far more television viewers than television stars. Not every Christian could be the heroic Polycarp, but many Christians wanted to know the details of the martyr's heroism, and wanted to "see," textually, the suffering for themselves.

Like Revelation, martyrologies fashioned a viewing self. Indeed, the

Martyrdom of Polycarp shares many of the features that this analysis has highlighted in the Apocalypse, including a diverse set of textual "Others." As a story of masculinity, the Martyrdom of Polycarp is a tale of two martyrs, or, to be precise, a tale of one "almost" martyrdom and of one "authentic" martyrdom. Before Polycarp even appears, we encounter a failed martyr, a Christian named Quintus who "came forward" but then "saw the wild animals and turned cowardly."[15] Rather than meet his maker, the cowardly, "unmanly" Quintus interrupts the martydom in the making and chooses instead to swear by the gods and to offer sacrifice to them. Polycarp, in contrast, is surrounded by signs of masculinity: at his trial he hears a voice out of the heavens exhorting him, "Be strong Polycarp, and be manly."[16] When the soldiers attempt to nail him to the stake, Polycarp waves them off: "Leave me thus. For he who has given me the strength to endure the flames will grant me to remain without flinching in the fire even without the nails."[17] Watching the contrasting examples of Quintus and Polycarp, the audience learns not only that the suffering self is "manly" but also that the practice of "voluntary martyrdom" is "unmanly."[18] As the Christianity represented by Jezebel is "unmanned" in Revelation, so that of Quintus is "unmanned" by the *Martyrdom of Polycarp*.

Beyond these shared elements, both texts expose the passionate character of viewing through the narrative spectators.[19] The narrator of the *Martyrdom of Polycarp* reports that "we have been preserved to report to others what befell."[20] The affection produced in the spectacle is explicitly described: the suffering Christ "we worship as the Son of God, but the martyrs we love (ἀγαπῶμεν) as disciples and imitators of the Lord; and rightly, because of their unsurpassable affection (εὐνοίας) toward their own King and Teacher. God grant that we too may be their companions and fellow-disciples."[21] Beholding the spectacle of the martyr was part of a love affair, an affair similar to the one that Revelation engendered between its audience and the monstrous Lamb. The *Martyrdom of Polycarp*, like Revelation, invites the audience to gaze on a beloved.

But danger lurked in this production of desire: Christians like Quintus, presumably inspired to martyrdom by the tales of other martyrs, could find themselves overwhelmed by those passions, turning "cowardly," effeminate, at the moment of truth. The risk of viewing, I have argued, was central to the attraction of spectacle under the Roman Empire, catching the audience in the slippage between viewer and viewed, affording spectators moments of testing and masculinity. This is precisely the kind of ambivalence that postcolonial critics such as Homi Bhabha might recognize as an effect of empire, in which structure culture and identity are fractured for both the dominant and the subaltern: "the observer becomes the observed and 'partial' representation rearticulates the whole notion of *identity* and alienates it from essence."[22] Spectacle in the Roman world destabilized the authoritative gaze, allowing for new forms of culture to surface when other discourses, such as the penetration grid, could no longer be relied upon to address the needs of Mediterranean populations. If, as Averil Cameron suggests, "it is still useful and important to ask how Christians, the quintessential outsiders as they appeared to men like Nero, Pliny, Tacitus, and Suetonius, talked and wrote themselves into a position where they spoke and wrote the rhetoric of empire," then the textual spectacles of ancient Christians, the accounts of martyrs, should be part of the discussion.[23] Like the Greek romance and the imperial cult, such martyr accounts—more effectively, perhaps, than contemporaneous cultural products—engaged the audience in relations of viewing and thus in the labor of self-fashioning.

The appeal of the Apocalypse, I have argued, must also be located here, in the power of spectacle. For all of its martial imagery, the new heavens and new earth that Revelation finally envisions is not an empire of warriors but one of viewers. "But the throne of God and of the Lamb will be in it," declares John, "and his servants will worship him; they will see his face, and his name will be on their foreheads" (Rev. 22: 3–4). Far from spinning an original yarn, Revelation tells a version of an already popular tale about spectacle and spectators. And this was a story that subjects of the Roman Empire loved, for they knew it well.

Notes

Chapter 1. Gods, Monsters, and Martyrs

1. See Robert M. Royalty, Jr.'s conclusion in *The Streets of Heaven: The Ideology of Wealth in the Apocalypse of John* (Macon, Ga.: Mercer University Press, 1998), 246.

2. See Richard Bauckham, *The Theology of the Book of Revelation*, New Testament Theology (New York: Cambridge University Press, 1993), 45. But cf. David E. Aune's presentation of similarities in the imagery of Revelation and Roman imperial ceremonies, "The Influence of Roman Imperial Court Ceremonial on the Apocalypse of John," *Papers of the Chicago Society of Biblical Research* 28 (1985): 5–26. An incisive analysis of scholarship on the issue can be found in Stephen D. Moore, *God's Gym: Divine Male Bodies of the Bible* (London: Routledge, 1996), 126–30.

3. Said, *Orientalism* (New York: Pantheon, 1978), 32.

4. For a survey, see Eugen Weber, *Apocalypses: Prophecies, Cults, and Millennial Beliefs Through the Ages* (Cambridge, Mass.: Harvard University Press, 1999).

5. J. A. T. Robinson, *Redating the New Testament* (Philadelphia: Westminster, 1976), 230–31.

6. Irenaeus, *Adversus haereses* 5.30.3.

7. Tacitus, *Annales* 15.38, 44. See T. D. Barnes, "Legislation Against the Christians," *Journal of Roman Studies* 58 (1968): 34–36.

8. Like Robinson, others have argued for a date under Nero's reign: see J. Chris Wilson, "The Problem of the Domitianic Date of Revelation," *New Testament Studies* 39 (1993): 587–605. Cf. John W. Marshall, *Parables of War: Reading John's Jewish Apocalypse*, Studies in Judaism and Christianity 10 (Toronto: Wilfred Laurier University Press, 2001), 88–97, who argues for a date of 69 C.E. (Tacitus's "long year"). Adela Yarbro Collins offers perhaps the most compelling defense of a date under Domitian's reign in "Myth and History in the Book of Revelation: The Problem of Its Date," in *Traditions in Transformation: Turning Points in Biblical Faith*, ed. Baruch Halpern and Jon D. Levenson (Winona Lake, Ind.: Eisenbrauns, 1981), 377–403. For a recent authoritative statement of evidence and arguments, see David E. Aune, *Revelation 1–5*, Word Biblical Commentary 52A (Dallas: Word, 1997), lvii–lxx.

9. See John J. Collins, "Introduction: Towards the Morphology of a Genre," *Semeia* 14 (1979): 1–19. Cf. E. P. Sanders, "The Genre of Palestinian Jewish Apocalypses," in *Apocalypticism in the Mediterranean World and the Near East:*

Proceedings of the International Colloquium on Apocalypticism, Uppsala, August 12–17, 1979, ed. David Hellholm (Tübingen: Mohr-Siebeck, 1983), 447–59. Adela Yarbro Collins modifies the definition to include function: an apocalypse is "intended to present earthly circumstances in light of the supernatural world and of the future, and to influence both the understanding and the behavior of the audience by means of divine authority." "Introduction: Early Christian Apocalypticism," *Semeia* 36 (1986): 7. See also David E. Aune, "The Apocalypse of John and the Problem of Genre," *Semeia* 36 (1986): 65–96.

10. Gager, *Kingdom and Community: The Social World of Early Christianity* (Englewood Cliffs, N.J.: Prentice-Hall, 1975), 51. But see Jonathan Z. Smith's criticism in "Too Much Kingdom, Too Little Community," *Zygon* 13 (1978): 120–35.

11. Collins, *Crisis and Catharsis: The Power of the Apocalypse* (Philadelphia: Westminster, 1984), 141. *Crisis and Catharsis* has proven to be the more significant of the two treatments, if at least one measure of significance is the number of times a work is cited by scholars.

12. Ibid., 84.

13. The seer tapped into both a general antipathy to Romans in the Greek East and his own personal trauma of being banished to the island of Patmos (Rev. 1:9). Collins, *Crisis and Catharsis*, 88–106.

14. Collins, *Crisis and Catharsis*, 141.

15. Schüssler Fiorenza, *The Book of Revelation: Justice and Judgment*, 2nd ed. (Philadelphia: Fortress, 1998). First published 1985.

16. Thompson, *The Book of Revelation: Apocalypse and Empire* (New York: Oxford University Press, 1990).

17. Royalty, *Streets of Heaven*, 28. See also Paul Duff, *Who Rides the Beast? Prophetic Rivalry and the Rhetoric of Crisis in the Churches of the Apocalypse* (New York: Oxford University Press, 2001), 13–14; and David A. Desilva, "The Revelation to John: A Case Study in Apocalyptic Propaganda and the Maintenance of Sectarian Identity," *Sociological Analysis* 53 (1992): 375–95. Royalty and Duff extend the earlier work of Schüssler Fiorenza, *Justice and Judgment* (114–32); and David E. Aune, "The Social Matrix of the Apocalypse of John," *Biblical Research* 26 (1981): 16–32. But cf. the new epilogue in Schüssler Fiorenza, *Justice and Judgment* (207), which is highly critical of the recent focus on a sectarian background to Revelation.

18. Robert Royalty suggests that the audience of Revelation "was probably very much like the Pauline churches . . . [it] was urban and was socially and culturally diverse." *Streets of Heaven*, 19. The book names seven cities in Asia Minor: Ephesus, Smyrna, Pergamum, Thyatira, Sardis, Philadelphia, and Laodicea (Rev. 2–3). On the composition of the Pauline churches, see the now classic treatment by Wayne A. Meeks, *The First Urban Christians: The Social World of the Apostle Paul* (New Haven, Conn.: Yale University Press, 1983), esp. 51–73.

19. It is significant that other Christians in the same region—as 1 Pet. 2:13–17, 1 Tim. 2:1–4, and Titus 3:1 indicate—promoted a far more conciliatory stance toward Roman authority than the book of Revelation. See Royalty, *Streets of Heaven* (33–34), and Adela Yarbro Collins, "Oppression from Without: The

Symbolisation of Rome as Evil in Early Christianity," *Concilium* 200 (1988): 66–74.

20. But see the questions raised about such approaches by Wayne A. Meeks, "Apocalyptic Discourse and Strategies of Goodness," *Journal of Religion* 80 (2000): 464–65.

21. Thompson, *Apocalypse and Empire*, 195.

22. See Collins, *Crisis and Catharsis* (89–90), which cites Harald Fuchs, *Der geistige Widerstand gegen Rom in der antiken Welt* (Berlin: Walter de Gruyter, 1938), on widespread, "intellectual opposition" to Rome in the Greek East, but later identifies the "trauma" and ostracization felt specifically by ancient Christians as the leading factor in the "perceived crisis" (98–104).

23. See John J. Collins, *The Apocalyptic Imagination: An Introduction to the Jewish Matrix of Christianity*, 2nd. ed. (Grand Rapids, Mich.: Eerdmans, 1998), 269–79.

24. See Tina Pippin's contention: "Although the Lamb and the Son of Man, creatures that represent Jesus Christ are pure and 'good,' as opposed to evil impure beasts, I want to argue that they, along with all the heavenly creatures, are also terrifying monsters." *Apocalyptic Bodies: The Biblical End of the World in Text and Image* (London: Routledge, 1999), 89.

25. Collins, *Crisis and Catharsis*, 102. Allison A. Trites concludes that while Revelation associates death with ὁ μάρτυς, the term's basic meaning in the book remains "forensic," that is, of a "witness" at a trial. "Μάρτυς and Martrydom in the Apocalypse," *Novum Testamentum* 15 (1973): 72–80. See too B. Dehandschutter, "The Meaning of Witness in the Apocalypse," in *L'Apocalypse johannique et l'Apocalyptique dans le Nouveau Testament*, ed. Jan Lambrecht, Bibliotheca ephemeridum theologicarum lovaniensium 53 (Leuven: Leuven University Press, 1980), 283–88.

26. Jung, "Answer to Job," in *The Portable Jung*, ed. Jospeh Campbell (New York: Penguin, 1971), 519–650; on Revelation, see pp. 607–19. First published as a monograph, *Answer to Job*, trans. R. F. C. Hull (London: Routledge and Kegan Paul, 1954).

27. "Psychologizing portait," as Jung, "Answer to Job" (621), plainly acknowledges. A recent attempt to recover Jung's analysis for the study of Revelation is Jacques M. Chevalier, *A Postmodern Revelation: Signs of Astrology and the Apocalypse* (Toronto: University of Toronto Press, 1997).

28. The study of "monsters" has of late gathered a great deal of scholarly steam; I list here a few works that have proven helpful: Lorraine Daston and Katherine Park, *Wonders and the Order of Nature* (New York: Zone Books, 1998), esp. 173–201; Jeffrey Jerome Cohen, "Monster Culture (Seven Theses)," in *Monster Theory*, ed. Cohen (Minneapolis: University of Minnesota Press, 1996), 3–25; John Block Friedman, *The Monstrous Races in Medieval Art and Thought* (Cambridge, Mass.: Harvard University Press, 1981); and Geoffrey Galt Harpham, *On the Grotesque: Strategies of Contradiction in Art and Literature* (Princeton, N.J.: Princeton University Press, 1982), esp. 3–22. Rudolf Wittkower, "Marvels of the East: A Study in the History of Monsters," *Journal of the Wartburg and Courtauld Institutes* 5 (1942): 159–87, is a classic investigation of mythic origins. For

biblical studies, in addition to Pippin, *Apocalyptic Bodies*, see Timothy K. Beal, *Religion and Its Monsters* (New York: Routledge, 2002), esp. 71–85, and Fiona C. Black, "The Beauty or the Beast? The Grotesque Body in the Song of Songs," *Biblical Interpretation* 8 (2000): 302–23.

29. See discussion of Gunkel and the *religionsgeschichtliche Schule* in Collins, *Apocalyptic Imagination*, 16–17.

30. See also R. H. Charles, *A Critical and Exegetical Commentary on the Revelation of St. John*, 2 vols., International Critical Commentary (Edinburgh: T & T Clark, 1920), whose complex "source analysis" of Revelation was influenced by the history-of-religions school. Aune, *Revelation 1–5*, cv–cxxxiv, offers a "two-version" theory, in which the final "Domitianic" edition of Revelation incorporates an earlier version written under Nero's reign. The present study is not redactional in approach, and will not attempt to identify sources in the book.

31. Wilhelm Bousset, *The Antichrist Legend: A Chapter in Christian and Jewish Folklore*, trans. A. H. Keane (London: Hutchinson, 1896), 6.

32. Gunkel, *Schöpfung und Chaos in Urzeit und Endzeit: Eine religionsgeschichtliche Untersuchung über Gen 1 und Ap Joh 12* (Göttingen: Vandenhoeck und Ruprecht, 1895), esp. 41–69, 315–18, 336–78. Biblical references include Job 40–41, Isa. 27:1, 59:1; for apocalypses, see 1 Enoch 60:9, 4 Ezra 6:49–52, and 2 Baruch 29:4. For an insightful treatment of "God's primordial enemies" and the "survival of chaos," see Jon D. Levenson, *Creation and the Persistence of Evil: The Jewish Drama of Divine Omnipotence* (San Francisco: Harper and Row, 1988), esp. 3–25.

33. Bousset, *Antichrist Legend*, 15. Bousset also wrote a commentary on Revelation, *Die Offenbarung des Johannes*, 6th ed., Kritisch-exegetischer Kommentar über das Neue Testament (Meyer-Kommentar) 16 (Göttingen: Vandenhoeck und Ruprecht, 1906).

34. A battle examined by Adela Yarbro Collins, *The Combat Myth in the Book of Revelation*, Harvard Dissertations in Religion 9 (Missoula, Mont.: Scholars Press, 1976).

35. Bousset, *Antichrist Legend*, 8–12, expresses dissatisfaction with Gunkel's approach, turning instead to a "less remote tradition." He also disagrees with Gunkel's rejection of the "contemporary-historical" method, arguing that symbols in Revelation may refer to tradition and simultaneously to contemporary history.

36. "Grand Central Station," Hal Lindsey's phrase. He writes: "Nearly every symbol in it is used somewhere else in the Bible, but finds its ultimate fulfillment and explanation in this final prophetic book of the Bible." Hal Lindsey, *There's a New World Coming* (New York: Bantam, 1973), xiv. Lindsey's Christian evangelical viewpoint is here quite apparent.

37. Recent treatments that adopt this approach include G. K. Beale, *The Book of Revelation: A Commentary on the Greek Text*, New International Greek Testament Commentary (Grand Rapids, Mich.: 1999), and Jan Fekkes III, *Isaiah and Prophetic Traditions in the Book of Revelation*, Journal for the Study of the New Testament Supplement Series 93 (Sheffield: Journal for the Study of the Old Testament Press, 1994).

38. To use a specific example: "I will throw filth at you / and treat you with contempt / and make you a spectacle" (παράδειγμα in the Septuagint; Nah. 3:6). Knowing that this text, an oracle against Ninevah, and countless other prophetic passages serve in some fashion as sources for John's visions tells us virtually nothing about the meaning of spectacle in the book's contemporary Roman environment. Nor, I suggest, does it throw much light upon the focus of this study: the portrayal of viewing in Revelation. Two recent treatments, in my view, follow fruitful lines of inquiry into John's use of Scripture: Steve Moyise, *The Old Testament in the Book of Revelation*, Journal for the Study of the New Testament Supplement Series 115 (Sheffield: Sheffield Academic Press, 1995), and Allen Dwight Callahan, "The Language of the Apocalypse," *Harvard Theological Review* 88 (1995): 453–70.

39. Smith, "The Image of God: Notes on the Hellenization of Judaism, with Especial Reference to Goodenough's Work on Jewish Symbols," *Bulletin of the John Rylands Library* 40 (1958): 481 (Smith's italics).

40. See Royalty, *The Streets of Heaven* (80, 194–97), and Schüssler Fiorenza, *Justice and Judgment* (135–36). Precisely which text of the Scriptures John employed remains a debated topic: see Collins, *Crisis and Catharsis* (48), which argues for the "*kaige*" recension of the Septuagint.

41. See Edward Said's related point: "The point is that texts have ways of existing that even in their most rarefied form are always enmeshed in circumstance, time, place, and society—in short, they are in the world, and hence worldly." *The World, the Text, and the Critic* (Cambridge, Mass.: Harvard University Press, 1983), 35.

42. Barton, *The Sorrow of the Ancient Romans: The Gladiator and the Monster* (Princeton, N.J.: Princeton University Press, 1993), 101. See also David Gilmore's observation: "For most people monsters are sources of identification and awe as well as of horror," *Monsters: Evil Beings, Mythical Beasts, and All Manner of Imaginary Terrors* (Philadelphia: University of Pennsylvania Press, 2003), 5.

43. O'Brien, "Michel Foucault's History of Culture," in *The New Cultural History*, ed. Lynn Hunt (Berkeley: University of California Press, 1989), 25, 33.

44. That power does not proceed from the top down, but is always relational, has remained one of Foucault's most influential formulations. See Michel Foucault, "Afterword: The Subject and Power," in *Michel Foucault: Beyond Structuralism and Hermeneutics*, ed. Hubert L. Dreyfus and Paul Rabinow (Chicago: University of Chicago Press, 1983), 216–26; and Foucault, *The History of Sexuality*, vol. 1, *An Introduction*, trans. Robert Hurley (New York: Vintage, 1980), 92–102.

45. On the discourse of sexuality Foucault writes: "The essential features of this sexuality are not the expression of a representation that is more or less distorted by ideology, or a misunderstanding caused by taboos; they correspond to the functional requirements of a discourse that must produce its truth." Foucault, *History of Sexuality*, vol. 1, 68. Foucault's fullest elaboration of "discourse" is in *The Archaeology of Knowledge*, trans. A. M. Sheridan Smith (New York: Pantheon, 1972).

46. An important example of the intersection between religious studies and postcolonial studies is David Chidester, *Savage Systems: Colonialism and Compar-*

ative Religion in Southern Africa (Charlottesville: University of Virginia Press, 1996), esp. 1–33. Chidester's work takes for granted a nexus of power and knowledge, on which see Foucault, *The Order of Things: An Archaeology of the Human Sciences,* trans. Alan Sheridan (New York: Random House, 1978).

47. Said, *Orientalism,* 22. Cf. Bill Ashcroft, Gareth Griffiths, and Helen Tiffin, *The Empire Writes Back: Theory and Practice in Post-Colonial Literatures,* New Accents (New York: Routledge, 1989).

48. Said, *Orientalism,* 9.

49. Said, *Orientalism,* 7. See also Said, *Culture and Imperialism* (New York: Knopf, 1994), 3–14.

50. See James Clifford's criticism that Said's shift from Foucauldian discourse analysis to a consideration of Orientalism as a tradition of stereotyping results in another stereotype, "Occidentalism." *The Predicament of Culture: Twentieth-Century Ethnography, Literature, and Art* (Cambridge, Mass.: Harvard University Press, 1988), 255–276.

51. Robert J. C. Young, *Postcolonialism: An Historical Introduction* (Oxford: Blackwell, 2001), 392. See also Bart Moore-Gilbert's extension of this criticism to Said, *Culture and Imperialism. Postcolonial Theory: Contexts, Practices, Politics* (New York: Verso, 1997), 61–73.

52. See, e.g., Bhabha, *The Location of Culture* (New York: Routledge, 1994), 73–75. A helpful introduction to Bhabha's work can be found in Moore-Gilbert, *Postcolonial Theory,* 114–51.

53. Bhabha, *Location of Culture,* 86 (Bhabha's italics).

54. Moore-Gilbert, *Postcolonial Theory,* 120.

55. Bhabha, *Location of Culture,* 89 (Bhabha's italics).

56. Bhabha, *Location of Culture,* 88.

57. As do other Bhabhian terms such as "hybridity"; see *Location of Culture,* 109–11.

58. Bhabha has not been without his critics. Benita Parry, "Problems in Current Theories of Colonial Discourse," *Oxford Literary Review* 9 (1987): 43, finds that Bhabha neglects the oppressive force of colonial institutions. See too Robert Young on "hybridity" and "an implicit politics of heterosexuality." *Colonial Desire: Hybridity in Theory, Culture, and Race* (New York: Routledge, 1995), 25–26.

59. Friesen, *Imperial Cults and the Apocalypse of John: Reading Revelation in the Ruins* (New York: Oxford University Press, 2001). See also my review of Friesen, *Reading Revelation in the Ruins, Journal of Biblical Literature* 121 (2002): 575–78.

60. Friesen, *Reading Revelation in the Ruins,* 21. Cf. Allen Brent's thesis, which reveals a similar dichotomy: Revelation constitutes a "Judaeo-Christian reconstruction of the values of pagan culture in which the impress of the culture is re-expressed in a reversed form." *The Imperial Cult and the Development of Church Order: Concepts and Images of Authority in Paganism and Early Christianity Before the Age of Cyprian,* Vigiliae Christianae Supplements 45 (Leiden: Brill, 1999), 208.

61. Friesen, *Reading Revelation in the Ruins,* 19, 165.

62. In some ways, the very structure of Friesen's study, split into two parts, establishes this dichotomy, treating consecutively imperial cults (pp. 23–132), then Revelation (pp. 133–217).

63. Leading practitioners would doubtless argue that there is no single methodology that can accurately be said to embody all of postcolonial studies. For further methodological considerations, see Moore-Gilbert, *Postcolonial Theory*, 152–84; and Patrick Wolfe, "History and Imperialism: A Century of Theory, from Marx to Postcolonialism," *American Historical Review* 102 (1997): 388–420, esp. 418–20.

64. For example, an anonymous reader for the press pointed to the presence of "New Historicism" in the book, especially as practiced by Stephen Greenblatt. For a helpful discussion of this "brand" of theory, see Louise Montrose, "New Historicisms," in *Redrawing the Boundaries: The Transformation of English and American Literary Studies*, ed. Stephen Greenblatt and Giles Gunn (New York: The Modern Language Association of America, 1992), 392–418. Interestingly, Greenblatt has been cited as an example of a scholar "influenced" by postcolonial studies; see Moore-Gilbert, *Postcolonial Theory*, 204 n. 3.

65. Moore-Gilbert, *Postcolonial Theory*, 12.

Chapter 2. Merely Players

1. In Suetonius, *Twelve Caesars* (trans. Graves).

2. The original *Res Gestae* stood in front of the emperor's mausoleum in Rome; copies were posted in Asia Minor. On the date, see Edwin S. Ramage, *The Nature and Purpose of Augustus' "Res Gestae"* (Stuttgart: Franz Steiner, 1987), 132–35.

3. Syme, *The Roman Revolution* (Oxford: Clarendon Press, 1939). See W. Eder, "Augustus and the Power of Tradition: The Augustan Principate as Binding Link Between Republic and Empire," in *Between Republic and Empire: Interpretations of Augustus and His Principate*, ed. Kurt A. Raaflaub and Mark Toher (Berkeley: University of California Press, 1990), 71–122, esp. 75.

4. N. H. Baynes, *The Speeches of Adolph Hitler*, 2 vols. (New York, 1969), 2: 1498, quoted by Jaś Elsner, "Inventing *Imperium*: Texts and the Propaganda of Monuments in Augustan Rome," in Elsner, *Art and Text in Roman Culture*, ed. Elsner (Cambridge: Cambridge University Press, 1996), 32.

5. Elsner, "Inventing *Imperium*," 34 (graffiti: fig. 8).

6. On the concept of *imperium*, see J. S. Richardson, "*Imperium Romanum*: Empire and the Language of Power," *Journal of Roman Studies* 81 (1991): 1–9. Claude Nicolet suggests that the title "Roman Empire" is a modern "play on words": an "empire of Rome" existed under the Roman Republic. *Space, Geography, and Politics in the Early Roman Empire*, trans. Hélène Leclerc, Jerome Lectures 19 (Ann Arbor: University of Michigan Press, 1991), 15.

7. Florence Dupont, *L'acteur-roi ou le théâtre dans la Rome antique* (Paris: Les Belles Lettres, 1985), 19–40.

8. Bartsch, *Actors in the Audience: Theatricality and Doublespeak from*

Nero to Hadrian (Cambridge, Mass.: Harvard University Press, 1994), 38. Bartsch credits three works in particular for developing this model: Barbara Freedman, *Staging the Gaze: Postmodernism, Psychoanalysis, and Shakespearean Comedy* (Ithaca, N.Y.: Cornell University Press, 1991), Ervin Goffman, *Strategic Interaction* (Philadelphia: University of Pennsylvania Press, 1969), and James C. Scott, *Domination and the Arts of Resistance: Hidden Transcripts* (New Haven, Conn.: Yale University Press, 1990).

9. Cassius Dio, *Historia romana* 63.15.2–3, quoted in Bartsch, *Actors in the Audience*, 5.

10. Bartsch, *Actors in the Audience*, 11.

11. Augustus, *Res Gestae* 12.

12. See Vivian Nutton, "The Beneficial Ideology," in *Imperialism in the Ancient World*, ed. Peter D. A. Garnsey and C. R. Whittaker (Cambridge: Cambridge University Press, 1978), 209–22, esp. 210–11. On the Roman emperor as benefactor, see Peter Garnsey and Richard P. Saller, *The Roman Empire: Economy, Society, and Culture* (Berkeley: University of California Press, 1987), 149–50.

13. Zanker, *The Power of Images in the Age of Augustus*, trans. Alan Shapiro, Jerome Lectures 16 (Ann Arbor: University of Michigan Press, 1988). Zanker's book, according to Andrew Wallace-Hadrill, "can be welcomed without exaggeration as the most significant contribution to the understanding of Augustan Rome since *The Roman Revolution*." "Rome's Cultural Revolution," *Journal of Roman Studies* 79 (1989): 157–61.

14. Zanker, *Power of Images*, 172–73.

15. Similar iconography decorates the cuirass of the Prima Porta Augustus, but the central scene is of the Parthian surrender of the standards to Mars; see Augustus, *Res Gestae* 13 on "peace through victory." Discussion (with plates) in Karl Galinsky, *Augustan Culture: An Interpretive Introduction* (Princeton, N.J.: Princeton University Press, 1996), 155–64.

16. Plutarch, *Praecepta gerendae rei publicae* 19; Aristides, *To Rome* 29 (*Orationes* 26.29, trans. Behr). On benefits of empire, see J. P. V. D. Balsdon, *Romans and Aliens* (London: Duckworth, 1979), 193–213, esp. 204–10. But see also Garnsey and Saller on Aristides' persistent "Hellenocentricity" in *To Rome* (*Orationes* 26). *Roman Empire*, 15.

17. For an overview, see Erich S. Gruen, *The Hellenistic World and the Coming of Rome*, 2 vols. (Berkeley: University of California Press, 1984), 2: 529–610, and David Magie, *Roman Rule in Asia Minor*, 2 vols. (Princeton, N.J.: Princeton University Press, 1950), 1: 468–90. For Greek opposition to Rome, see Harald Fuchs, *Der geistige Widerstand gegen Rom in der antiken Welt* (Berlin: de Gruyter, 1938), 45–57, and Glen Bowersock, *Augustus and the Greek World* (Oxford: Clarendon Press, 1965), 101–11. See also the account of Greek self-definition by Guy M. Rogers, *The Sacred Identity of Ephesos* (London: Routledge, 1991), esp. 136–51. But cf. Mary T. Boatwright's critique of Rogers in *Hadrian and the Cities of the Roman Empire* (Princeton, N.J.: Princeton University Press, 2000), 96–99.

18. Brian D. Shaw, "The Divine Economy: Stoicism as Ideology," *Latomus* 44 (1985): 39.

19. Shaw, "Divine Economy," 22.

20. Ewen L. Bowie, "Greeks and Their Past in the Second Sophistic," in *Studies in Ancient Society*, ed. Moses I. Finley, Past and Present Series (Boston: Routledge and Kegan Paul, 1974), 166–211.

21. Simon Swain, *Hellenism and Empire: Language, Classicism, and Power in the Greek World, A.D. 50–250* (Oxford: Oxford University Press, 1996), 113.

22. For a critique of the scholarly propensity to affirm or reproduce this opposition, see Tim Whitmarsh, *Greek Literature and the Roman Empire: The Politics of Imitation* (New York: Oxford University Press, 2001), 17–20.

23. Horace, *Epistulae* 2.1.156 (trans. Fairclough).

24. See David Castriota, *The Ara Pacis Augustae and The Imagery of Abundance in Later Greek and Early Roman Imperial Art* (Princeton, N.J.: Princeton University Press, 1995), 13–57. On the Hellenization of Italian artists, see Diane Atnally Conlin, *The Artists of the Ara Pacis: The Process of Hellenization in Roman Relief Sculpture* (Chapel Hill: University of North Carolina Press, 1997).

25. Zanker, *Power of Images*, 239, quotes Dionysius. See also Andrew Wallace-Hadrill, "*Mutatio Morum*: The Idea of a Cultural Revolution," in *The Roman Cultural Revolution*, ed. Thomas Habinek and Alessandro Schiesaro (Cambridge: Cambridge University Press, 1997), 7–11.

26. Castriola, *Ara Pacis Augustae*, 124–44.

27. Zanker, *Power of Images*, 129.

28. See Wallace-Hadrill, "*Mutatio Morum*," 12.

29. Cicero, *De haruspicum responso* 19 (trans. Watts). See also See Horace *Odes* 3.6.3.

30. Balsdon, *Romans and Aliens*, 2.

31. Vergil, *Eclogues* 4.28–29. See also the language of fertility in Horace, *Carmen Saeculare*, composed for the Secular Games of 17 B.C.E. On the book of Revelation and the eschatological transformation of nature in Roman literature, see both Dieter Georgi, "Who Is the True Prophet?," *Harvard Theological Review* 79 (1986): 100–26, and Sean M. McDonough, "Of Beasts and Bees: The View of the Natural World in Virgil's *Georgics* and John's Apocalypse," *New Testament Studies* 46 (2000): 227–44. See also F. Gerald Downing, "Common Strands in Pagan, Jewish, and Christian Eschatologies in the First Century," *Theologische Zeitschrift* 51 (1995): 196–211.

32. Vergil, *Aeneid* 6.791–94 (trans. Goold). On the *aurea saecula*, see Galinsky, *Augustan Culture*, 106–28.

33. That is, Cicero's *orbis terrarum* and Polybius's οἰκουμένη. See P. A. Brunt, "*Laus Imperii*," in *Imperialism in the Ancient World*, ed. Peter D. A. Garnsey and C. R. Whittaker (Cambridge: Cambridge University Press, 1978), 159–91, esp. 168.

34. Brunt, *Roman Imperial Themes* (Oxford: Oxford University Press, 1990), 440. On conceptualizing "global" conquest in this period, see Nicolet, *Space*, 29–56, 95–122. For "defensive imperialism," see E. Badian, *Roman Imperialism in the Late Republic* (Oxford: Oxford University Press, 1968).

35. Augustus, *Res Gestae* 67 (trans. Brunt and Moore).

36. Jaś Elsner suggests that when Romans encountered this priestly depiction of Augustus, they "saw a cultural process in which they themselves became involved." "Cult and Sculpture: Sacrifice in the Ara Pacis Augustae," *Journal of Roman Studies* 81 (1991): 52.

37. Augustus, *Res Gestae* 8 (trans. Brunt and Moore).

38. Velleius Paterculus, *Compendium of Roman History* 2.126 (trans. Shipley).

39. For ancient references, see Maud W. Gleason, *Making Men: Sophists and Self-Presentation in Ancient Rome* (Princeton, N.J.: Princeton University Press, 1995), 63 n. 38, and Dale B. Martin, "Contradictions of Masculinity: Ascetic Inseminators and Menstruating Men in Greco-Roman Culture," in *Generation and Degeneration: Tropes of Reproduction in Literature and History from Antiquity through Early Modern Europe*, ed. Valeria Finucci and Kevin Brownlee (Durham, N.C.: Duke University Press, 2001), 81 n. 1.

40. Beacham, *Spectacle Entertainments of Early Imperial Rome* (New Haven, Conn.: Yale University Press, 1999), ix; Cassius Dio, *Historia romana* 52.34.2 is quoted here.

41. The Roman emperors, Peter Brown explains, "were careful to show their power in the approved manner." *Power and Persuasion in Late Antiquity: Towards a Christian Empire* (Madison: University of Wisconsin Press, 1992), 58. Further, he notes, this late antique expectation dates back to the Augustan regime. See too Ramsay MacMullen, *Roman Social Relations, 50 B.C. to A.D. 284* (New Haven, Conn.: Yale University Press, 1974), 110.

42. See W.K. Lacey, "*Patria Potestas*," in *The Family in Ancient Rome: New Perspectives*, ed. Beryl Rawson (London: Croom Helm, 1986), 125. On "barbarians" as children, see Sarah Currie, "The Empire of Adults: The Representation of Children on Trajan's Arch at Beneventum," in Elsner, *Art and Text in Roman Culture*, 153–81. See further references in my " 'For My Child, Onesimus': Paul and Domestic Power in Philemon," *Journal of Biblical Literature* 119 (2000): 93–97.

43. The classic statement remains M. P. Charlesworth, "The Virtues of a Roman Emperor: Propaganda and the Creation of Belief," *Proceedings of the British Academy* 23 (1937): 105–33. See the more recent treatment by J. Rufus Fears, "The Cult of Virtues and Roman Imperial Ideology," *Aufstieg und Niedergang der römischen Welt* 2.17.2 (1981): 827–948.

44. Apuleius, *Metamorphoses* 3.29 (trans. Walsh).

45. Boatwright, *Hadrian and the Cities*, 14.

46. See Rogers, *Sacred Identity*, 80–127.

47. See Susan E. Alcock, *Graecia Capta: The Landscapes of Roman Greece* (Cambridge: Cambridge University Press, 1993), 198.

48. Pliny, *Epistulae* 10.74.

49. See Simon R. F. Price, *Rituals and Power: The Roman Imperial Cult in Asia Minor* (Cambridge: Cambridge University Press, 1984), 191–206.

50. Boatwright, *Hadrian and the Cities*, 14.

51. No emperor visited Asia Minor in the first century C.E., according to Price, *Rituals and Power*, 1. See the list of emperor statues from Ephesus in Sjef van Tilborg, *Reading John in Ephesus* (Leiden: Brill, 1996), 194–96.

52. See Steven J. Friesen, *Twice Neokoros: Ephesus, Asia and the Cult of the Flavian Imperial Family*, Etudes préliminaires aux religions orientales dans l'empire romain 116 (Leiden: Brill, 1993), 76–113.

53. Price, *Rituals and Power*, 206. A recent overview of "imperial rituals" throughout the Roman Empire may be found in Mary Beard, John North, and Simon Price, *Religions of Rome*, 2 vols. (Cambridge: Cambridge University Press, 1998), 1: 348–62.

54. See Price, *Rituals and Power*, 65–77.

55. The imperial cult "lacked all genuine religious content," according to M. P. Nilsson, *Greek Piety* (Oxford: Clarendon, 1948), 178. See also Glen W. Bowersock, "Greek Intellectuals and the Imperial Cult in the Second Century A.D.," in *Le culte des souverains dans l'empire romain*, ed. W. Den Boer, Entretiens Hardt 19 (Geneva: Entretiens Hardt, 1973), 177–212. For a critique, see Philip A. Harland, "Honors and Worship: Emperors, Imperial Cults and Associations at Ephesus (First to Third Centuries C.E.)," *Studies in Religion/Sciences Religieuses* 25 (1996): 319–34, esp. 320–24.

56. Suetonius, *Vespasianus* 23.4, in Suetonius, *Twelve Caesars* (trans. Graves). "A huge joke": Kenneth Scott, "Humor at the Expense of the Ruler Cult" *Classical Philology* 27 (1932): 317, quoted by Price, *Rituals and Power*, 114 who rejects this view.

57. See Price, *Rituals and Power*, 126–32, and Robin Lane Fox, *Pagans and Christians* (San Francisco: Harper and Row, 1986), 46–63. Cities with temples adopted the title of νεωκόρος ("temple warden") and printed it on coins: "Pergamum, Metropolis of Asia and the first city to be Twice Temple Warden." Friesen, *Twice Neokoros*, 58.

58. Stephen Mitchell, *Anatolia: Lands, Men, and Gods in Asia Minor*, 2 vols. (Oxford: Clarendon Press, 1993), 1: 133. See also Susan E. Alcock, "Archaeology and Imperialism: Roman Expansion and the Greek City," *Journal of Mediterranean Archaeology* 2 (1989): 87–135. On Roman temples generally, see John E. Stambaugh, "The Functions of Roman Temples," *Aufstieg und Niedergang der römischen Welt* 2.16.1 (1978): 580–85.

59. See Tacitus, *Annales* 4.55–56, and Friesen, *Twice Neokoros*, 17–19.

60. Friesen, *Twice Neokoros*, 75.

61. "Faith of fifty million," Clifford Ando's phrase in *Imperial Ideology and Provincial Loyalty in the Roman Empire* (Berkeley: University of California Press, 2000), 336.

62. Lily Ross Taylor, *The Divinity of the Roman Emperor* (Middletown, Conn.: American Philological Association, 1931), 1–35.

63. See Price, *Rituals and Power*, 43, and Douglas R. Edwards, *Religion and Power: Pagans, Jews, and Christians in the Greek East* (Oxford: Oxford University Press, 1996), 49.

64. This stele is now part of the J. Paul Getty Museum in Malibu; see the text in P. Hodot, "Decret de Kyme en l'honneur du prytane Kleanax," *J. Paul Getty Museum Journal* 10 (1982): 165–80. Analysis by Richard Gordon, "The Veil of Power: Emperors, Sacrificers and Benefactors," in Beard and North, *Pagan Priests*, ed. Mary Beard and John North (Ithaca, N.Y.: Cornell University Press, 1990), 225–28.

65. See Gordon, "The Veil of Power," 228. See also Shaw, "Divine Economy," 18, on the contribution of Stoicism to euergetism. On euergetism generally in the Roman world, see Paul Veyne, *Bread and Circuses: Historical Sociology and Political Pluralism*, trans. Brian Pearce (New York: Allen Lane, 1990), 10–13.

66. Were sacrifices offered directly to the emperors—as indicated by the Kyme stele—or to the gods on behalf of the emperors? For Price, there is a contradiction between these two kinds of sacrifices. *Rituals and Power*, 247–48. See also Price, "Between Man and God: Sacrifice in the Roman Imperial Cult," *Journal of Roman Studies* 70 (1990): 28–43, and J. Pollini, "Man or God: Divine Assimilation and Imitation in the Late Republic and Early Principate," in *Between Republic and Empire*, ed. Kurt A. Raaflaub and Mark Toher (Berkeley: University of California Press, 1990), 334–63. Friesen argues instead that the question itself is inappropriate and that no contradiction exists between sacrifices to or on behalf of the emperor. *Twice Neokoros*, 150. For a prayer to both emperor and gods, see Aristides, *To Rome* 32 (*Orationes* 26:32).

67. Aristides, *To Rome* 104 (*Orationes* 26.104).

68. For the panels and commentary, see R. R. R. Smith, "The Imperial Reliefs from the Sebasteion at Aphrodisias," *Journal of Roman Studies* 77 (1987): 88–138, esp. 135–37, which compares the south portico's imperial panels to the Ara Pacis. See also Smith, "*Simulacrum Gentium*: The *Ethne* from the Sebasteion at Aphrodisias," *Journal of Roman Studies* 78 (1988): 50–77, and Joyce M. Reynolds, "Ruler Cult at Aphrodisias in the Late Republic and Under the Julio-Claudian Emperors," in *Subject and Ruler: The Cult of the Ruling Power in Classical Antiquity*, ed. Alastair Small, Journal of Roman Archaeology Supplements 17 (Ann Arbor, Mich.: Journal of Roman Archaeology, 1996), 41–50.

69. Smith, "Imperial Reliefs," 101–4, 115–17.

70. Smith, "*Simulacrum Gentium*", 59.

71. Smith, "*Simulacra Gentium*", 71. Cf. Friesen, *Reading Revelation in the Ruins*, 77–95, which points up Hellenizing tendencies in the Sebasteion.

72. See Suetonius, *Nero* 46, on Nero's dream about the images in Pompey's theater.

73. Smith, "*Simulacra Gentium*", 77 (my italics).

74. Augustus, *Res Gestae* 26–33. On Augustus's "international exploits," see Ramage, *Nature and Purpose*, 54–58.

75. Mary Louise Pratt, *Imperial Eyes: Travel Writing and Transculturation* (New York: Routledge, 1992), 7. "Autoethnography" seems closely related to Homi Bhabha's notion of "hybridity." See Bhabha, *Location of Culture*, 84–92.

76. Hopkins, *Conquerors and Slaves* (Cambridge: Cambridge University Press, 1978), 210; cf. Friesen's remark: "A municipal cult could absorb local piety and bring the imperial family closer to the subjects but at the same time avail itself of intercultural influences (from Rome and elsewhere) that are an unavoidable byproduct of imperialism." *Reading Revelation in the Ruins*, 95.

77. Quotations taken from *Martyrdom of Pionius* 20 (trans. Musurillo).

78. Marcus Aurelius, *Meditations* 10.3.

79. Brown, *The Making of Late Antiquity* (Cambridge, Mass.: Harvard University Press, 1978), 55.

80. See Augustine, *Confessions* 6.7–8. See also Tertullian, *De spectaculis* 29 (trans. Glover), on the fan "who shudders at the corpse of someone who has died a natural death, [but] lingers with the most patient eyes in the amphitheater on bodies that have been gnawed and torn apart and are still with their own blood." See also Shelby Brown, "Death as Decoration: Scenes from the Arena on Roman Domestic Mosaics," in *Pornography and Representation in Ancient Rome*, ed. Amy Richlin (Oxford: Oxford University Press, 1992), 180–211.

81. Gunderson, "The Ideology of the Arena," *Classical Antiquity* 15 (1996): 149. A social-historical assessment of the spectacles can be found in Keith Hopkins's chapter, "Murderous Games," in *Death and Renewal* (Cambridge: Cambridge University Press, 1983), 1–30. An evocative but outdated treatment may be found in Roland Auguet, *Cruelty and Civilization: The Roman Games* (London: Allen and Unwin, 1972), 184–99.

82. Juvenal, *Satirae* 10.81. See Eckart Köhne, "Bread and Circuses: The Politics of Entertainment," in *Gladiators and Caesars: The Power of Spectacle in Rome*, ed. Eckart Köhne and Cornelia Ewigleben, trans. A. Bell (Berkeley: University of California Press, 2000), 8–30, and Veyne, *Bread and Circuses*, 399–403.

83. Fronto, *Epistulae* 2.216 (trans. Haines).

84. Welch, "Roman Amphitheaters Revived," *Journal of Roman Archaeology* (1991): 273. See also Matthew Leigh on arena "poetics" in *Lucan: Spectacle and Engagement* (Oxford: Clarendon Press, 1997), 282–91.

85. Apuleius, *Metamorphoses* 4.13 (trans. Walsh); see too 10.18.

86. On special seating, see Suetonius, *Divus Augustus* 44 and Cassius Dio, *Historia romana* 55.22. For discussion, see J. C. Edmondson, "Dynamic Arenas: Gladiatorial Presentations in the City of Rome and the Construction of Roman Society During the Early Empire," in *Roman Theater and Society*, ed. William J. Slater (Ann Arbor: University of Michigan Press, 1996), 85–87, and J. Kolendo, "La répartition des places aux spectacles et la stratification sociale dans l'Empire romain," *Ktema* 6 (1981): 301–15. That such segregation held true for the province of Asia Minor is maintained by Charlotte Roueché, *Performers and Partisans at Aphrodisias in the Roman and Late Roman Periods*, Journal of Roman Studies Monographs 6 (London: Society for the Promotion of Roman Studies, 1992), 120.

87. Edmondson, "Dynamic Arenas," 94.

88. See Sabine MacCormack, *Art and Ceremony in Late Antiquity*, Transformation of the Classical Heritage 1 (Berkeley: University of California Press, 1981), 17–22.

89. Mitchell, *Anatolia*, 1.110, and Hopkins, *Death and Renewal*, 13 n. 21. Friesen, *Twice Neokoros*, 77, nuances this point, arguing against the common view that "Asiarch" was another name for the provincial high priest of the imperial cult. Nevertheless, "Asiarchs" were certainly responsible for sponsoring spectacles: see *Martyrdom of Polycarp* 12:2.

90. Robert writes: "Les combats de gladiateurs, d'origine romaine, ne sont pas restés, dans l'Orient grec, une coutume réservée aux romains établis là: la population grecque se l'est assimilée." *Les gladiateurs dans l'Orient grec* (Amsterdam: Hakkert, 1971), 239. For the western provinces, see Georges Ville, *La gladiateure en Occident des origenes à la mort de Domitien* (Rome: Palais Farnese, 1981). See

Thomas Wiedemann on Lucian's essay *Demonax*, which suggests that gladiatorial displays arrived in the Greek East out of civic rivalry between Athens and Corinth. *Emperors and Gladiators* (London: Routledge, 1992), 144–45. See also Minos Kokolakis, "Gladiatorial Games and Animal-Baiting in Lucian," *Plataon* 10 (1958): 328–51. For gladiators and wild-beast hunts in Aphrodisias, see Roueché, *Performers and Partisans*, 61–80.

91. While remains from Roman Asia Minor indicate "the mutual assimilation of Hellenistic and Roman building techniques," Marc Waelkens maintains that "the Hellenistic tradition seems to have been stronger, sometimes absorbing new ideas from Italy, but almost always giving them a new direction, more suited to local taste." "Hellenistic and Roman Influence in the Imperial Architecture of Roman Asia Minor," in *The Greek Renaissance in the Roman Empire: Papers from the Tenth British Museum Classical Colloquium*, ed. Susan Walker and Averil Cameron, Bulletin Supplement 55 (London: University of London, 1989), 88. See also J. C. Moretti, "L'adaption des théâtres de Gréce aux spectacles impèriaux," in *Spectacula*, vol. 2, *Le théâtre antique et ses spectacles*, ed. C. Landes and V. Kramérérovskis (Lattes: Le Musé, 1992), 179. On Roman imperial architecture in Asia Minor, see Cornelius C. Vermeule, *Roman Imperial Art in Greece and Asia Minor* (Cambridge, Mass.: Harvard University Press, 1968), 15–38. On "Romanization," see Richard Hingley, "The 'Legacy' of Rome: The Rise, Decline, and Fall of the Theory of Romanization," in *Roman Imperialism: Post-Colonial Perspectives*, ed. Jane Webster and Nicolas J. Cooper (Leicester: School of Archaeological Studies, 1996), 35–48.

92. Woolf, "Becoming Roman, Staying Greek: Culture, Identity, and the Civilizing Process in the Roman East," *Proceedings of the Cambridge Philological Society* 40 (1994): 130. See further Valerie M. Hope, "Negotiating Identity and Status: The Gladiators of Roman NÔmes," in *Cultural Identity in the Roman Empire*, ed. Ray Laurence and Joanne Berry (London: Routledge, 1998), 179–95. See Tacitus, *Annales* 14.20, on Roman "gladiatorial" morality versus "soft" Greek entertainment, cited by Welch, "Amphitheatres Revived," 276 n. 8.

93. Martial, *Spectacula* 20 (trans. Shackleton Bailey). See also Pliny, *Naturalis historia* 8.19. On the domination of the natural world, see Monique Clavel-Lévíque, "L'espace des jeux dans le monde romain: hégémonie, symbolique et pratique sociale," *Aufstieg und Niedergang der Römischen Welt* 2.16.3 (1986): 2405–563, esp. 2470. See J. M. C. Toynbee, *Animals in Roman Life and Art* (London: Thames and Hudson, 1973), 46–49, on Pompey's infamous slaughter of elephants, which elicited sympathy for the beasts, according to Cicero, *Tusculanae Disputationes* 7.1.3.

94. Pliny, *Naturalis historia* 8.6, 17.

95. Cassius Dio, *Historia romana* 66.25, and Augustus, *Res Gestae* 22. On *venationes* in Aphrodisias, see Roueché, *Performers and Partisans*, 61–80.

96. Hippo: Pliny, *Naturalis historia* 8.96; rhinoceros: 8.71. On Pliny's view of the natural world as a spectacle, see M. Beagon, *Roman Nature: The Thought of Pliny the Elder* (Oxford: Oxford University Press, 1992), 153–56. On the "Grand Procession" of Ptolemy Philadelphus in Alexandria in the third century B.C.E. and the Roman *venationes*, see Kathleen M. Coleman, "Ptolemy Philadelphus and the Roman Amphitheater," in Slater, *Roman Theater*, 49–68.

97. Pliny, *Naturalis historia* 9.15, discussed by Coleman, "Ptolemy Philadelphus," 63. See also Suetonius, *Divus Claudius* 21, on the panther hunt for the palace guard.

98. Donald G. Kyle, *Spectacles of Death in Ancient Rome* (New York: Routledge, 1998), 91.

99. Coleman, "Fatal Charades: Roman Executions Stage as Mythological Enactments," *Journal of Roman Studies* 80 (1990): 44–73.

100. Tertullian *Apologeticus* 15.4–5, and Martial *Spectacula* 8. See Coleman, "Fatal Charades," 63. But cf. the different interpretation in W. O. Moeller, "Juvenal and Martial *De Spectaculis* 8," *Classical Journal* 62 (1967): 369–70.

101. Bartsch, *Actors in the Audience*, 54. See also Keith R. Bradley, "The Significance of the *Spectacula* in Suetonius' *Caesares*," *Rivista Storica dell'"Antichità* 11 (1981): 129–37.

102. Potter and Mattingly, *Life, Death, and Entertainment in the Roman Empire* (Ann Arbor: University of Michigan Press, 1999), 303. Potter and Mattingly include a reproduction of Jean Léon Gérôme's famous *Pollice verso* (named for the audience gesture—"thumbs down" or possibly, according to Potter, "thumbs up"), which depicts just this scene; see 304 fig. 27.

103. Hopkins, *Death and Renewal*, 7–10. See also n. 109 below.

104. See Ville, *Gladiateure*, 365–66, which cites Plutarch's essay, *Non posse suaviter vivi secundum Epicurum* 1099B.

105. See Robert, *Gladiateurs*, 64–73, and Wiedemann, *Emperors and Gladiators*, 55–59.

106. Wiedemann, *Emperors and Gladiators*, 120–22.

107. For sources, see Magnus Wistrand, *Entertainment and Violence in Ancient Rome: The Attitudes of Roman Writers of the First Century A.D.* (Goteborg, Sweden: Acta Universitatis Gothoburgensis, 1992), 15–29.

108. Martial, *Spectacula* 31 (trans. Shackleton Bailey).

109. On gladiators and status, see Wiedemann, *Emperors and Gladiators*, 102–27; and Hopkins, *Death and Renewal*, 22–25. On free persons volunteering to fight, see Petronius, *Satyricon* 45, and discussion in Potter and Mattingly, *Life, Death, and Entertainment*, 312. See also Shelby Brown, "Explaining the Arena: Did the Romans 'Need' Gladiators?" *Journal of Roman Archaeology* 8 (1995): 382.

110. Tacitus, *Annales* 1.76.3 and 11.21.1, cited by Wiedemann, *Emperors and Gladiators*, 27–28.

111. Pliny, *Panegyricus* 33.1 (trans. Radice).

112. Cicero, *Tusculanae disputations* 2.41, translated and discussed in Toner, *Leisure and Ancient Rome* (Cambridge: Polity Press, 1995), 41. See also Cicero's dissatisfaction with Pompey's shows in *Epistulae ad familiares* 7.1.1–3.

113. Barton, *Sorrow of the Ancient Romans*, 28.

114. But see Katherine Welch's critique in her review of Barton, *The Sorrow of the Ancient Romans: The Gladiator and the Monster, Journal of Social History* (1993): 430–33.

115. Implied by Barton, "Savage Miracles: The Redemption of Lost Honor in Roman Society and the Sacrament of the Gladiator and the Martyr," *Representations* 45 (1994): 53–54.

116. Seneca, *Epistulae* 7.5 (trans. Gummere).

117. Welch, review of Barton, *Sorrow of the Ancient Romans*, 431. In the midst of a fairly harsh assessment of Barton's book, Welch unwittingly confirms Barton's thesis. See Barton, "Savage Miracles," 55: "The witness who senses that another is acting freely has the sense that the other is 'authentically' there, that the action is 'real'."

118. Ovid, *Ars amatoria* 1.141–46 (trans. Melville). On gender and artifice in *Ars Armatoria*, see Eric Downing, "Anti-Pygmalion: The *Praeceptor in Ars amatoria*, Book 3," in the *Constructions of the Classical Body*, ed. James I. Porter (Ann Arbor: University of Michigan Press, 1999), 235–51.

119. Ovid, *Amores* 3.2 (trans. Melville).

120. Ovid, *Ars amatoria* 1.170 (trans. Melville).

121. Ovid, *Ars amatoria* 1.97–100 (trans. Melville).

122. Elsner, *Imperial Rome and Christian Triumph: The Art of the Roman Empire, AD 100–450* (Oxford: Oxford University Press, 1998), 11.

123. Ovid, *Fasti* 5.567–68 (trans. Frazer), cited by Wallace-Hadrill, "Rome's Cultural Revolution," 162.

124. Suetonius, *Gaius Cailigula* 54, on which see Paul Plass, *The Game of Death in Ancient Rome: Arena Sport and Political Suicide* (Madison: University of Wisconsin Press, 1995), 74–77.

125. Suetonius, *Divus Titus* 8.2 and *Tiberius* 8.2. See discussion in Ando, *Imperial Ideology and Provincial Loyalty*, 373–85.

126. Cameron, *Circus Factions: Blues and Greens at Rome and Byzantium* (Oxford: Clarendon Press, 1976), 162. The bulk of this volume concerns the circus factions of the late Roman Empire, but see his discussion of "The Emperor and His People at the Games," 157–92.

127. Pliny, *Panegyricus* 51.4–5 (trans. Radice).

128. Suetonius, *Domitianus* 10 and Cassius Dio, *Historia romana* 59.10. See Hopkins, *Death and Renewal*, 10.

129. Cameron, *Christianity and the Rhetoric of Empire: The Development of Christian Discourse*, Sather Classical Lectures 55 (Berkeley: University of California Press, 1991), 79.

130. Dupont, *L'acteur-roi*, 23.

131. Suetonius, *Domitianus* 4, in Suetonius, *Twelve Caesars* (trans. Graves). See Robert Garland, *The Eye of the Beholder: Deformity and Disability in the Graeco-Roman World* (Ithaca, N.Y.: Cornell University Press, 1995), 45–58.

132. Suetonius, *Domitianus* 23, in Suetonius, *Twelve Caesars* (trans. Graves).

133. Virginia Burrus, *"Begotten, Not Made": Conceiving Manhood in Late Antiquity* (Stanford, Calif.: Stanford University Press, 2000), 21.

Chapter 3. A Vast Spectacle

1. Quotations taken from Philo, *De Abrahamo* 149–53 (trans. Colson). On this passage, see Georgia Frank, *The Memory of the Eyes: Pilgrims to Living Saints in Christian Late Antiquity*, Transformation of the Classical Heritage 30 (Berkeley: University of California Press, 2000), 122–24. See Aristotle, *De anima* 2.7–11, on the senses.

2. Augustine, *Confessions* 10.35 (trans. Boulding).

3. Revelation uses ὁράω fifty-five times (normally in the second aorist). Cf. James L. Resseguie, *Revelation Unsealed: A Narrative Critical Approach to John's Apocalypse* (Leiden: Brill, 1998), 33, on the priority of hearing in the book.

4. Keller, *Apocalypse Now and Then: A Feminist Guide to the End of the World* (Boston: Beacon, 1996), 42–43. Keller observes that earlier, "eschatological" examples of a shift from hearing to seeing, orality to writing, include Jer. 30:2–3 and Hab. 2:2. The story of Daniel and the "writing on the wall" (Dan. 5) comes to mind as well.

5. On "vision" in apocalyptic literature, see Collins, *Apocalyptic Imagination*, 5.

6. Catherine Keller suggests that these "eye-studded bodies . . . signify multiplicity itself," inviting reflection upon the act of interpretation and "the endless plurality of viewpoints." "Eyeing the Apocalypse," in *Postmodern Interpretations of the Bible: A Reader*, ed. A. K. M. Adam (St. Louis: Chalice, 2001), 254.

7. Harry O. Maier, "Staging the Gaze: Early Christian Apocalypses and Narrative Self-Representation," *Harvard Theological Review* 92 (1997): 131–54. Many of this article's insights appear now in Maier, *Apocalypse Unveiled: The Book of Revelation after Christendom* (Minneapolis: Fortress, 2002), esp. 64–90. I regret that here I have been unable to engage more fully with this recent publication. See also Thompson, *Apocalypse and Empire*, 52, on "script" and "play" in his analysis. In an older study, J. L. Bowman has compared Revelation and the Greco-Roman stage. "The Revelation to John: Its Dramatic Setting and Message," *Interpretation* 9 (1955): 436–53.

8. Maier, "Staging the Gaze," 146–48.

9. See studies listed in Chapter 1, n. 17, and Heikki Räisänen, "The Clash Between Christian Styles of Life in the Book of Revelation," in *Mighty Minorities? Minorities in Early Christianity: Positions and Strategies. Essays in Honour of Jacob Jervell on his Seventieth Birthday, 21 May 1995*, ed. David Hellholm, Halvor Moxnes, and Turid Karlsen Seim (Oslo: Scandinavian University Press, 1995), 151–66.

10. See also Duff, *Who Rides the Beast*, 127–33. But cf. Schussler Fiorenza's criticism of the "sectarian rivalry" thesis in *Justice and Judgment*, 207. The classic, still relevant, discussion of early Christian diversity is Walter Bauer, *Orthodoxy and Heresy in Earliest Christianity*, ed. Robert A. Kraft and Gerhard Krodel, trans. Kraft et al. (Philadelphia: Fortress, 1971), esp. 77–89. Translation of *Rechtgläubigkeit und Ketzerei im ältesten Christentum*, ed. Georg Strecker, 2nd ed. (Tübingen: Mohr-Siebeck, 1964). First published 1934. See also Robert A. Markus, "The Problem of Self-Definition: From Sect to Church," in *Jewish and Christian Self-Definition*, vol. 1: *The Shaping of Christianity in the Second and Third Centuries*, ed. E. P. Sanders (Philadelphia: Fortress, 1992), 1–15.

11. Maier, "Staging the Gaze," 151. On Revelation and the Bakhtinian category "carnivalesque," see Tina Pippin, *Death and Desire: The Rhetoric of Gender in the Apocalypse of John* (Louisville: Westminster/John Knox Press, 1992), 65–67. The book's portrayal of textual spectators rarely finds parallels in contemporary apocalypses, but see the "man from the sea" who appears before bellicose and peaceable multitudes in 4 Ezra 13.

12. "Culture of viewing": Simon Goldhill, "The Naive and Knowing Eye:

Ecphrasis and the Culture of Viewing in the Hellenistic World," in *Art and Text in Ancient Greek Culture*, ed. Simon Goldhill and Robin Osborne (Cambridge: Cambridge University Press, 1994), 197–223. See also Halvor Moxnes, "'He Saw That the City Was Full of Idols' (Acts 17:16): Visualizing the World of the First Christians," in Hellholm, Moxnes, and Seim, *Mighty Minorities*, 107–31.

13. An allusion to Tertullian's ironic description of judgment day in *De spectaculis* 30.

14. On "paradoxography" and ancient travel writing, see Georgia Frank, "The *Historia Monachorum in Aegypto* and Ancient Travel Writing," *Studia Patristica* 30 (1997): 191–95, and, a longer essay, Frank, "Miracles, Monks, and Monuments," in *Pilgrimage and Holy Space in Late Antique Egypt*, ed. David Frankfurter (Leiden: Brill, 1998), 484–504. No longer extant, the earliest known paradoxography (third century B.C.E.) is Kallimachos of Cyrene, *A Collection of Wonders from the Entire Earth Arranged by Locality* (Phlegon, *Book of Marvels*, [trans. Hansen] 3). Extant examples include Apollonios, *Wondrous Researches*, and Antigonus of Karystos, *A Collection of Marvellous Researches*. Greek texts (with Latin translations) of the paradoxographers can be found in Alessandro Giannini, ed., *Paradoxographorum Graecorum Reliquiae* (Milan, 1965).

15. Phlegon, *Book of Marvels* 34 (trans. Hansen).

16. Phlegon, *Book of Marvels* 20 (trans. Hansen). For classical Greeks, Dominique Lenfant observes, monsters were "beings who do not resemble their parents, in that they deviate from the characteristics of their species." "Monsters in Greek Ethnography and Society in the Fifth and Fourth Centuries B.C.E.," in *From Myth to Reason? Studies in the Development of Greek Thought*, ed. Richard Buxton (New York: Oxford University Press, 1999), 198.

17. Twenty children: Phlegon, *Book of Marvels* 26; hippocentaurs: 34.

18. James S. Romm, *The Edges of the Earth in Ancient Thought: Geography, Exploration, and Fiction* (Princeton, N.J.: Princeton University Press, 1992), 82–120; and Romm, "Novels Beyond Thule: Antonius Diogenes, Rabelais, Cervantes," in *The Search for the Ancient Novel*, ed. James Tatum (Baltimore: Johns Hopkins University Press, 1994), 101–16, esp. 103–8. On later traditions about the edges of civilization see Daston and Park, *Wonders and the Order of Nature*, 25–39, Stephen Greenblatt, *Marvelous Possessions: The Wonder of the New World* (Chicago: University of Chicago Press, 1991).

19. Snake-children: Phlegon, *Book of Marvels* 24 (trans. Hansen); four-headed child: 20.

20. Two marvels occur in Rome: an animal child (Phlegon, *Book of Marvels* 20) and a two-headed baby (25).

21. Pliny, *Naturalis historia* 7.3.

22. Phlegon, *Book of Marvels* 35 (trans. Hansen).

23. On lists of prodigies in the middle republican period, see Bruce MacBain, *Prodigy and Expiation: A Study in Religion and Politics in Republican Rome* (Brussels: Latamus, 1982).

24. Lucretius, *De rerum natura* 2.700 (trans. Rouse); Vitruvius, *De architectura* 7.5 (trans. Granger).

25. J. H. W. G. Liebeschuetz, *Continuity and Change in Roman Religion* (Oxford: Clarendon Press, 1979), 199.

26. Lane Fox, *Pagans and Christians*, 107. Livy, *History of Rome* 22.1.11. For recent discussions of the broader issues of vision, authority, and narrative in Livy's historiography, see both Andrew Feldherr, *Spectacle and Society in Livy's History* (Berkeley: University of California Press, 1998), 1–50; and Mary Jaeger, *Livy's Written Rome* (Ann Arbor: University of Michigan Press, 1997), 15–29.

27. See Liebeschuetz, *Continuity and Change*, 9. See also John North, "Diviners and Divination at Rome," in Beard and North, *Pagan Priests*, 54.

28. Phlegon, *Book of Marvels* 25.

29. Suetonius, *Divus Augustus* 34 (trans. Graves); Pausanias, *Graeciae description* 10.7.1; Josephus, *Bellum judaicum* 7.160. See Alcock's discussion in *Graecia Capta*, 175–80. On Gaius's failed attempt to bring the statue of Olympian Zeus to Rome, see Glen W. Bowersock, "The Mechanics of Subversion in the Roman Provinces," in *Oppostion et résistances a l'empire d'Auguste à Trajan*, ed. Adalbeto Giovannini, Entretiens Hardt 33 (Geneva: Entretiens Hardt, 1987), 297–98.

30. Mitchell, *Colonising Egypt* (Cambridge: Cambridge University Press, 1988), 1–33.

31. "Imperial eyes," "transculturation," "autoethnography": see Pratt, *Imperial Eyes*, 1–11. See also Philip de Souza, " 'They Are the Enemies of All Mankind': Justifying Roman Imperialism in the Late Republic," in Webster and Cooper, *Roman Imperialism*, 125–34, and Balsdon, *Romans and Aliens*, 18–29.

32. See Gleason on Favorinus, who "resurrects his statue . . . by the power of words alone" (*Making Men*, 20). For an overview of the period, see the survey in Graham Anderson, *The Second Sophistic: A Cultural Phenomenon in the Roman Empire* (London: Routledge, 1993). See also Margaret Miles, "Image," in *Critical Terms in Religious Studies*, ed. Mark Taylor (Chicago: University of Chicago Press, 1997), 160–72, for insights into representation and interpretation in antiquity.

33. Philostratus, *Imagines* 1.295. Other formal examples of ecphrasis include the writings of Callistratus and Philostratus the Younger. See D. P. Fowler, "Narrate and Describe: The Problem of Ekphrasis," *Journal of Roman Studies* 81 (1991): 25–35, and Jaś Elsner, *Art and the Roman Viewer: The Transformation of Art from the Pagan World to Christianity* (Cambridge: Cambridge University Press, 1995), 21–48.

34. Nicolaus 3:491. Translation and discussion in Shadi Bartsch, *Decoding the Ancient Novel: The Reader and the Role of Description in Heliodorus and Achilles Tatius* (Princeton, N.J.: Princeton University Press, 1989), 111; see also 3–39. See texts in Leonard Spengel, ed., *Rhetores Graeci*, 3 vols. (Leipzig, 1883–86). On ecphrasis, see Hermogenes 2:16–17; Aphthonius 2:46–49; Theon 2:118–20; and Nicolaus 3:491–93.

35. Elsner, *Art and the Roman*, 49.

36. On the shield of Achilles, see Murray Krieger, *Ekphrasis: The Illusion of the Natural Sign* (Baltimore: Johns Hopkins, 1992), xv; on Euripides, see Froma I. Zeitlin, "Ecphrasis and Spectacle in Euripides," in Goldhill and Osborne, *Art and Text in Ancient Greek*, 138–96.

37. Peacock mating: Achilles Tatius, *Leukippe and Kleitophon* 1.16; "festival of the Nile": Heliodorus, *Ethiopian Tale* 9.9. Bartsch, *Decoding*, 36.

38. Brigand's sword: Achilles Tatius, *Leukippe and Kleitophon* 2.23; ruse: 3.15. On Pantheia's dream, see Bartsch, *Decoding*, 87–89.

39. Bartsch, *Decoding*, 39.

40. On travel writing: in addition to Pratt, *Imperial Eyes*, see Jaś Elsner and Joan-Pau Rubiés, eds., *Voyages and Visions: Towards a Cultural History of Travel* (London: Reaktion Books, 1999), 1–56, and Mary B. Campbell, *The Witness and the Other World: Exotic European Travel Writing, 400–1600* (Ithaca, N.Y.: Cornell University Press, 1988). See also Michel de Certeau, "Ethnography: Speech, or the Space of the Other," in *The Writing of History*, trans. Tom Conley (New York: Columbia University Press, 1988), 209–43.

41. A useful discussion of travel in ancient literature (including the book of Acts) is Daniel Marguerat, "Voyages et voyageurs dans le Livre des Actes et la culture gréco-romaine," *Revue d'histoire et de philosophie religieuses* 78 (1998): 33–59. Marguerat argues that the travel theme in Acts reflects a wide range of traditions and ancient literatures, not just the Greek romance.

42. Cooper, *The Virgin and the Bride: Idealized Womanhood in Late Antiquity* (Cambridge, Mass.: Harvard University Press, 1996), 34. Other scholars have suggested the same re-articulation of the travel motif in *Daphnis and Chloe*; see B. P. Reardon, "The Greek Novel," *Phoenix* 23 (1969): 301. Konstan argues for a "loosening of local ties" in *Sexual Symmetry: Love in the Ancient Novel and Related Genres* (Princeton, N.J.: Princeton University Press, 1994), 225–31. But cf. Cooper's arguments for the deep conservatism of the romance in *Virgin and the Bride*, 36–37.

43. That ancient travel accounts bore the weight of "facticity" for many ancients is demonstrated, I suggest, by Lucian, *Vera historiae*: this story, which takes readers to the moon, among other places, makes sense as a parody only because other travel accounts were esteemed as "real." An epitome by Photius of the most far-reaching novel, *The Wonders Beyond Thule*, which includes, like the *Verae historiae*, a trip to the moon, suggests that it might be the primary target of Lucian's parody; see J. R. Morgan, "Lucian's *True Histories* and the *Wonders Beyond Thule* of Antonius Diogenes," *Classical Quarterly* 35 (1985): 475–90.

44. A strange world "out there," but not a necessarily inferior one: see Jaś Elsner on the implications of Apollonius's pilgrimage to imperial borderlands such as India and Egypt (dangerous but also, in contradistinction to Domitian's Rome, the domain of true philosophy). "Hagiographic Geography: Travel and Allegory in the *Life of Apollonius of Tyana*," *Journal of Hellenic Studies* 67 (1997): 22–37. On the Asian provenance of Greek romances, see Ewen L. Bowie, "The Readership of Greek Novels in the Ancient World," in Tatum, *Search for the Ancient Novel*, 435–59, esp. 450–51, and Thomas Hägg, *The Novel in Antiquity* (Oxford: Oxford University Press, 1983), 98.

45. Achilles Tatius, *Leukippe and Kleitophon* 4.19 (trans. Winkler).

46. Bartsch, *Decoding*, 110, see also Leigh, *Lucan*, 282–90.

47. Bartsch, *Decoding*, 115. On sophistic deportment, see Gleason, *Making Men*, 21–54.

48. Heliodorus, *Ethiopian Story* 1.2; Achilles Tatius, *Leukippe and Kleitophon* 2.24.

49. See Virginia Burrus, "Torture and Travail: Producing the Christian Martyr," in *Feminist Companion to the New Testament*, ed. Amy-Jill Levine (Sheffield: Sheffield Academic Press, forthcoming), 10, on this aspect of Cooper's argument in *Virgin and the Bride*, 37–38.

50. But cf. Royalty, *Streets of Heaven*, 125–33.

51. On the term "*angelus intepres*," see Hansgünter Reichelt, *Angelus Interpres-Texte in der Johannes-Apokalypse: Strukturen, Aussagen, und Hintergründe* (Frankfurt am Main: Lang, 1994), 101–36. The otherworldly mediator is a typical feature of ancient apocalypses; see Collins, *Apocalyptic Imagination*, 1–14, and Aune, *Revelation* 1–5, 12–16. On Rev. 17–18 as ecphrasis, see Aune, *Revelation* 17–22, Word Biblical Commentary 52C (Waco, Tex.: Word, 1998), 919–28.

52. Cf. Rev. 1:17; see also Dan. 7:15 and 4 Ezra 13:11. On emotional reactions of seers in apocalyptic narratives, see Richard J. Bauckham, *The Climax of Prophecy: Studies in the Book of Revelation* (Edinburgh: T and T Clark, 1993), 118–49; on the related topic of apocalypses reflecting the emotional experiences of their authors, see Christopher Rowland, *The Open Heaven: A Study of Apocalyptic in Judaism and Early Christianity* (New York: Crossroad, 1982), 214–47. On the puzzled narrator and ecphrasis in Greco-Roman literature, see Bartsch, *Decoding*, 25–27, and Aune, *Revelation* 17–22, 927.

53. Timothy Dwyer, *The Motif of Wonder in the Gospel of Mark*, Journal for the Study of the New Testament: Supplement Series 128 (Sheffield: Sheffield Academic Press, 1996), 82. Dwyer further notes a similar "negative" questioning of wonder in the Gospel of John (see 3:7 and 5:28).

54. These "positive" moments in Revelation capture the kind of amazement that is elicited by the authority and miracles of Jesus in the Gospels; see the several examples in the Gospel of Luke (8:25, 11:14, 24:41).

55. See Leigh, *Lucan*, 276–77, on "pathetic" and "thaumastic" viewing in the Roman arena.

56. See Frank, *Memory of the Eyes*, 18–19.

57. Longinus, *De sublimitate* 15.1–2 (trans. Russell).

58. Narcissus: see Ovid, *Metamorphoses* 3.344. On "transfixion," see Barton, *Sorrows of the Ancient Romans*, 105–6.

59. Plutarch, *De curiositate* 520C–D (trans. Helmbold).

60. See also the story of the curious Aristomenes and the witches in Apuleius, *Metamorphoses* 1.12–13.

61. Augustine, *Confessions* 6.7–8 (trans. Boulding). On Augustine and curiosity, see Barton, *Sorrows of the Ancient Romans*, 87–90. See also Tertullian, *De spectaculis* 15 (trans. Glover): "There is no public spectacle without violence to the spirit."

62. I prefer "extratextual audience" to "implied reader" or other, comparable terms; but see Stanley K. Stowers's careful discussion of "the empirical reader, the encoded explicit reader, and the encoded implicit reader. *A Rereading of Romans: Justice, Jews, and Gentiles* (New Haven, Conn.: Yale University Press, 1994), 21–22.

63. See Collins, *Crisis and Catharsis*, 150–52, on the "combat myth" here. On source theories and interpretations of Rev. 11:1–2, see Aune, *Revelation 6–16*, Word Biblical Commentary 52B (Waco, Tex.: Word, 1998), 588–98.

64. On two eschatological figures, see John J. Collins, *The Scepter and the Star: The Messiahs of the Dead Sea Scrolls* (New York: Doubleday, 1997), 71–90, and Richard J. Bauckham, "The Martyrdom of Enoch and Elijah: Jewish or Christian?" *Journal of Biblical Literature* 95 (1976): 447–58.

65. For parallels to these plagues in pagan and Jewish sources, see Aune, *Revelation 6–16*, 615. C. H. Giblin suggests that the prophets' testimony is emotionally unbearable. "Revelation 11:1–13: Its Form, Function, and Contextual Integration," *New Testament Studies* 30 (1984): 444.

66. On this "polemical parallelism," see Paul Barnett, "Polemical Parallelism: Some Further Reflections on the Apocalypse," *Journal for the Study of the New Testament* 35 (1989): 111–20, and Royalty, *Streets of Heaven*, 129. For "conquer," see Rev. 2:7, 11, 17, 26, and 3:5, 12, 21.

67. On the dishonor and pollution associated with the unburied dead, see Robert Parker, *Miasma: Pollution and Purification in Early Greek Thought* (Oxford: Clarendon Press, 1983), 45–46.

68. While some interpreters take "the dwellers of the earth" here to refer exclusively to Jews, Schüssler Fiorenza rightly rejects this view in *Justice and Judgement*, 63 n. 91; see also Aune, *Revelation 1–5*, 240. On earthquakes in the Bible, see Bauckham, *Climax of Prophecy*, 199–209.

69. See Rev. 16:19, 17:18, 18:10, 16, 18–21, where "the great city" is unquestionably Rome. For analysis, see William W. Reader, "The Riddle of the Identification of the Polis in Rev. 11:1–13," *Studia Evangelica* 7 (1982): 407–14, and Robert H. Mounce's outline of the scholarly discussion. *The Book of Revelation*, New International Commentary on the New Testament (Grand Rapids, Mich.: Eerdmans, 1977), 226–27.

70. Sodom and idolatry (see Isa.1:10, Jer. 23:14, Ezek. 16:46), and Egypt and slavery (Isa. 19:1, Ezek. 20:7). On this passage, see P. G. R. de Villiers, "The Lord Was Crucified in Sodom and Egypt: Symbols in the Apocalypse of John," *Neotestementica* 22 (1988): 125–38, and David E. Aune, "Charismatic Exegesis in Early Judaism and Early Christianity," in *The Pseudepigrapha and Early Biblical Interpretation*, ed. James H. Charlesworth and Craig A. Evans (Sheffield: JSOT, 1993), 126–50.

71. Carey, *Elusive Apocalypse: Reading Authority in the Revelation to John*. Studies in American Biblical Hermeneutics 15 (Macon, Ga.: Mercer University Press, 1999), 144.

72. Said, *Orientalism*, 85. See Michel Foucault's discussion of "heterotopic" sites. "Of Other Spaces," *Diacritics* 16 (1986): 22–27. On "biblicizing" (as opposed to typology), see Miriam Peskowitz, "Tropes of Travel," *Semeia* 75 (1996): 177–96, and Frank, *Memory of the Eyes*, 17–19.

73. The Devil deceives "the whole world" (ἡ οἰκουμένη ὅλη; Rev. 3:10, 12:9, 16:14), or "the whole earth" (ὅλη ἡ γῆ; Rev. 13:3).

74. See the terse command issued in a contemporaneous text: "Fear God. Honor the emperor" (1 Pet. 2:17).

75. See Gunkel, *Schöpfung und Chaos*, 336–78, and Collins, *Combat Myth in the Book of Revelation*, 161–65.

76. Charles, *Revelation*, 1:348. On Revelation's "glass sea" (4:6; 15:2–3; cf. Exod. 15:8) and "the primeval ocean of Ancient Near Eastern mythology," see David J. Halperin, *Faces of the Chariot: Early Jewish Responses to Ezekiel's Vision*, Texte und Studien zum antiken Judentum 16 (Tübingen: Mohr-Siebeck, 1988), 93–96.

77. Carey, *Elusive Apocalypse*, 153. See also Barnett, "Polemical Parallelism," 115.

78. See Aune, *Revelation 6–16*, 738–40, and Bauckham, *Climax of Prophecy*, 423–31.

79. *Sibylline Oracles* 8:68–72 (trans. Collins).

80. Cf. Matt. 7:15. Revelation's parody of the Roman imperial cult here has often been noted by scholars. Steven Friesen offers the most recent, most sophisticated look at the issue in *Reading Revelation in the Ruins*, esp. 77–95, 201–4. See also Thompson, *Apocalypse and Empire*, 158–64.

81. See Steven J. Scherrer, "Signs and Wonders in the Imperial Cult: A New Look at a Roman Religious Institution in the Light of Rev. 13:13–15," *Journal of Biblical Literature* 104 (1984): 599–610.

82. Royalty argues: "Revelation 18 sounds like 'biblical' language because it is just that—phrases, words, and images taken from the Hebrew scriptures and crafted into a new, highly rhetorical *psogos* or invective against Babylon." *Streets of Heaven*, 196. See also Friesen, *Reading Revelation in the Ruins*, 204–9. On this passage as an angelic dirge, see Adela Yarbro Collins, "Revelation 18: Taunt-Song or Dirge?" in Lambrecht, *L'Apocalypse johannique*, 185–204.

83. For a technical discussion of the identification of Rome with Babylon, see C.-H. Hunzinger, "Babylon als Deckname für Rom und die Datierung des I. Petrusbriefes," in *Gottes Wort und Gottes Land: Hans-Wilhelm Hertzberurg zum 70. Geburtstag*, ed. H. G. Reventlow (Göttingen: Vandenhoeck & Ruprecht, 1965), 67–77. Revelation, 4 Ezra, 2 Baruch, 1 Peter, and the Sibylline Oracles establish a discursive "Babylon" as a key component in an "endless exhibition" of Jewish apocalyptic historiography. On Rome and Babylon, see Royalty, *Streets of Heaven*, 177–209. See also Collins, "The Political Perspective of the Revelation to John," *Journal of Biblical Literature* 96 (1977): 241–56, and *Crisis and Catharsis*, 121–24.

84. Royalty, *Streets of Heaven*, 196.

85. Cf. Martha Himmelfarb on "vertical" travel in apocalyptic literature. *Ascent to Heaven in Jewish and Christian Apocalypses* (Oxford: Oxford University Press, 1993).

86. The wealth of these spectators has received much comment: see Royalty, *Streets of Heaven*, 188, Bauckham, *Climax of Prophecy*, 338–83, and J. Nelson Kraybill, *Imperial Cult and Commerce in the Book of Revelation*, Journal for the Study of the New Testament: Supplement Series 132 (Sheffield: Sheffield Academic Press, 1996), who argues that merchants were part of a coercive, imperial cult environment in Asia Minor.

87. Collins, *Crisis and Catharsis*, 119.

88. See Collins, *Apocalyptic Imagination*, 214.

89. See also Rev. 5:9, 7:9, 11:9, 13:7, 14:6, and 19:1; on this crowd, see Carey, *Elusive Apocalypse*, 140, and Charles, *Revelation*, 1:201, which identifies this "great multitude" with the sealed 144,000. Others, like Collins, contend that "this is the vision of the ultimate, complete salvation and triumph of all the faithful." *The Apocalypse*, New Testament Message 22 (Collegeville, Minn.: Liturgical Press, 1979), 53.

90. *Sibylline Oracles* 8.130 (trans. Collins). Being made into a "spectacle" is of course a traditional threat: see, for example, the oracle against Ninevah (Nah. 3:5–7). For discussion, see Collins, *Crisis and Catharsis*, 92–93, and Larry T. Kreitzer's interesting article, "Sibylline Oracles 8, the Roman Imperial Adventus Coinage of Hadrian, and the Apocalypse of John," *Journal for the Study of the Pseudepigrapha* 4 (1989): 69–85.

91. Tertullian, *De spectaculis* 30 (trans. Glover).

92. Tertullian, *De spectaculis* 20 (trans. Glover).

93. Maier, "Staging the Gaze," 153; Maier cites as well Minucius Felix, *Octavius* 10.3–5.

94. Simon Goldhill, "The Erotic Eye: Visual Stimulation and Cultural Conflict," in *Being Greek under Rome: Cultural Identity, the Second Sophistic and the Development of Empire*, ed. Simon Goldhill and Robin Osborne (Cambridge: Cambridge University Press, 2001), 182–84. See also Barton, *Sorrow of the Ancient Romans*, 91–95.

95. Tertullian, *De spectaculis* 30 (trans. Glover). Just prior, Tertullian defines these "things of greater joy" by alluding to 1 Cor. 2:19: "What no eye has seen, nor ear heard, nor the human heart conceived, what God has prepared for those who love him."

96. Tertullian, *De spectaculis* 16 (trans. Glover).

97. Tertullian, *De spectaculis* 30 (trans. Glover).

98. See also Rev. 16:6, and Tina Pippin's discussion of the "ideology of desire" in *Death and Desire*, 69–86.

Chapter 4. As If Slain

1. See Stephen Greenblatt, *Renaissance Self-Fashioning: From More to Shakespeare* (Chicago: University of Chicago Press, 1984), 9.

2. Shaw, "Divine Economy," 54. See also Catharine Edwards's observation: "Roman expositions of virtuous behaviors do not differ very substantially from Greek." *The Politics of Immorality in Ancient Rome* (Cambridge: Cambridge University Press, 1993), 21.

3. Shaw, "Divine Economy," 29, quotes Epictetus (Arrian, *Epicteti dissertationes* 1.9.3): "Never say 'I am an Athenian' or 'I am a Corinthian,' but rather 'I am of cosmic'."

4. Famously mapped in Foucault, *The History of Sexuality*, vol. 2, *The Use of Pleasure*, trans. Robert Hurley (New York: Pantheon, 1985), and vol. 3, *The Care of the Self*, trans. Robert Hurley (New York: Pantheon, 1986). Veyne argues that

the valorization of domesticity in this period follows from the "emasculation" of male Roman aristocrats in the political sphere by the institution of the principate. "La famille et l'amour sous le Haut-Empire romain," *Annales E.S.C.* 33 (1978): 36–63. Cf. Susan Treggiari, *Roman Marriage: Iusti Coniuges from the Time of Cicero to the Time of Ulpian* (Oxford: Clarendon Press, 1991), 185–228. In *Care of the Self*, 43, Foucault avers that the "cultivation of the self has a rather large historical range, but reached its peak at that particular moment," that is, under the Roman principate. See the summary in Elizabeth A. Clark, "Foucault, the Fathers, and Sex," *Journal of American Academy of Religion* 56 (1988): 622–27, and Averil Cameron, "Redrawing the Map: Early Christian Territory after Foucault," *Journal of Roman Studies* 76 (1986): 266–71.

    5. Foucault, *Care of the Self*, 84.

    6. Dale B. Martin, *The Corinthian Body* (New Haven, Conn.: Yale University Press, 1995), 207. See Foucault, *Care of the Self*, 112–23.

    7. Plutarch, *Conjugalia Praecepta* 138C, quoted by Andrew S. Jacobs, "A Family Affair: Marriage, Class, and Ethics in the Apocryphal Acts of the Apostles," *Journal of Early Christian Studies* 7 (1999): 116; see pp. 109–23 for a careful analysis of evidence relating to "conjugal morality" under the Roman Empire.

    8. Amy Richlin registers deep dissatisfaction with Foucault in several places. She launches an opening salvo in "Zeus and Metis: Foucault, Feminism, Classics," *Helios* 18 (1991): 160–80, but perhaps the best introduction to her negative assessment of Foucault is "The Ethnographer's Dilemma and the Dream of a Lost Golden Age," in *Feminist Theory and the Classics*, ed. Nancy Rabinowitz and Amy Richlin (New York: Routledge, 1993), 272–304. In an otherwise balanced and highly important work on Roman sexuality Richlin opines: "In the confines of this endnote I suggest that Foucault's work on antiquity is so ill-informed that it is not really worth reading." *The Garden of Priapus: Sexuality and Aggression in Roman Humor*, rev. ed. (Oxford: Oxford University Press, 1992), xxix n. 2. For an admirable attempt to bridge the gap between Foucauldian and anti-Foucauldian classicists, see Marilyn B. Skinner, "Zeus and Leda: The Sexuality Wars in Contemporary Classical Scholarship," *Thamyris* 3 (1996): 103–23. Foucault's specific interpretations may be problematic, but his general argument, and his treatment of sex as a discourse of power, like the work of Paul Veyne that inspires it, remains *very much* "worth reading."

    9. Cooper, "Insinuations of Womanly Influence: An Aspect of the Christianization of the Roman Aristocracy," *Journal of Roman Studies* 82 (1992): 151, and Cooper, *Virgin and the Bride*, 11–17.

    10. See Jo-Ann Shelton, "Pliny the Younger and the Ideal Wife," *Classica et Medievalia* 41 (1990): 163–86, and works listed in n. 8 above.

    11. Cooper, "Womanly Influence," 152–53. See also John J. Winkler's conclusion: "most of [ancient Mediterranean] men's observations and moral judgments about women and sex and so forth have minimal descriptive validity and are best understood as coffeehouse talk, addressed to men themselves." *The Constraints of Desire: The Anthropology of Sex and Gender in Ancient Greece* (New York: Routledge, 1990), 6 and 70.

    12. Burrus, "Begotten, Not Made," 21; pp. 18–35 of this book offer an effi-

cient survey of problems and "solutions" of masculinity in the ancient and late-ancient Roman world. See also Gleason, *Making Men*, 159–68. A groundbreaking anthropology of masculinity in diverse settings is David Gilmore, *Manhood in the Making: Cultural Concepts of Masculinity* (New Haven, Conn.: Yale University Press, 1990). On the stake of gender studies, see Daniel Boyarin, *Unheroic Conduct: The Rise of Heterosexuality and the Invention of the Jewish Man*, Controversies: Critical Studies in Jewish Literature, Culture, and Society 8 (Berkeley: University of California Press, 1997), 1–29; for the ancient context, see esp. 1–13. See too Boyarin, "Gender," in Taylor, *Critical Terms*, 117–59.

13. Goldhill, *Foucault's Virginity: Ancient Erotic Fiction and the History of Sexuality* (Cambridge: Cambridge University Press, 1995), 110–11.

14. See *Constraints of Desire*, 101–26, esp. 125, on "serious" and "play" at the beginning and end of *Daphnis and Chloe*. See also Cooper, *Virgin and the Bride*, 23: "But romance . . . spoke in a voice both light-hearted and acutely serious to the men and women of the ancient polis." Goldhill, *Foucault's Virginity*, 6–30, offers an extended meditation on the "pleasures" of the story.

15. On the novel's bucolic atmosphere, see B. P. Reardon, "Μῦθος οὐ λόγος: Longus's Lesbian Pastorals," in Tatum, *Search for the Ancient Novel*, 135–47.

16. "Lycaenion" is the feminine diminutive form of λύκος: the prowling Lycaenion is a "she-wolf." There is also a real "she-wolf" (*Daphnis and Chloe* 1.11), and Dorcon, who disguises himself in a wolf's hide in order to deceive and rape Chloe (*Daphnis and Chloe* 1.20). See discussion in Winkler, *Constraints of Desire*, 118.

17. *Daphnis and Chloe* 3.15 (trans. Gill).

18. *Daphnis and Chloe* 3.19 (trans. Gill, slightly modified).

19. Winkler, *Constraints of Desire*, 118–22.

20. *Daphnis and Chloe* 4.40 (trans. Gill).

21. *Daphnis and Chloe* 4.40 (trans. Gill, modified). Gill, following the text of M. D. Reeve's Teubner edition (1982), has "shepherd's games" (ποιμένων παίγνια) rather than "children's games." I follow instead the text of Edmonds. Winkler's chapter also favors the variant of "children's games": see *Constraints of Desire*, 230 n. 1.

22. Winkler, *Constraints of Desire*, 124.

23. Ibid., 122. Cf. David Konstan's contention: "The judgment of the text, then, is that Lycaenium's teachings are suitable to marriage, rather than to the premarital sexual play of Daphnis and Chloe." *Sexual Symmetry*, 89. Konstan views Daphnis's "amnesia," the goatherd's repression of Lycaenion's lecture, as the expression of the genre's interest in maintaining "mutuality" in the central love relationship. According to Konstan, the text invites the reader to imagine that this first coital encounter was not violent.

24. Winkler, *Constraints of Desire*, 117. Further on "nature" versus "nuture" in the novel, see Froma I. Zeitlin, "Gardens of Desire in Longus's *Daphnis and Chloe*: Nature, Art, and Imitation," in Tatum, *Search for the Ancient Novel*, 148–70.

25. Winkler, *Constraints of Desire*, 124.

26. This is not to say that Winkler's reading is the final interpretation of *Daphnis and Chloe*. Rather, the brilliance of Winkler's treatment is that it leaves open the possibility of different readings, a reflection of the manner in which the Greek romance raised problems rather than finally solving them. For a careful assessment of Winkler's interpretation, see Goldhill, *Foucault's Virginity*, 30–45.

27. Holt N. Parker, "The Teratogenic Grid," in *Roman Sexualities*, ed. Judith P. Hallet and Marilyn B. Skinner (Princeton, N.J.: Princeton University Press, 1997), 48. Much of the scholarship on Roman sexuality and gender appropriates work on classical Greece, especially the contributions of David M. Halperin, *One Hundred Years of Homosexuality and Other Essays on Greek Love* (New York: Routledge, 1990), 15–40. See Stephen D. Moore's recent overview of scholarship on ancient sexuality and gender, noting especially the work of Halperin, Winkler, and Foucault, in *God's Beauty Parlor: And Other Queer Spaces in and Around the Bible*, Contraversions: Jews and Other Differences (Stanford, Calif.: Stanford University Press, 2001), 135–46.

28. Brooten, *Love Between Women: Early Christian Responses to Female Homoeroticism* (Chicago: University of Chicago Press, 1996), 116. Maud Gleason writes: "The essential idea here is that there exist masculine and feminine 'types' that do not necessarily correspond to the anatomical sex of the person in question." "The Semiotics of Gender: Physiognomy and Self-Fashioning in the Second Century C.E.," in *Before Sexuality: The Construction of Erotic Experience in the Ancient Greek World*, ed. David M. Halperin, John J. Winkler, and Froma I. Zeitlin (Prinecton, N.J.: Princeton University Press, 1990), 390. See also Thomas Laquer, *Making Sex: Body and Gender from the Greeks to Freud* (Cambridge, Mass.: Harvard University Press, 1990), 25–62.

29. See Jonathan Walters, " 'No More Than a Boy': The Shifting Construction of Masculinity from Ancient Greece to the Middle Ages," *Gender and History* 5 (1993): 20–33, esp. 26.

30. See Richlin, *Garden of Priapus*, 105–33. Cf. Anthony Corbeill's argument that the consistent derision of "homosexual" effeminacy in Roman sources indicates that, for Romans, "effeminacy connotes a specific sexuality." "Dining Deviants in Roman Political Invective," Hallett and Skinner, *Roman Sexualities*, 116. Reflecting on the same sources, Richlin, *Garden of Priapus*, 222, observes: "effeminate men are often claimed to be not homosexual, but bisexual, in fact, overtly active with both sexes." To seek, as Corbeill does, something akin to a modern "sexual orientation" in the Roman world leads him to the strange and problematic conclusion that the "pathic" (*cinaedus*) stereotype arises from a prior actuality: "we must expect there to be some truth behind these constructions of effeminacy." "Dining Deviants," 117. In a separate essay (cited approvingly by Corbeill), Richlin proves herself not wholly unsympathetic to this perspective. "Not Before Homosexuality: The Materiality of the *Cinaedus* and the Roman Law Against Love Between Men," *Journal of the History of Sexuality* 3 (1993): 523–73.

31. See Brooten, *Love Between Women*, 29–72.

32. Jonathan Walters, "Invading the Roman Body: Manliness and Impenetrability in Roman Thought," in Hallett and Skinner, *Roman Sexualities*, 37. The

notable exception, Walters observes, is the Roman soldier, whose body was subjected to corporal punishment.

33. As Stephen D. Moore and Janice Capel Anderson observe: "Mastery is synonymous with masculinity in most of the Greek and Latin texts that survive from antiquity. Such mastery could be directed outward as the domination of others or inward as domination of oneself." "Taking It Like a Man: Masculinity in 4 Maccabees," *Journal of Biblical Literature* 117 (1998): 272.

34. See Foucault, *Care of the Self*, 4–36, and Winkler, *Constraints of Desire*, 17–44.

35. Quotations from Artemidorus, *Oneirocritica* 78 (trans. White).

36. Parker, "Teratogenic Grid," 53.

37. Martin, *Corinthian Body*, 177. See also Winkler, *Constraints of Desire*, 39.

38. Loraux distinguishes between two modes of death, by the sword and by the rope, manly and womanly, respectively. The sword is privileged without qualification, and the "virile" women in the plays of Euripides choose to throw themselves on the sharp instrument rather than accept the feminine noose. *Tragic Ways of Killing a Woman*, trans. A. Forster (Cambridge, Mass.: Harvard University Press, 1987), 14–15. See the suicide by sword of Charite, whose "manly spirit" (*animam virilem*) expires (Apuleius, *Metamorphoses* 8.14).

39. Apuleius, *Metamorphoses* 2.17 (trans. Walsh).

40. Apuleius, *Metamorphoses* 3.20 (trans. Walsh, slightly modified).

41. Winkler, *Auctor and Actor: A Narratological Reading of Apuleius' Golden Ass* (Berkeley: University of California Press, 1985), 175.

42. The formative moment for this topic was Laura Mulvey's essay, "Visual Pleasure and Narrative Cinema," *Screen* 16 (1975): 6–18; repr. in *Visual and Other Pleasures*, ed. Laura Mulvey (Bloomington: University of Indiana Press, 1989), 14–26. Criticism of Mulvey's essentialist male-female dichotomy has not diminished this signal contribution: see Teresa de Lauretis, *Technologies of Gender: Essays on Theory, Film, and Fiction* (Bloomington: Indiana University Press, 1987), 127–48. For a useful introduction to the "gaze" and film criticism, see "Introduction" in *Feminism and Film*, ed. E. Ann Kaplan, Oxford Readings in Feminism (Oxford: Oxford University Press, 2000), 1–16.

43. Mulvey, "Visual Pleasure," 11. See Goldhill, *Foucault's Virginity*, 72, and Francoise Frontisi Ducroux, "Eros, Desire, and the Gaze," trans. Kline, in *Sexuality in Ancient Art*, ed. Natalie Boymel Kampen (Cambridge: Cambridge University Press, 1996), 81–100, esp. 95.

44. E. Ann Kaplan, "Is the Gaze Male?" in *Women and Film: Both Sides of the Camera* (New York: Methuen, 1983), 31. See also Blake Leyerle's remark: "The gendered gaze ensures a hierarchical positioning of male and female encoded in terms such as active/passive and subjective/objective." "John Chrysostom on the Gaze," *Journal of Early Christian Studies* 1 (1993): 159.

45. Frank, *Memory of the Eyes*, 124. See also Shadi Bartsch, "The Philosopher as Narcissus: Vision, Sexuality, and Self-Knowledge in Classical Antiquity," in Elsner, *Visuality Before*, 70–97, esp. 74–77, on Plato's *Phaedrus*.

46. Rousselle, *Porneia: On Desire and the Body in Antiquity*, trans. Felicia Pheasant (New York: Basil Blackwell, 1988), 65.

47. Achilles Tatius, *Leukippe and Kleitophon* 1.9 (trans. Winkler). See the famous antithesis of Jesus that associates sight and intercourse (Matt. 5:27–29a). See also *Daphnis and Chloe* 1.13–14: Chloe stares at Daphnis well in advance of the "wedding night."

48. Achilles Tatius, *Leukippe and Kleitophon* 1.19 (trans. Winkler).

49. See Royalty, *Streets of Heaven*, 223–24, on Revelation's vice list and parallels in Pauline (esp. 1 Cor. 6:9–10; Gal. 5:19–21; and Eph. 5:3–5) and moral philosophical traditions. See also Aune, *Revelation 17–22*, 1132.

50. See Edwards, *Politics of Immorality*, 124–25, and Stowers, *Rereading Romans*, 53.

51. MacMullen, *Enemies of the Roman Order: Treason, Unrest, and Alienation in the Empire* (Cambridge, Mass.: Harvard University Press, 1966), 95–127.

52. Greeks, of course, had their own views, and ἀνδρεία ("manliness") remained a cardinal virtue for them, despite Roman defamation to the contrary. On the Greek counterparts—ἀνήρ and ἀνδρεία—see Moore and Anderson, " 'Taking It like a Man," 253, and Halvor Moxnes, "Conventional Values in the Hellenistic World," in *Conventional Values of the Hellenistic Greeks*, ed. Per Bilde et al., Studies in Hellenistic Civilization 8 (Aarhus: University of Aarhus Press, 1997), 263–84.

53. Martial, *Epigrams* 2.86; Cicero, *Tusculanae disputationes* 1.1.2. Woolf observes that the ideal Roman governor was "to safeguard the good that remained of Greek civilization by saving imperial Greeks from their characteristic vices." "Becoming Roman, Staying Greek," 125. See also Edwards, *Politics of Immorality*, 95.

54. The present treatment of gender and sexuality in Revelation is greatly indebted to Stephen D. Moore, "Revolting Revelations," in *The Personal Voice in Biblical Interpretation*, ed. Inga Rosa Kitzberger (London: Routledge, 1999), 183–98. See now Moore, *God's Beauty Parlor*, 173–99.

55. The comparative particle ὡς "does not mean that the Lamb only *appeared* to have been slaughtered but rather that the Lamb had been slaughtered and was alive"; see Aune, *Revelation 1–5*, 353. Note the description of the "amazing" beast with seven heads, one of which appears "as if slain" (ὡς ἐσφαγμένην). Unlike the Lamb, which remains "as if slain," the beast is miraculously healed (Rev. 13:3); see John Court, *Myth and History in the Book of Revelation* (Atlanta: John Knox Press, 1979), 133.

56. J. A. du Rand, "The Imagery of the Heavenly Jerusalem (Revelation 21:9–22:5)," *Neotestementica* 22 (1988): 73.

57. On the throne room imagery, see Aune, "Roman Imperial Court," 14–22; Leonard Thompson, *Apocalypse and Empire*, 53–73; and Royalty, *Streets of Heaven*, 97–101. Further on the Lamb, see Sophie Laws, *In the Light of the Lamb: Image, Parody, and Theology in the Apocalypse of John*, Good News Studies 31 (Wilmington, Del.: Michael Glazier, 1988), 27–31. For a recent overview of studies of the Lamb and the Christology of Revelation, see Thomas B. Slater, *Christ and Community: A Socio-Historical Study of the Christology of Revelation*. Journal for the Study of the New Testament: Supplement Series 178 (Sheffield: Sheffield Aca-

demic Press, 1999), 57–61. Slater argues that the slain Lamb reflects the oppression experienced by John's community. Of earlier studies of Revelation's Christology, see T. Holtz, *Die Christologie der Offenbarung Johannis*, Texte und Untersuchungen 85 (Berlin: Akademie Verlag, 1971).

58. William Klassen comments: "To be sure, the Lamb appearing as if slain is no weakling." "Vengeance in the Apocalypse of John," *Catholic Biblical Quarterly* 28 (1966): 305. G. R. Beasley-Murray charts three stages in Revelation 5's "royal investiture" of the Lamb: exaltation, presentation, and enthronement. *The Book of Revelation*, New Century Bible (London: Oliphants, 1974), 110–11. See also Slater, *Christ and Community*, 168–74.

59. On parallels to this narrative setting in the Hellenistic theater, see T. C. Voortman and J. A. du Rand, "The Worship of God and the Lamb: Exploring the Liturgical Setting of the Apocalypse of John," *Ekklesiatikos Pharos* 80 (1998): 56–67.

60. In Greek tragedy, σφάζω is the verb of virgin sacrifice; see Loraux, *Tragic Ways of Killing*, 31–48.

61. Bauckham, *Climax of Prophecy*, 183. Cf. Laws, who suggests that the blood of the Lamb not sacrificial but "the means of freedom and purchase." *Light of the Lamb*, 30.

62. Moore, "Revolting Revelations," 197 n. 8.

63. The classic "liberationist" treatment of Revelation remains Allan A. Boesak, *Comfort and Protest: Reflections on the Apocalypse of John of Patmos* (Philadelphia: Westminster, 1987). Boesak dedicates his book to "all those who . . . have struggled . . . They are seeing the power of the beast. They shall see the victory of the Lamb" (*Comfort and Protest*, 5). For an overview of liberationist treatments, see Carey, *Elusive Apocalypse*, 32–43. See also, for example, Collins, "Political Perspective," 273, which argues that Revelation encourages "a passive acceptance of suffering" and expresses "a fundamental critique of the rule of Rome"; see also Collins, *Crisis and Catharsis*, 124–31.

64. Aune, *Revelation 6–16*, 835, argues that "and before the Lamb" is a gloss of a later editor, "since the Lamb is in effect subordinated to the angels." The present analysis remains concerned with the final form of the text, which, according to Aune, would have included this "gloss."

65. For a helpful survey of "attitudes to the damned" in ancient apocalypses, see Richard J. Bauckham, "The Conflict of Justice and Mercy: Attitudes to the Damned in Apocalyptic Literature," *Apocrypha* 1 (1990): 181–96. Commentators on Revelation sometimes construe Rev. 14:9–10 as a warning to the faithful rather than "gloating": see, for example, Schüssler Fiorenza, *Revelation: Vision of a Just World*, Proclamation (Minneapolis: Fortress, 1991), 89. Others argue that the desire for revenge is "understandable": Adela Yarbro Collins observes that "the violent deeds of the Roman Empire called forth a desire for vengeance." *Crisis and Catharsis*, 144. See also Slater, *Christ and Community*, 205, and David L. Barr, *Tales of the End: A Narrative Commentary on the Book of Revelation* (Santa Rosa, Calif.: Polebridge Press, 1988), 86, on "avenge" in Rev. 6:10: "Retribution is a very important theme in the Apocalypse . . . perhaps not a noble sentiment but one understandable by anyone who has witnessed any great evil."

66. This passage and several sections of chapter 7 are absent from the oldest manuscripts. See also 1 Enoch 27:2–3; Luke 16:23; and Rev. 9:2.

67. The parallels are legion: see, for example, 2 Clement 7:6 and 17:5.

68. Moore, *God's Gym*, 20.

69. Michel Foucault, *Discipline and Punish: The Birth of the Prison*, trans. Alan Sheridan (New York: Vintage, 1979), 32–69. On tattoos in the ancient world, see Christopher P. Jones, "*Stigma*: Tatooing and Branding in Graeco-Roman Antiquity," *Journal of Roman Studies* 77 (1987): 139–55. See also Aune, *Revelation 6–16*, 456–59, on "Marking, Branding, and Tattooing in the Ancient World."

70. Wiedemann, *Emperors and Gladiators*, 138. See Livy, *Roman History* 41.20.10–12, in which Antiochus imports gladiator shows to rouse enthusiasm in men.

71. Pliny the Younger, *Panegyricus* 33.1 (trans. Radice).

72. Apuleius, *Metamorphoses* 10:23–35.

73. Lucian, *De morte Peregrini* 9 (trans. Harmon). Cited by and discussed in K. J. Dover, *Greek Homosexuality* (Cambridge, Mass.: Harvard University Press, 1989), 106–7.

74. An important difference exists here between the "branding" of the beast and the "sealing" of the servants of God in Revelation 7. As Aune notes, branding was nearly always a sign of degradation in antiquity; seals, in contrast, "represent the authority and power of its owner." *Revelation 6–16*, 457–58.

75. Aune, *Revelation 6–16*, 835.

76. The book here conflates two figures from Daniel 7 and 10: "one like a son of man" and "the ancient of days"; see Laws, *Light of the Lamb*, 25. Adela Yarbro Collins argues convincingly that the book's "son of man" tradition reflects an early Palestinian Christianity and is independent of the one found in the Synoptics. "The 'Son of Man' Tradition and the Book of Revelation," in *Cosmology and Eschatology in Jewish and Christian Apocalypticism*, ed. John J. Collins, Journal for the Study of Judaism: Supplement Series 50 (Leiden: Brill, 1996), 159–97.

77. On the female body in Christian martyr accounts, see Margaret M. Miles, *Carnal Knowing: Female Nakedness and Religious Meaning in the Christian West* (New York: Vintage, 1989), 53–80.

78. *Acts of Paul and Thecla* 34 (trans. Elliott). Virginia Burrus notes: "a fire blazes around the young virgin Thecla protecting her body not only from bestial attack but also from the intrusive male gaze." "Word and Flesh: The Bodies and Sexuality of Ascetic Women in Christian Antiquity," *Journal of Feminist Studies in Religion* 10 (1994): 29.

79. On Revelation's influence on this martyr account's conception of heaven, see R. Petraglio, "Des influences de l'Apocalypse dans la 'Passio Perpetuae' 11–13," in *L'Apocalypse de Jean: Traditions exégetiques et iconographiques*, ed. Y. Christie (Geneva: Librairie Droz, 1979), 43–56.

80. *Martyrdom of Perpetua and Felicitas* 20 (trans. Musurillo). See *Martyrdom of Perpetua and Felicitas* 18.2 (trans. Musurillo): "Perpetua went along . . . putting down everyone's stare by her own intense gaze."

81. *Martyrdom of Perpetua and Felicitas* 21 (trans. Musurillo).

82. If this discussion of the two martyr accounts places too much emphasis

on the passivity of Thecla and Perpetua, it does so to describe one dimension of the violence of the arena so as to highlight the hierarchy of domination and submission that materializes in Rev. 14:9–10. A full treatment would have to take into consideration the "gender-bending" in both accounts, and the ramifications of this for power relations. See Virginia Burrus, "Torture and Travail," 20–24; Patricia Cox Miller, *Dreams in Late Antiquity: Studies in the Imagination of a Culture* (Princeton, N.J.: Princeton University Press, 1994), 148–84; and Elizabeth Castelli, " 'I Will Make Mary Male': Pieties of the Body and Gender Transformation of Christian Women in Late Antiquity," in *Body Guards: The Cultural Politics of Gender Ambiguity*, ed. Julia Epstein and Kristina Straub (New York: Routledge, 1991), 29–49.

83. See Maier, "Staging the Gaze," 140–43.

84. See Collins, "The 'Son of Man' Tradition," 189–94, and Slater, *Christ and Community*, 108–61.

85. But see Moore, "Revolting Revelations," 186–87.

86. See 4 Ezra 13:10–18.

87. Whether this figure is to be identified with the rider in Rev. 6:2 remains an open question. A recent proposal that this rider is a "counterfeit," a "false messiah," is found in Allen Kerkeslager, "Apollo, Greco-Roman Prophecy, and the Rider on the White Horse in Rev. 6:2," *Journal of Biblical Literature* 112 (1993): 116–21. For an overview of alternative interpretations, see Slater, *Christ and Community*, 175; on the figure generally, see pp. 209–35.

88. Strangely, this anonymity seems deeply compromised in v. 14: "his name is called The Word of God," and then again in v. 16: "On his robe and on his thigh he had a name inscribed, 'King of Kings and Lord of lords." On this passage as an account of the messianic "parousia," see Schüssler Fiorenza, *Vision of a New World*, 105. Aune makes the salutary observation: "The blood mentioned here is not primarily a metaphor for the atoning death of Christ but rather a literal reference to the heavenly warrior whose garment is stained *with the blood of those he has slain*." *Revelation 17–22*, 1057 (my italics).

89. See also 2 Baruch 29:4 and 4 Ezra 6:52. On the victory feast and its roots in traditions about the armies of Yahweh consuming the dead carcasses of Behemoth and Leviathan, see Aune, *Revelation 6–16*, 1033.

90. See Collins, "Political Perspective," 247.

91. Moore, "Revolting Revelations," 188. This allusion to Ps. 2:9 also appears in Rev. 12:5: "And she gave birth to a son, a male child, who is to rule all nations with a rod of iron."

92. The manly figure also, it should be noted, usurps the place of "one like a son of man," treading the wine press (Rev. 19:5).

93. This wedding imagery with "Christ as bridegroom" stems perhaps from Psalm 45. On the chorus, see T. C. Voortman and J. A. du Rand. "The Worship of God and the Lamb: Exploring the Liturgical Setting of the Apocalypse of John." *Ekklesiatikos Pharos* 80 (1998): 56–67.

94. *Daphnis and Chloe* 4.40 (trans. Gill).

Chapter 5. Wherever the Lamb Goes

1. On this passage, see Bartsch, *Decoding*, 55–57. Simon Goldhill observes that the novel provides "the first example in Western art history of a pair of paintings being analyzed precisely as a diptych with significant links, which shows well Achilles' interest in using such images as productive of further readings for the reader." *Foucault's Virginity*, 72.

2. Ecphrasis of Andromeda: Achilles Tatius, *Leukippe and Kleitophon* 3.7 (trans. Winkler).

3. Cf. the tale of Psyche in Apuleius, *Metamorphoses* 4.33, who is left on a rock to await the arrival of her "husband," a "snake-like monster" she must "marry" to fulfill a prophecy. But the monster never arrives, and Psyche is carried off by the winds to Cupid.

4. Cf. the ecphrasis of Philemola's rape: Achilles Tatius, *Leukippe and Kleitophon* 5.3–5.

5. The ecphrasis of Prometheus is found in Achilles Tatius, *Leukippe and Kleitophon* 3.8 (trans. Winkler).

6. On Revelation 12, see Aune, *Revelation 6–16*, 647–712. The discussion of this episode has been singularly impacted by Collins's work on the "combat myth." Following patristic authors, some have identified the woman with Mary; for a critique, see Court, *Myth and History*, 106–8. See further Aune, *Revelation 6–16*, 667–76, for a critical survey of scholarship on Revelation 12, including work by Collins and J. Fontenrose, *Python: A Study in Delphic Myth* (Berkeley: University of California Press, 1959).

7. Collins, *Combat Myth*, 101–56. See also Edith McEwan Humphrey on the "sun woman" and the "bride-city" of New Jersalem. *The Ladies and the Cities* (Sheffield: Sheffield Acadmic Press, 1995), 103–15.

8. Aune, *Revelation 6–16*, 665.

9. Elsner, "Between Mimesis and Divine Power: Visuality in the Greco-Roman World," in Nelson, *Visuality Before and Beyond the Renaissance: Seeing as Others Was*, ed. Robert S. Nelson (Cambridge: Cambridge University Press, 2000), 49.

10. But cf. David J. Halperin's suggestion: "But, when I hear of a dream or vision or fantasy in which a snake chases a woman and squirts water at her out of his mouth, I cannot doubt that one of the things the dreamer or visionary has on his mind is sex." "Heavenly Ascension in Ancient Judaism: The Nature of the Experience," *SBL Seminar Papers, 1987* (Atlanta: Scholars Press, 1987), 228.

11. Cooper, "Voice of the Victim: Gender, Representation, and Early Christian Martyrdom," *Bulletin of the John Rylands Library* 80 (1999): 155.

12. Burrus, "An Immoderate Feast: Augustine Reads John's Apocalypse," in *History, Apocalypse, and the Secular Imagination: New Essays on Augustine's City of God*, ed. Mark Vessey, Karla Pollmann, and Allan D. Fitzgerald (Bowling Green, Ohio: Philosophy Documentation Center, 1999), 189.

13. Ibid., 188–89, 192.

14. Achilles Tatius, *Leukippe and Kleitophon* 3.8 (trans. Winkler).

15. On the cluster of notions relating sexuality to martyrdom and asceticism

in early Christianity, see Gillian Clark, "Bodies and Blood: Late Antique Debate on Martyrdom, Virginity, and Resurrection," in *Changing Bodies, Changing Meanings: Studies on the Human Body in Antiquity*, ed. Dominic Montserrat (London: Routledge, 1998), 99–115.

16. Rev. 14:4 and *Martyrs of Lyons* 1.10 (trans. Musurillo).

17. Halperin, "Why Is Diotima a Woman?" in *One Hundred Years of Homosexualiy*, 113–52, from which I cite here. (A shorter version appeared first in Halperin, Winkler, and Zeitlin, *Before Sexuality*, 257–308.) Quotations in this paragraph: Halperin, "Diotima," 113–14. On Halperin and Eilberg-Schwartz, discussed below, see Elizabeth A. Clark, "The Lady Vanishes: Dilemmas of a Feminist Historian after the 'Linguistic Turn'," *Church History* 67 (1998): 1–31.

18. Halperin, "Diotima," 117.

19. Ibid., 147.

20. Ibid.

21. Ibid., 151. Cf. the alternative reading of Burrus, "*Begotten, Not Made*," 117–20.

22. A phrase I borrow from Eve Sedgewick, *Between Men: English Literature and Male Homosocial Desire* (New York: Columbia University Press, 1985); see esp. 25–27 on the groundbreaking essay by Gayle Rubin, "The Traffic in Women: Notes Toward a Political Economy of Sex," in *Toward an Anthropology of Women*, ed. Rayna Reiter (New York: Monthly Review Press, 1975), 157–210. See also Elizabeth A. Clark, "Early Christian Women: Sources and Interpretation," in *That Gentle Strength: Historical Perspectives on Women in Christianity*, ed. Lynda L. Coon, Katherine J. Haldane, and Elisabeth W. Sommer (Charlottesville: University of Virginia Press, 1990), 29–30.

23. See Howard Eilberg-Schwartz, *God's Phallus: And Other Problems for Men and Monotheism* (Boston: Beacon, 1994) and Eilberg-Schwartz, "The Nakedness of a Woman's Voice, the Pleasure in a Man's Mouth: An Oral History of Ancient Judaism," in *Off with Her Head! The Denial of Women's Identity in Myth, Religion, and Culture*, ed. Eilberg-Schwartz and Wendy Doniger (Berkeley: University of California Press, 1995), 165–84.

24. Eilberg-Schwartz, *God's Phallus*, 144–45.

25. Ibid., 130–32.

26. Eilberg-Schwartz, "Nakedness of a Woman's Voice," 180.

27. See Peter Brown, *The Body and Society: Men, Women, and Sexual Renunciation in Early Christianity* (New York: Columbia University Press, 1988), 153–59; Brown acknowledges at n. 57 his debt to Claude Lévi-Strauss for the notion.

28. See, e.g., Cameron, *Rhetoric of Empire*, 171–80, and Cooper, *Virgin and the Bride*, 116–43.

29. Burrus, "Reading Agnes: The Rhetoric of Gender in Ambrose and Prudentius," *Journal of Early Christian Studies* 3 (1995): 39.

30. Ibid., 41–42.

31. *Peristephanon* 14:69–80 (trans. Clark).

32. Burrus, "Reading Agnes," 42.

33. Gleason, *Making Men*, 160.

34. Polemo, *De physiognomia* (1.160–64), translated by Gleason, *Making Men*, 7.

35. Gleason, *Making Men*, 162.

36. Where Gleason, *Making Men*, 162, attributes such risk-taking to the "immense security of the *Pax Romana*," Burrus, *"Begotten, Not Made"*, 21, cites instead both the "waning of civic autonomy" and the place of fragility in "the habitual structure of masculine subjectivity."

37. Frend, *Martyrdom and Persecution in the Early Church: A Study of Conflict from the Maccabees to the Donatists* (Oxford: Blackwell, 1965), 1.

38. Roman citizenship: *Martyrs of Lyons* 1.47 (trans. Musurillo).

39. *Martyrs of Lyons* 1.40 (trans. Musurillo).

40. See David S. Potter, "Martyrdom as Spectacle," in *Theater and Society in the Classical World*, ed. Ruth Scodel (Ann Arbor: University of Michigan Press, 1993), 53–88. On 4 Maccabees generally, see John M. G. Barclay, *Jews in the Mediterranean Diaspora: From Alexander to Trajan (323 BCE–117 CE)* (Edinburgh: T and T Clark, 1996), 369–80, and David DeSilva, *4 Maccabees* (Sheffield Academic Press, 1998). On dating the book, see J. W. van Henten, "Datierung und Herkunft des Vierten Makkabäerbuches," in *Tradition and Reinterpretation in Jewish and Early Christian Literature: Essays in Honor of Jürgen C. H. Lebraum*, ed. Henten and H. J. de Jonge (Leiden: Brill, 1987), 137–45. The goal here is not to trace lines of literary dependence but a common cultural sensibility. See Judith M. Lieu's similar approach in *Image and Reality: The Jews in the World of the Christians in the Second Century* (Edinburgh: T and T Clark, 1996), 80.

41. For suggestive insights into the complex of intersecting themes that characterized ancient Jewish and Christian martyr accounts, see Daniel Boyarin, *Dying for God: Martyrdom and the Making of Christianity and Judaism*, Figurae: Reading Medieval Culture (Stanford, Calif.: Stanford University Press, 1999), 93–126, esp. 117–25.

42. Eusebius, *Historia ecclesiastica* 5.1.3–2.8. *The Martyrs of Lyons* is also known as *The Letter of the Churches of Lyons and Vienne*.

43. Quotations in this paragraph are taken from *Martyrs of Lyons* 1.5–19 (trans. Musurillo).

44. Ashes: *Martyrs of Lyons* 1.62.

45. "Self-control" (ἐγκράτεια) is also a key term: see 4 Macc. 5:33–34. For discussion, see DeSilva, *4 Maccabees*, 51–75, and David C. Aune, "Mastery of the Passions: Philo, 4 Maccabes and Earliest Christianity," in *Hellenization Revisited: Shaping a Christian Response within the Greco-Roman World*, ed. Wendy E. Helleman (Lanham, Md.: University Press of America, 1994), 125–58.

46. Moore and Anderson, "Taking It Like a Man," 273. Cf. Brian D. Shaw, "Body/Power/Identity: Passions of the Martyrs," *Journal of Early Christian Studies* 4 (1996): 269–312. Moore and Anderson dispute Shaw's elevation of "endurance" in this text as to "preeminence" in the book. Rather than distinct from traditional notions of masculinity (as Shaw proposes), endurance, according to Moore and Anderson, is to be viewed as subsumed under self-mastery and masculinity (see 257 n. 22).

47. *Martyrs of Lyons* 1.17–19 (trans. Musurillo). For an interesting discussion

of the relation of ascetic training and the endurance of Christian martyrs, see Maureen A. Tilley, "The Ascetic Body and the (Un)making of the World of the Martyr," *Journal of the American Academy of Religion* 59 (1991): 467–79.

48. *Martyrs of Lyons* 1.57–58 (trans. Musurillo).

49. Moore and Anderson, "Taking It Like a Man," 255. Further on the "self-mastery" of rulers, see Stanley K. Stowers, *A Rereading of Romans: Justice, Jews, and Gentiles* (New Haven, Conn.: Yale University Press, 1994), 56–58.

50. *Martyrs of Lyons* 1.55 (trans. Musurillo).

51. See Teresa Rajak, "Dying for the Law: The Martyr's Portait in Jewish-Greek Literature," in *Biographical Representation in the Greek and Latin Literature of the Roman Empire*, ed. M. J. Edwards and Simon Swain (Oxford: Clarendon Press, 1997), 39–68.

52. Despite Eleazar's deeply emotional speech, Frend, *Martyrdom and Persecution* (67), maintains that "for all this, martyrdom in Judaism remained something of a *Hamlet* without a Prince. . . . The Law remained God-created and majestic, but impersonal, and for deep-thinking minds an 'occasion for sin' rather than a means of salvation." See now Boyarin's incisive critique in *Dying for God*, 127–30. See also Jan Willem van Henten, *The Maccabean Martyrs as Saviors of the Jewish People: A Study of 2 and 4 Maccabees*, Supplements to the Journal for the Study of Judaism 57 (Leiden: Brill, 1997), 298.

53. See Robin Darling Young, "The 'Woman with the Soul of Abraham': Traditions about the Mother of the Maccabean Martyrs," in *"Women like This": New Perspectives on Jewish Women in the Greco-Roman World*, ed. Amy-Jill Levine (Atlanta: Scholars Press, 1991), 67–81.

54. Young, " 'Woman,' " 77–78.

55. Moore and Anderson, "Taking It Like a Man," 269–72.

56. See Elizabeth Castelli, "Visions and Voyeurism: Holy Women and the Politics of Sight in Early Christianity," in *Protocol of the Colloquy of the Center for Hermeneutical Studies, 6 December 1992*, new series 2, ed. Christopher Ocker (Berkeley, Calif.: Center for Hermeneutical Studies, 1994), 18–19. On Blandina and the "Maccabean mother," see Stuart G. Hall, "Women Among the Early Martyrs," in *Martyrs and Martyrologies*, ed. Diana Wood (London: Blackwell, 1993), 14–15.

57. *Martyrs of Lyons* 1.41 (trans. Musurillo); cf. Sanctus: *Martyrs of Lyons* 1.23. See Miles, Carnal Knowing, 57.

58. *Martyrs of Lyons* 1.55–57 (trans. Musurillo). See Burrus, "Torture and Travail," 19.

59. *Martyrs of Lyons* 1.41 (trans. Musurillo).

60. See Bruce Metzger, *The Canon of the New Testament: Its Origin, Development, and Significance* (Oxford: Clarendon Press, 1987), 96–98.

61. *Martyrs of Lyons* 1.58 (trans. Musurillo).

62. Aune, *Revelation 6–16*, 708, identifies the anger of the dragon with the fury of pagan persecutors in Jewish and Christian martyr accounts.

63. By contrast, throughout Revelation, the wrathful God is simultaneously an "achieving" God.

64. Many recent studies of the prostitute Babylon make the issue of gender

a central topic. One that does not is Mathias Rissi, *Die Hure Babylon and die Verführung der Heiligen: Eine Studie zur Apokalypse des Johannes*, Beiträge zur Wissenschaft vom Alten (und Neuen) Testament 7/16 (Stuttgart: Kohlhammer, 1995), which understands the figure to be symbolic of ancient religious syncretism.

65. For a careful assessment of the debate over the violence of Revelation, see Keller, "Eyeing," 269–71. Keller (271) memorably labels the two "postions" in the debate as "liberation neoapocalypse" and "feminist antiapocalypse."

66. Pippin, *Death and Desire*, 103. See also Pippin, "Eros and the End: Reading for Gender in the Apocalypse of John," *Semeia* 59 (1992): 193–210, and Gail Corrington Street's assessment: Babylon is "stripped naked, sexually humiliated, tortured, and burned—to the exultation of the righteous—under the unblinking gaze of the thunderstruck 'seer'." *The Strange Woman: Power and Sex in the Bible* (Louisville: Westminster/John Knox, 1997), 158.

67. Schüssler Fiorenza, *Vision of a Just World*, 89–90, 106.

68. Rossing, *A Choice Between Two Cities: Whore, Bride, and Empire in the Apocalypse*, Harvard Theological Studies (Harrisburg, Pa.: Trinity, 1999), 15. "Disconnects": see, for example, p. 89: Rev. 17:16 "is not an *ekphrasis* of the woman's tortured body on which the viewer's gaze lingers."

69. Adela Yarbro Collins, "Feminine Symbolism in the Book of Revelation," *Biblical Interpretation* 1 (1993): 27. David Barr likewise objects to those who find misogyny in Revelation: the images are meant to persuade Revelation's audience to resist abusive Roman power. "Towards an Ethical Reading of the Apocalypse: Reflections on John's Use of Power, Violence, and Misogyny," *Society of Biblical Literature Seminar Papers* 36 (1997): 373.

70. Collins, *Crisis and Catharsis*, 172.

71. Schüssler Fiorenza, *Justice and Judgment*, 199.

72. See Greg Carey's criticism of this view in *Elusive Apocalypse*, 180.

73. Exum, *Plotted, Shot, and Painted: Cultural Representations of Biblical Women*, Journal for the Study of the Old Testament: Supplement Series 215, Gender, Culture, Theory 3 (Sheffield: Sheffield Academic Press, 1996), 120–21. My approach runs parallel to and has been informed by Pippin's work, as well as Mary Wilson Carpenter, "Representing Apocalypse: Sexual Politics and the Violence of Revelation," in *Postmodern Apocalypse*, ed. Richard Dellamora (Philadelphia: University of Pennsylvania Press, 1995), 107–35, esp. 111–17, and J. K. Kim, " 'Uncovering Her Wickedness': An Inter(con)textual Reading of Revelation 17 from a Postcolonial Feminist Perspective," *Journal for the Study of the New Testament* 73 (1999): 61–81. See also Maria Selvidge, "Powerful and Powerless Women in the Apocalypse," *Neotestamentica* 26 (1992): 161–78.

74. See Pippin, *Death and Desire*, 66–67, which takes θαυμάζω here to indicate sexual arousal, a proposal rejected by Barr in "Towards an Ethical Reading," 360.

75. See Duff, *Who Rides the Beast*, 108–11.

76. On the "dangers" of the adorned body, see Maria Wyke, "The Rhetoric of Adornment in the Roman World," in *Women in Ancient Societies: An Illusion of the Night*, ed. Léonie Archer, Susan Fischler, and Wyke (London: Macmillan, 1994), 134–51.

77. See Pablo Richard, *Apocalypse: A People's Commentary on the Book of Revelation* (Maryknoll, N.Y.: Orbis, 1995), 100. On the disdain for commercial wealth, depicted, for example, in Petronius's Trimalchio, as opposed to inherited wealth, see Royalty, *The Streets of Heaven*, 102–11. But cf. Duff's criticism of Royalty in *Who Rides the Beast*, 62–64.

78. Royalty, *Streets of Heaven*, 209.

79. Cf. Ezek. 23:25–29.

80. See Edwards, *Politics of Immorality*, 81–84, and Dale B. Martin, "*Arsenokoitĺs* and *Malakos*: Meanings and Consequences," in *Biblical Ethics and Homosexuality: Listening to Scripture*, ed. Robert L. Brawley (Louisville, Ky.: Westminster/John Knox, 1996), 126.

81. See Carey, *Elusive Apocalypse*, 138–41.

82. See, for example, Jude 11; 2 Pet. 2:15–16.

83. See Aune, "Social Matrix, 27.

84. Some scholars believe Jezebel and the Nicolatians to belong to the same group: see Adela Yarbro Collins, "Villification and Self-Definition," 316, and Aune, "Social Matrix," 28.

85. See Duff, *Who Rides the Beast*, 89–92, on Jezebel and Babylon.

86. Carey, *Elusive Apocalypse*, 157.

87. See Collins, "Villification and Self-Definition," 313, and Shaye D. Cohen, *The Beginning of Jewishness: Boundaries, Varieties, Uncertainties*, Hellenistic Culture and Society 31 (Berkeley: University of California Press, 1999), 25–26.

88. See Stephen G. Wilson, *Related Strangers: Jews and Christians, 60–170 C.E.* (Minneapolis: Fortress, 1995), 162–63.

89. Derrida, "No Apocalypse, Not Now (Full Speed Ahead, Seven Missiles, Seven Missives)," *Diacritics* 14 (1984): 20–31.

90. On the success of John's rivals, see Royalty, *Streets of Heaven*, 31–33.

91. Aune has argued that these "letters" conform in structure and tone to Roman imperial edicts. "The Form and Function of the Proclamations to the Seven Churches (Rev. 2–3)," *New Testament Studies* 36 (1990): 182–204.

92. Quotations taken from *Martyrs of Lyons* 1:10–11 (trans. Musurillo). The following discussion complements the suggestive essay of Mitchell G. Reddish, "Martyr Christology in the Apocalypse," *Journal for the Study of the New Testament* 33 (1988): 85–95.

93. Halperin, "Heavenly Ascension," 229.

94. See Victor Saxer, "The Influence of the Bible in Early Christian Martyrology," in *The Bible in Greek Christian Antiquity*, ed. and trans. Paul M. Blowers, Bible Through the Ages 1 (Notre Dame, Ind.: University of Notre Dame Press, 1997): 342–74.

95. See Paula Fredriksen, "Apocalypse and Redemption in Early Christianity: From John of Patmos to Augustine of Hippo," *Vigiliae Christianae* 45 (1991): 151–83.

96. Irenaeus, *Adversus haereses* 5.33, and Justin Martyr, *Dialogus cum Tryphone* 81.

97. See Humphries, *The Ladies and the Cities*, 103–18.

98. Royalty, *Streets of Heaven*, 226.

99. See William W. Reader, "The Twelve Jewels of Revelation 21:19–20: Tradition, History, and Modern Interpretations," *Journal of Biblical Literature* 100 (1981): 433–57.

100. Royalty, *Streets of Heaven*, 236.

101. Kraybill, *Imperial Cult and Commerce*, 23. See also Schüssler Fiorenza, *Vision of a Just World*, 113: "Revelation never pictures any serfs and subjects of this reign. Not oppressive rulership and subordination but the life-giving and life-sustaining power of God characterizes God's eschatological reign and empire."

102. Collins, *Crisis and Catharsis*, 144. See also Klaus Wengst, "Babylon the Great and the New Jerusalem: The Visionary View of Political Reality in the Revelation of John," in *Politics and Theopolitics in the Bible and Postbiblical Literature*, ed. H. Grad Reventlow, Yair Hoffman, and Benjamin Uffenheimer, Journal for the Study of the Old Testament: Supplement Series 171 (Sheffield: Sheffield Academic Press, 1994), 195–210.

103. See Ezek. 37:27.

104. See Moore, *God's Gym*, 129, and 4 Ezra 10:54: "For no work of man's building could endure in a place where the city of the Most High was to be revealed."

105. For a different reading, see David E. Aune, "Following the Lamb: Discipleship in the Apocalypse," in *Patterns of Discipleship in the New Testament*, ed. Richard N. Longenecker (Grand Rapids, Mich.: Eerdmans, 1996), 271.

106. See Aune, *Revelation 17–22*, 1181, which leaves the ambiguity undecided.

107. See Barr's compelling suggestion that Revelation incorporates the "mythology of war" only to "remythologize the war" so as to make the "death of the warrior" (figured by the Lamb), and not the victory of the warrior, the turning point. *Tales of the End*, 146. But cf. Moore, *God's Beauty Parlor* (180), which, identifying the creature with the "rider" of Rev. 19:11–21, labels the Lamb a "superwarrior."

108. See Aune, "Roman Imperial Court," 24–25.

Chapter 6. Epilogue: A Well-Known Story

1. Donald W. Riddle has argued that the "apocalypse directed its attention to a social unit, while the martyrology attempted to control the individual." "From Apocalypse to Martyrology," *Harvard Theological Review* 9 (1927): 267. Cf. Reddish, "Martyr Christology," 91–92.

2. See Moore, *God's Beauty Parlor*, 190–96, who arrives at a similar conclusion.

3. For an overview of the pagan persecution of Christians, see Lane Fox, *Pagans and Christians*, 419–92. Older but still useful for its careful survey of the evidence (if not for its analysis) is Frend, *Martyrdom and Persecution*.

4. *Acts of the Scillitan Martyrs* 3 (trans. Musurillo).

5. See Robert L. Wilken, "The Piety of the Persecutors," in *The Christians as the Romans Saw Them* (New Haven, Conn.: Yale University Press, 1984), 48–67.

6. See the debate between A. N. Sherwin White and G. E. M. de Ste.

Croix. Sherwin-White maintains that Christians were punished for specific crimes, or *flagitia*. "Early Persecutions and Roman Law Again," *Journal of Theological Studies* 3 (1952): 199–213, and "Why Were the Early Christians Persecuted?— An Amendment," *Past and Present* 27 (1964): 23–27. Ste. Croix's position is that Christians were prosecuted simply for the name "Christian." "Why Were the Early Christians Persecuted?" *Past and Present* 26 (1963): 6–31, and "Why Were the Christians Persecuted?—A Rejoinder," *Past and Present* 27 (1964): 28–33.

7. Ramsay MacMullen, *Christianizing the Roman Empire, A.D. 100–400* (New Haven, Conn.: Yale University Press, 1984), 32 n. 26.

8. Peter Brown remarks: "As for the emperors, they were too preoccupied with the frontiers to care about the Christians." *The World of Late Antiquity, AD 150–750* (New York: Norton, 1989), 68.

9. T. D. Barnes, "Legislation Against the Christians," *Journal of Roman Studies* 58 (1968): 32–50.

10. Ste. Croix, "Aspects of the 'Great Persecution'," *Harvard Theological Review* 47 (1954): 104.

11. See the pagan complaint reported by Minucius Felix in *Octavius* 12 (trans. Rendall): "You do not go to our shows, you take no part in our processions, you are not present at our public banquets, you shrink in horror from our sacred games."

12. Pliny the Younger, *Epistulae* 10.96.

13. Perkins, *The Suffering Self: Pain and Narrative Representation in the Early Christian Era* (New York: Routledge, 1995), 11.

14. Ibid., 3.

15. *Martyrdom of Polycarp* 4 (trans. Musurillo).

16. *Martyrdom of Polycarp* 9 (trans. Musurillo).

17. *Martyrdom of Polycarp* 13 (trans. Musurillo).

18. On this theme in second-century Christian texts, see Steve Young, "Being a Man: The Pursuit of Manliness in *The Shepherd of Hermas*," *Journal of Early Christian Studies* 2 (1993): 237–55.

19. On eroticism in ancient martyr accounts, see Castelli, "Visions and Voyeurism," and Boyarin, *Dying for God*, esp. 95–96, 101–14.

20. *Martyrdom of Polycarp* 15 (trans. Musurillo).

21. *Martyrdom of Polycarp* 17.3 (trans. Musurillo).

22. Bhabha, *Location of Culture*, 89.

23. Cameron, *Rhetoric of Empire*, 14.

Selected Bibliography

I most often quote biblical texts, including the Apocrypha/Deuterocanon, from the translation of the New Revised Standard Version. Further, I have quoted from the twenty-seventh edition of Nestle-Aland's *Novum Testamentum Graece* and from Rahlf's *Septuaginta*. For other ancient sources, I include here editions of works that have been consulted only when such contain passages that are quoted at length. For secondary sources, this selected bibliography lists works that have left the deepest impression on the present study. The endnotes provide documentation for every cited secondary source.

PRIMARY SOURCES

Achilles Tatius. *Leukippe and Kleitophon.* In *Achilles Tatius.* Edited by S. Gaselee. Loeb Classical Library. Cambridge, Mass.: Harvard University Press, 1917. Translated by John J. Winkler. "Leucippe and Clitophon." In Reardon, *Collected Ancient Greek Novels,* 170–284.

Acts of Paul and Thecla. Translated by J. K. Elliott. In *The Apocryphal New Testament: A Collection of Apocryphal Christian Literature in an English Translation based on M. R. James,* edited by J. K. Elliott, 364–88. Oxford: Clarendon Press, 1993.

Acts of the Scillitan Martyrs. In Musurillo, *Acts of the Christian Martyrs,* 86–89.

Aelius Aristides. *To Rome (Orationes 26).* Translated by Charles A. Behr. "Regarding Rome." In vol. 2 of *P. Aelius Aristides: The Complete Works.* 2 vols. Leiden: Brill, 1981.

Apuleius. *Metamorphoses.* In *Metamorphoses.* Edited by J. Arthur Hanson. 2 vols. Loeb Classical Library. Cambridge, Mass.: Harvard University Press, 1989. *The Golden Ass.* Translated by P. G. Walsh. Oxford: Oxford University Press, 1994.

Artemidorus. *Oneirocritica.* Translated by Robert J. White. *The Interpretation of Dreams.* Park Ridge, N.Y.: Noyes Press, 1975.

Augustine. *Confessions.* Translated by Maria Boulding. *Saint Augustine's Confessions.* New York: Vintage, 1998.

Augustus. *Res Gestae Divi Augusti.* In *Documents Illustrating the Reigns of Augustus and Tiberius,* edited by V. Ehrenberg and A. H. M. Jones, 1–32. 2nd ed. Oxford: Clarendon Press, 1955. Translated by P. A. Brunt and J. M. Moore. *Res Gestae Divi Augusti; The Achievements of the Divine Augustus.* London: Oxford University Press, 1967.

Cassius Dio. *Historia romana.* Translated by E. Cary. 9 vols. Loeb Classical Library. Cambridge, Mass.: Harvard University Press, 1914–1927.

Cicero. *De haruspicum responso.* Translated by N. H. Watts. In *Cicero,* vol. 11. Loeb Classical Library. Cambridge, Mass.: Harvard University Press, 1953.

———. *Tusculanae disputationes.* Translated by J. E. King. In *Cicero,* vol. 18. Loeb Classical Library. Cambridge, Mass.: Harvard University Press, 1927.

Fronto. *Correspondence.* Translated by C. H. Haines. 2 vols. Loeb Classical Library. Cambridge: Harvard University Press, 1919.

Horace. *Epistulae.* Translated by H. R. Fairclough. In *Satires, Epistles, and Ars Poetica.* Loeb Classical Library. Cambridge, Mass.: Harvard University Press, 1932.

Longinus. *De sublimitate.* Revised translation by Donald Russell. In *Aristotle,* vol. 22. Loeb Classical Library. Cambridge, Mass.: Harvard University Press, 1953.

Longus. *Daphnis and Chloe.* Edited by J. M. Edmonds. Loeb Classical Library. Cambridge, Mass.: Harvard University Press, 1916. Translated by Christopher Gill. "Daphnis and Chloe." In Reardon, *Collected Ancient Greek Novels,* 285–348.

Lucian. *De morte Peregrini.* Translated by A. M. Harmon. In *Lucian,* vol. 5. Loeb Classical Library. Cambridge, Mass.: Harvard University Press, 1962.

Lucretius. *De rerum natura.* Translated by W. H. D. Rouse. Loeb Classical Library. Cambridge, Mass.: Harvard University Press, 1975.

Martial. *Spectacula.* Translated by D. R. Shackleton Bailey. In *Epigrams.* 3 vols. Loeb Classical Library. Cambridge, Mass.: Harvard University Press, 1993.

Martyrdom of Perpetua and Felicitas. In Musurillo, *Acts of the Christian Martyrs,* 106–31.

Martyrdom of Pionius. In Musurillo, *Acts of the Christian Martyrs,* 136–67.

Martyrdom of Polycarp. In Musurillo, *Acts of the Christian Martyrs,* 2–21.

Martrys of Lyons. In Musurillo, *Acts of the Christian Martyrs,* 62–85.

Minucius Felix. *Octavius.* Translated by G. H. Rendall. In *Apology and De Spectaculis; Mincius Felix.* Loeb Classical Library. New York: G.P. Putnam, 1931.

Musurillo, Herbert, ed. and trans. *The Acts of the Christian Martyrs.* London: Oxford University Press, 1972.

Ovid. *Amores.* Translated by A. D. Melville. In *Ovid: The Love Poems.* Oxford: Oxford University Press, 1990.

———. *Ars amatoria.* Translated by A. D. Melville. In *Ovid: The Love Poems.* Oxford: Oxford University Press, 1990.

———. *Fasti.* Translated by Sir James Frazer. Loeb Classical Library. Cambridge, Mass.: Harvard University Press, 1931.

Philo. *De Abrahamo.* Translated by F. H. Colson. In *Philo,* vol. 6. Loeb Classical Library. Cambridge, Mass.: Harvard University Press, 1939.

Phlegon of Tralles. *Book of Marvels.* In *Paradoxographorum Graecorum Reliquiae,* edited by Alessandro Giannini, 169–219. Milan, 1965. *Phlegon of Tralles' Book of Marvels.* Translated by William Hansen. Exeter Studies in History. Exeter: University of Exeter Press, 1996.

Pliny the Younger. *Panegyricus.* Translated by Betty Radice. In *Letters and Panegyricus of Pliny,* vol. 2. Loeb Classical Library. Cambridge, Mass.: Harvard University Press, 1975.

Plutarch. *De curiositate.* Translated by W. C. Helmbold. "On Being a Busybody."

In *Plutarch's Moralia*, vol. 6. Loeb Classical Library. Cambridge, Mass.: Harvard University Press, 1939.

Prudentius. *Peristephanon* 14. Translated by Elizabeth A. Clark. In Clark, *Women in the Early Church*, 109–14. Wilmington, Del.: Michael Glazier, 1983.

Reardon, B. P., ed. *Collected Ancient Greek Novels.* Berkeley: University of California Press, 1989.

Rhetores Graeci. Edited by Leonard Spengel. 3 vols. Leipzig, 1883–86.

Seneca. *Epistulae.* Translated by R. M. Gummere. In *Epistulae Morales.* 3 vols. Loeb Classical Library. Cambridge, Mass.: Harvard University Press, 1917–1925.

Suetonius. *Twelve Caesars.* Translated by Robert Graves. New York: Penguin, 1957.

Sybilline Oracles. Translated by John J. Collins. In *The Old Testament Pseudepigrapha*, vol. 2, edited by James H. Charlesworth. Garden City, N.Y.: Doubleday, 1985.

Tertullian. *De spectaculis.* Translated by T. R. Glover. In *Apology and De Spectaculis; Mincius Felix.* Loeb Classical Library. Cambridge, Mass.: Harvard University Press, 1931.

Velleius Paterculus. *Compendium of Roman History.* Translated by F. W. Shipley. In *Velleius Paterculus.* Loeb Classical Library. Cambridge, Mass.: Harvard University Press, 1967.

Vergil. *Aeneid.* Revised translation by G. P. Goold. In Virgil. 2 vols. Loeb Classical Library. Cambridge, Mass.: Harvard University Press, 1999.

Vitruvius. *De architectura.* Translated by F. Granger. 2 vols. Loeb Classical Library. Cambridge, Mass.: Harvard University Press, 1931–34.

SECONDARY SOURCES

Alcock, Susan E. *Graecia Capta: The Landscapes of Roman Greece.* Cambridge: Cambridge University Press, 1993.

Anderson, Graham. *The Second Sophistic: A Cultural Phenomenon in the Roman Empire.* London: Routledge, 1993.

Ashcroft, Bill, Gareth Griffiths, and Helen Tiffin. *The Empire Writes Back: Theory and Practice in Post-Colonial Literatures.* New Accents. New York: Routledge, 1989.

Aune, David C. "Mastery of the Passions: Philo, 4 Maccabees, and Earliest Christianity." In *Hellenization Revisted: Shaping a Christian Response within the Greco-Roman World*, edited by Wendy E. Helleman, 125–58. Lanham, Md.: University Press of America, 1994.

Aune, David E. "Following the Lamb: Discipleship in the Apocalypse." In *Patterns of Discipleship in the New Testament*, edited by Richard N. Longenecker, 269–84. Grand Rapids, Mich.: Eerdmans, 1996.

———. "The Form and Function of the Proclamations to the Seven Churches (Rev 2–3)." *New Testament Studies* 36 (1990): 182–204.

———. "The Influence of Roman Imperial Court Ceremonial on the Apocalypse of John." *Papers of the Chicago Society of Biblical Research* 28 (1985): 5–26.

———. *Revelation 1–5*. Word Biblical Commentary 52A. Dallas: Word, 1997.

———. *Revelation 6–16*. Word Biblical Commentary 52B. Waco, Tex.: Word, 1998.

———. *Revelation 17–22*. Word Biblical Commentary 52C. Waco, Tex.: Word, 1998.

———. "The Social Matrix of the Apocalypse of John." *Biblical Research* 26 (1981): 16–32.

Balsdon, J. P. V. D. *Romans and Aliens*. London: Duckworth, 1979.

Barclay, John M. G. *Jews in the Mediterranean Diaspora: From Alexander to Trajan (323 BCE–117 CE)*. Edinburgh: T and T Clark, 1996.

Barnes, T. D. "Legislation Against the Christians." *Journal of Roman Studies* 58 (1968): 32–50.

Barnett, Paul. "Polemical Parallelism: Some Further Reflections on the Apocalypse." *Journal for the Study of the New Testament* 35 (1989): 111–20.

Barr, David L. *Tales of the End: A Narrative Commentary on the Book of Revelation*. Santa Rosa, Calif.: Polebridge Press, 1988.

———. "Towards an Ethical Reading of the Apocalypse: Reflections on John's Use of Power, Violence, and Misogyny." *Society of Biblical Literature Seminar Papers* 36 (1997): 358–73.

Barton, Carlin A. "Savage Miracles: The Redemption of Lost Honor in Roman Society and the Sacrament of the Gladiator and the Martyr." *Representations* 45 (1994): 41–71.

———. *The Sorrow of the Ancient Romans: The Gladiator and the Monster*. Princeton, N.J.: Princeton University Press, 1993.

Bartsch, Shadi. *Actors in the Audience: Theatricality and Doublespeak from Nero to Hadrian*. Cambridge, Mass.: Harvard University Press, 1994.

———. *Decoding the Ancient Novel: The Reader and the Role of Description in Heliodorus and Achilles Tatius*. Princeton, N.J.: Princeton University Press, 1989.

Bauckham, Richard J. *The Climax of Prophecy: Studies in the Book of Revelation*. Edinburgh: T and T Clark, 1993.

———. "The Conflict of Justice and Mercy: Attitudes to the Damned in Apocalyptic Literature." *Apocrypha* 1 (1990): 181–96.

———. *The Theology of the Book of Revelation*. New Testament Theology. New York: Cambridge University Press, 1993.

Beacham, Richard C. *Spectacle Entertainments of Early Imperial Rome*. New Haven, Conn.: Yale University Press, 1999.

Beard, Mary and John North, eds. *Pagan Priests*. Ithaca, N.Y.: Cornell University Press, 1990.

Beasley-Murray, G. R. *The Book of Revelation*. New Century Bible. London: Oliphants, 1974.

Bhabha, Homi K. *The Location of Culture*. New York: Routledge, 1994.

Boatwright, Mary T. *Hadrian and the Cities of the Roman Empire*. Princeton, N.J.: Princeton University Press, 2000.

Boesak, Allan A. *Comfort and Protest: Reflections on the Apocalypse of John of Patmos*. Philadelphia: Westminster, 1987.

Bousset, Wilhelm. *The Antichrist Legend: A Chapter in Christian and Jewish Folklore*. Translated by A. H. Keane. London: Hutchinson, 1896.

Bowersock, Glen. *Augustus and the Greek World*. Oxford: Clarendon Press, 1965.

———. "The Mechanics of Subversion in the Roman Provinces." In *Opposition et résistances à l'empire d'Auguste à Trajan*, edited by Adalbeto Giovannini, 285–320. Entretiens Hardt 33. Geneva: Entretiens Hardt, 1987.

Bowie, Ewen L. "Greeks and Their Past in the Second Sophistic." In *Studies in Ancient Society*, edited by Moses I. Finley, 166–211. Past and Present Series. Boston: Routledge and Kegan Paul, 1974.

Boyarin, Daniel. *Dying for God: Martyrdom and the Making of Christianity and Judaism*. Figurae: Reading Medieval Culture. Stanford, Calif.: Stanford University Press, 1999.

———. *Unheroic Conduct: The Rise of Heterosexuality and the Invention of the Jewish Man*. Controversions: Critical Studies in Jewish Literature, Culture, and Society 8. Berkeley: University of California Press, 1997.

Bradley, Keith R. "The Significance of the *Spectacula* in Suetonius' *Caesares*." *Rivista Storica dell"Antichità* 11 (1981): 129–37.

Brooten, Bernadette J. *Love Between Women: Early Christian Responses to Female Homoeroticism*. Chicago: University of Chicago Press, 1996.

Brown, Peter. *The Body and Society: Men, Women, and Sexual Renunciation in Early Christianity*. New York: Columbia University Press, 1988.

———. *The Making of Late Antiquity*. Cambridge, Mass.: Harvard University Press, 1978.

———. *Power and Persuasion in Late Antiquity: Towards a Christian Empire*. Madison: University of Wisconsin Press, 1992.

———. *The World of Late Antiquity, AD 150–750*. New York: Norton, 1989.

Brown, Shelby. "Death as Decoration: Scenes from the Arena on Roman Domestic Mosaics." In *Pornography and Representation in Ancient Rome*, edited by Amy Richlin, 180–211. Oxford: Oxford University Press, 1992.

———. "Explaining the Arena: Did the Romans 'Need' Gladiators?" *Journal of Roman Archaeology* 8 (1995): 382.

Brunt, P. A. *Roman Imperial Themes*. Oxford: Oxford University Press, 1990.

Burrus, Virginia. *"Begotten, Not Made": Conceiving Manhood in Late Antiquity*. Stanford, Calif.: Stanford University Press, 2000.

———. "An Immoderate Feast: Augustine Reads John's Apocalypse." In *History, Apocalypse, and the Secular Imagination: New Essays on Augustine's City of God*. Edited by Mark Vessey, Karla Pollmann, and Allan D. Fitzgerald, 183–94. Bowling Green, Ohio: Philosophy Documentation Center, 1999.

———. "Reading Agnes: The Rhetoric of Gender in Ambrose and Prudentius." *Journal of Early Christian Studies* 3 (1995): 25–46.

———. "Torture and Travail: Producing the Christian Martyr." In *Feminist Companion to the New Testament*, edited by Amy-Jill Levine. Sheffield: Sheffield Academic Press, forthcoming.

———. "Word and Flesh: The Bodies and Sexuality of Ascetic Women in Christian Antiquity." *Journal of Feminist Studies in Religion* 10 (1994): 27–51.

Cameron, Alan. *Circus Factions: Blues and Greens at Rome and Byzantium*. Oxford: Clarendon Press, 1976.

Cameron, Averil. *Christianity and the Rhetoric of Empire: The Development of Christian Discourse.* Sather Classical Lectures 55. Berkeley: University of California Press, 1991.

———. "Redrawing the Map: Early Christian Territory after Foucault." *Journal of Roman Studies* 76 (1986): 266–71.

Carey, Greg. *Elusive Apocalypse: Reading Authority in the Revelation to John.* Studies in American Biblical Hermeneutics 15. Macon, Ga.: Mercer University Press, 1999.

Carpenter, Mary Wilson. "Representing Apocalypse: Sexual Politics and the Violence of Revelation." In *Postmodern Apocalypse: Theory and Cultural Practice at the End,* edited by Richard Dellamora, 107–35. Philadelphia: University of Pennsylvania Press, 1995.

Castelli, Elizabeth. " 'I Will Make Mary Male': Pieties of the Body and Gender Transformation of Christian Women in Late Antiquity." In *Body Guards: The Cultural Politics of Gender Ambiguity,* edited by Julia Epstein and Kristina Straub, 29–49. New York: Routledge, 1991.

———. "Visions and Voyeurism: Holy Women and the Politics of Sight in Early Christianity." In *Protocol of the Colloquy of the Center for Hermeneutical Studies, 6 December 1992,* new series 2, edited by Christopher Ocker, 1–20. Berkeley, Calif.: Center for Hermeneutical Studies, 1994.

Charles, R. H. *A Critical and Exegetical Commentary on the Revelation of St. John.* 2 vols. International Critical Commentary. Edinburgh: T and T Clark, 1920.

Chidester, David. *Savage Systems: Colonialism and Comparative Religion in Southern Africa.* Charlottesville: University of Virginia Press, 1996.

Clark, Elizabeth A. "Early Christian Women: Sources and Interpretation." In *That Gentle Strength: Historical Perspectives on Women in Christianity,* edited by Lynda L. Coon, Katherine J. Haldane, and Elisabeth W. Sommer, 19–35. Charlottesville: University of Virginia Press, 1990.

———. "Foucault, the Fathers, and Sex." *Journal of the American Academy of Religion* 56 (1988): 619–41.

———. "The Lady Vanishes: Dilemmas of a Feminist Historian After the 'Linguistic Turn.' " *Church History* 67 (1998): 1–31.

Clark, Gillian. "Bodies and Blood: Late Antique Debate on Martyrdom, Virginity, and Resurrection." In *Changing Bodies, Changing Meanings: Studies on the Human Body in Antiquity,* edited by Dominic Montserrat, 99–115. London: Routledge, 1998.

Clifford, James. *The Predicament of Culture: Twentieth-Century Ethnography, Literature, and Art.* Cambridge, Mass.: Harvard University Press, 1988.

Cohen, Jeffrey Jerome. "Monster Culture (Seven Theses)." In *Monster Theory,* edited by Jeffrey Jerome Cohen, 3–25. Minneapolis: University of Minnesota Press, 1996.

Cohen, Shaye D. *The Beginning of Jewishness: Boundaries, Varieties, Uncertainties.* Hellenistic Culture and Society 31. Berkeley: University of California Press, 1999.

Coleman, K. M. "Fatal Charades: Roman Executions Stage as Mythological Enactments." *Journal of Roman Studies* 80 (1990): 44–73.

Collins, Adela Yarbro. *Crisis and Catharsis: The Power of the Apocalypse.* Philadelphia: Westminster, 1984.
———. "Feminine Symbolism in the Book of Revelation." *Biblical Interpretation* 1 (1993): 20–33.
———. "Myth and History in the Book of Revelation: The Problem of Its Date." In *Traditions in Transformation: Turning Points in Biblical Faith*, edited by Baruch Halpern and Jon D. Levenson, 377–403. Winona Lake, Ind.: Eisenbrauns, 1981.
———. "Oppression from Without: The Symbolisation of Rome as Evil in Early Christianity." *Concilium* 200 (1988): 66–74.
———. "The Political Perspective of the Revelation to John." *Journal of Biblical Literature* 96 (1977): 241–56.
———. "The 'Son of Man' Tradition and the Book of Revelation." In *Cosmology and Eschatology in Jewish and Christian Apocalypticism*, edited by John J. Collins, 159–97. Journal for the Study of Judaism Supplement Series 50. Leiden: Brill, 1996.
Collins, John J. *The Apocalyptic Imagination: An Introduction to the Jewish Matrix of Christianity.* 2d. ed. Grand Rapids, Mich.: Eerdmans, 1998.
———. "Introduction: Towards the Morphology of a Genre." *Semeia* 14 (1979): 1–19.
Cooper, Kate. "Insinuations of Womanly Influence: An Aspect of the Christianization of the Roman Aristocracy." *Journal of Roman Studies* 82 (1992): 150–64.
———. *The Virgin and the Bride: Idealized Womanhood in Late Antiquity.* Cambridge, Mass.: Harvard University Press, 1996.
———. "Voice of the Victim: Gender, Representation and Early Christian Martyrdom." *Bulletin of the John Rylands Library* 80 (1999): 147–57.
Court, John. *Myth and History in the Book of Revelation.* Atlanta: John Knox Press, 1979.
De Certeau, Michel. *The Writing of History.* Translated by Tom Conley. New York: Columbia University Press, 1988.
Dover, K. J. *Greek Homosexuality.* Cambridge, Mass.: Harvard University Press, 1989.
Duff, Paul B. *Who Rides the Beast? Prophetic Rivalry and the Rhetoric of Crisis in the Churches of the Apocalypse.* New York: Oxford University Press, 2001.
Dupont, Florence. *L'acteur-roi ou le théâtre dans la Rome antique.* Paris: Les Belles Lettres, 1985.
Dwyer, Timothy. *The Motif of Wonder in the Gospel of Mark.* Journal for the Study of the New Testament Supplement Series 128. Sheffield: Sheffield Academic Press, 1996.
Edwards, Catharine. *The Politics of Immorality in Ancient Rome.* Cambridge: Cambridge University Press, 1993.
Edwards, Douglas R. *Religion and Power: Pagans, Jews, and Christians in the Greek East.* Oxford: Oxford University Press, 1996.
Eilberg-Schwartz, Howard. *God's Phallus: And Other Problems for Men and Monotheism.* Boston: Beacon, 1994.

———. "The Nakedness of a Woman's Voice, the Pleasure in a Man's Mouth: An Oral History of Ancient Judaism." In *Off with Her Head! The Denial of Women's Identity in Myth, Religion, and Culture,* edited by Howard Eilberg-Schwartz and Wendy Doniger, 165–84. Berkeley: University of California, 1995.

Elsner, Jaś. *Art and the Roman Viewer: The Transformation of Art from the Pagan World to Christianity.* Cambridge: Cambridge University Press, 1995.

———, ed. *Art and Text in Roman Culture.* Cambridge: Cambridge University Press, 1996.

———. "Cult and Sculpture: Sacrifice in the Ara Pacis Augustae." *Journal of Roman Studies* 81 (1991): 50–61.

———. "Hagiographic Geography: Travel and Allegory in the *Life of Apollonius of Tyana.*" *Journal of Hellenic Studies* 67 (1997): 22–37.

Exum, J. Cheryl. *Plotted, Shot, and Painted: Cultural Representations of Biblical Women.* Journal for the Study of the Old Testament Supplement Series 215, Gender, Culture, Theory 3. Sheffield: Sheffield Academic Press, 1996.

Foucault, Michel. "Afterword: The Subject and Power." In *Michel Foucault: Beyond Structuralism and Hermeneutics,* edited by Hubert L. Dreyfus and Paul Rabinow, 216–26. Chicago: University of Chicago Press, 1983.

———. *Discipline and Punish: The Birth of the Prison.* Translated by Alan Sheridan. New York: Vintage, 1979.

———. *The History of Sexuality.* Vol. 1, *An Introduction.* Translated by Robert Hurley. New York: Vintage, 1980.

———. *The History of Sexuality.* Vol. 2, *The Use of Pleasure.* Translated by Robert Hurley. New York: Pantheon, 1985.

———. *The History of Sexuality.* Vol. 3, *The Care of the Self.* Translated by Robert Hurley. New York: Pantheon, 1986.

Frank, Georgia. "The *Historia Monachorum in Aegypto* and Ancient Travel Writing." *Studia Patristica* 30 (1997): 191–95.

———. *The Memory of the Eyes: Pilgrims to Living Saints in Christian Late Antiquity.* Transformation of the Classical Heritage 30. Berkeley: University of California Press, 2000.

Fredriksen, Paula. "Apocalypse and Redemption in Early Christianity: From John of Patmos to Augustine of Hippo." *Vigiliae Christianae* 45 (1991): 151–83.

Frend, W. H. C. *Martyrdom and Persecution in the Early Church: A Study of Conflict from the Maccabees to the Donatists.* Oxford: Blackwell, 1965.

Friesen, Steven J. *Imperial Cults and the Apocalypse of John: Reading Revelation in the Ruins.* New York: Oxford University Press, 2001.

———. *Twice Neokoros: Ephesus, Asia, and the Cult of the Flavian Imperial Family.* Etudes préliminaires aux religions orientales dans l'empire romain 116. Leiden: Brill, 1993.

Frilingos, Chris. " 'For My Child, Onesimus,': Paul and Domestic Power in Philemon." *Journal of Biblical Literature* 119 (2000): 93–97.

Frontisi-Ducroux, Francoise. "Eros, Desire, and the Gaze." Translated by N. Kline. In *Sexuality in Ancient Art,* edited by Natalie Boymel Kampen, 81–100. Cambridge: Cambridge University Press, 1996.

Gager, John. *Kingdom and Community: The Social World of Early Christianity.* Englewood Cliffs, N.J.: Prentice-Hall, 1975.

Galinsky, Karl. *Augustan Culture: An Interpretive Introduction.* Princeton, N.J.: Princeton University Press, 1996.

Garland, Robert. *The Eye of the Beholder: Deformity and Disability in the Graeco-Roman World.* Ithaca, N.Y.: Cornell University Press, 1995.

Garnsey, Peter D. A. and C. R. Whittaker, eds. *Imperialism in the Ancient World.* Cambridge: Cambridge University Press, 1978.

Garnsey, Peter and Richard P. Saller. *The Roman Empire: Economy, Society, and Culture.* Berkeley: University of California Press, 1987.

Gilmore, David. *Manhood in the Making: Cultural Concepts of Masculinity.* New Haven, Conn.: Yale University Press, 1990.

———. *Monsters: Evil Beings, Mythical Beasts, and All Manner of Imaginary Terrors.* Philadelphia: University of Pennsylvania Press, 2003.

Gleason, Maud W. *Making Men: Sophists and Self-Presentation in Ancient Rome.* Princeton, N.J.: Princeton University Press, 1995.

Goldhill, Simon, and Robin Osborne, eds. *Art and Text in Ancient Greek Culture.* Cambridge: Cambridge University Press, 1994.

———. "The Erotic Eye: Visual Stimulation and Cultural Conflict." In *Being Greek Under Rome: Cultural Identity, the Second Sophistic, and the Development of Empire,* edited by Simon Goldhill, 154–94. Cambridge: Cambridge University Press, 2001.

———. *Foucault's Virginity: Ancient Erotic Fiction and the History of Sexuality.* Cambridge: Cambridge University Press, 1995.

Greenblatt, Stephen. *Renaissance Self-Fashioning: From More to Shakespeare.* Chicago: University of Chicago Press, 1984.

Gunderson, Erik. "The Ideology of the Arena." *Classical Antiquity* 15 (1996): 113–51.

Gunkel, Hermann. *Schöpfung und Chaos in Urzeit und Endzeit: Eine religionsgeschichtliche Untersuchung über Gen 1 und Ap Joh 12.* Göttingen: Vandenhoeck und Ruprecht, 1895.

Hall, Stuart G. "Women Among the Early Martyrs." In *Martyrs and Martyrologies,* edited by Diana Wood, 1–21. London: Blackwell, 1993.

Hallett, Judith P., and Marilyn B. Skinner, eds. *Roman Sexualities.* Princeton, N.J.: Princeton University Press, 1997.

Halperin, David J. *Faces of the Chariot: Early Jewish Responses to Ezekiel's Vision.* Texte und Studien zum antiken Judentum 16. Tübingen: Mohr-Siebeck, 1988.

———. "Heavenly Ascension in Ancient Judaism: The Nature of the Experience." In *SBL Seminar Papers, 1987,* 218–32. Society of Biblical Literature Seminar Papers 26. Atlanta: Scholars Press, 1987.

Halperin, David M., John J. Winkler, and Froma I. Zeitlin, eds. *Before Sexuality: The Construction of Erotic Experience in the Ancient Greek World.* Princeton, N.J.: Princeton University Press, 1990.

———. *One Hundred Years of Homosexuality and Other Essays on Greek Love.* New York: Routledge, 1990.

Harland, Philip A. "Honors and Worship: Emperors, Imperial Cults and Associations at Ephesus (First to Third Centuries C.E.)." *Studies in Religion/Sciences Religieuses* 25 (1996): 319–34.

Harpham, Geoffrey Galt. *On the Grotesque: Strategies of Contradiction in Art and Literature*. Princeton, N.J.: Princeton University Press, 1982.

Hellholm, David, Halvor Moxnes, and Turid Karlsen Seim, eds. *Mighty Minorities? Minorities in Early Christianity: Positions and Strategies, Essays in Honour of Jacob Jervell on His 70th Birthday, 21 May 1995*. Oslo: Scandinavian University Press, 1995.

Henten, Jan Willem van. "Datierung und Herkunft des Vierten Makkabäerbuches." In *Tradition and Reinterpretation in Jewish and Early Christian Literature: Essays in Honor of Jürgen C. H. Lebraum*, edited by Jan Willem van Henten and H. J. de Jonge, 137–45. Leiden: Brill, 1987.

———. *The Maccabean Martyrs as Saviors of the Jewish People: A Study of 2 and 4 Maccabees*. Supplements to the Journal for the Study of Judaism 57. Leiden: Brill, 1997.

Himmelfarb, Martha. *Ascent to Heaven in Jewish and Christian Apocalypses*. Oxford: Oxford University Press, 1993.

Hope, Valerie M. "Negotiating Identity and Status: The Gladiators of Roman NÔmes." In *Cultural Identity in the Roman Empire*, edited by Ray Laurence and Joanne Berry, 179–95. London: Routledge, 1998.

Hopkins, Keith. *Conquerors and Slaves*. Cambridge: Cambridge University Press, 1978.

———. *Death and Renewal*. Cambridge: Cambridge University Press, 1983.

Hunzinger, C.-H. "Babylon als Deckname für Rom und die Datierung des I. Petrusbriefes." In *Gottes Wort und Gottes Land: Hans-Wilhelm Hertzberurg zum 70. Geburtstag*, edited by H. G. Reventlow, 67–77. Göttingen: Vandenhoeck and Ruprecht, 1965.

Jacobs, Andrew S. "A Family Affair: Marriage, Class, and Ethics in the Apocryphal Acts of the Apostles." *Journal of Early Christian Studies* 7 (1999): 105–38.

Jones, Christopher P. "*Stigma*: Tatooing and Branding in Graeco-Roman Antiquity." *Journal of Roman Studies* 77 (1987): 139–55.

Jung, Carl G. "Answer to Job." In *The Portable Jung*. Edited by Joseph Campbell, 519–650. New York: Penguin, 1971. Reprint of *Answer to Job*. Translated by R. F. C. Hull. London: Routledge and Kegan Paul, 1954.

Kaplan, E. Ann. *Women and Film: Both Sides of the Camera*. New York: Methuen, 1983.

Keller, Catherine. *Apocalypse Now and Then: A Feminist Guide to the End of the World*. Boston: Beacon, 1996.

———. "Eyeing the Apocalypse." In *Postmodern Interpretations of the Bible: A Reader*, edited by A. K. M. Adam, 253–77. St. Louis: Chalice, 2001.

Kerkeslager, Allen. "Apollo, Greco-Roman Prophecy, and the Rider on the White Horse in Rev. 6:2." *Journal of Biblical Literature* 112 (1993): 116–21.

Kim, J. K. " 'Uncovering Her Wickedness': An Inter(con)textual Reading of Revelation 17 from a Postcolonial Feminist Perspective." *Journal for the Study of the New Testament* 73 (1999): 61–81.

Klassen, William. "Vengeance in the Apocalypse of John." *Catholic Biblical Quarterly* 28 (1966): 300–11.

Köhne, Eckart. "Bread and Circuses: The Politics of Entertainment." In *Gladiators and Caesars: The Power of Spectacle in Rome*. Edited by Eckart Köhne and Cornelia Ewigleben, translated by A. Bell, 8–30. Berkeley: University of California Press, 2000.

Konstan, David. *Sexual Symmetry: Love in the Ancient Novel and Related Genres.* Princeton, N.J.: Princeton University Press, 1994.

Kraybill, J. Nelson. *Imperial Cult and Commerce in the Book of Revelation.* Journal for the Study of the New Testament Supplement Series 132. Sheffield: Sheffield Academic Press, 1996.

Kyle, Donald G. *Spectacles of Death in Ancient Rome.* London: Routledge, 1998.

Lambrecht, Jan, ed. *L'Apocalypse johannique et l'apocalyptique dans le Nouveau Testament.* Bibliotheca ephemeridum theologicarum lovaniensium 53. Leuven: Leuven University Press, 1980.

Lauretis, Teresa de. *Technologies of Gender: Essays on Theory, Film, and Fiction.* Bloomington: Indiana University Press, 1987.

Laws, Sophie. *In the Light of the Lamb: Image, Parody, and Theology in the Apocalypse of John.* Good News Studies 31. Wilmington, Del.: Michael Glazier, 1988.

Leigh, Matthew. *Lucan: Spectacle and Engagement.* Oxford: Clarendon Press, 1997.

Lenfant, Dominique. "Monsters in Greek Ethnography and Society in the Fifth and Fourth Centuries B.C.E." In *From Myth to Reason? Studies in the Development of Greek Thought*, edited by Richard Buxton, 197–214. New York: Oxford University Press, 1999.

Levenson, Jon D. *Creation and the Persistence of Evil: The Jewish Drama of Divine Omnipotence.* San Francisco: Harper and Row, 1988.

Leyerle, Blake. "John Chrysostom on the Gaze." *Journal of Early Christian Studies* 1 (1993): 159–74.

Liebeschuetz, J. H. W. G. *Continuity and Change in Roman Religion.* Oxford: Clarendon Press, 1979.

Lieu, Judith M. *Image and Reality: The Jews in the World of the Christians in the Second Century C.E.* Edinburgh: T and T Clark, 1996.

Loraux, Nicole. *Tragic Ways of Killing a Woman.* Translated by A. Forster. Cambridge, Mass.: Harvard University Press, 1987.

MacCormack, Sabine. *Art and Ceremony in Late Antiquity.* Transformation of the Classical Heritage 1. Berkeley: University of California Press, 1981.

MacMullen, Ramsay. *Christianizing the Roman Empire, A.D. 100–400.* New Haven, Conn.: Yale University Press, 1984.

———. *Enemies of the Roman Order: Treason, Unrest, and Alienation in the Empire.* Cambridge, Mass.: Harvard University Press, 1966.

———. *Roman Social Relations, 50 B.C. to A.D. 284.* New Haven, Conn.: Yale University Press, 1974.

Maier, Harry O. *Apocalypse Unveiled: The Book of Revelation after Christendom.* Minneapolis: Fortress, 2002.

———. "Staging the Gaze: Early Christian Apocalypses and Narrative Self-Representation." *Harvard Theological Review* 92 (1997): 131–54.

Marshall, John W. *Parables of War: Reading John's Jewish Apocalypse*. Studies in Judaism and Christianity 10. Toronto: Wilfred Laurier University Press, 2001.

Martin, Dale B. "Contradictions of Masculinity: Ascetic Inseminators and Menstruating Men in Greco-Roman Culture." In *Generation and Degeneration: Tropes of Reproduction in Literature and History from Antiquity through Early Modern Europe*, edited by Valeria Finucci and Kevin Brownlee, 81–108. Durham, N.C.: Duke University Press, 2001.

———. *The Corinthian Body*. New Haven, Conn.: Yale University Press, 1995.

Meeks, Wayne A. "Apocalyptic Discourse and Strategies of Goodness." *Journal of Religion* 80 (2000): 461–76.

———. *The First Urban Christians: The Social World of the Apostle Paul*. New Haven, Conn.: Yale University Press, 1983.

Metzger, Bruce. *The Canon of the New Testament: Its Origin, Development and Significance*. Oxford: Clarendon Press, 1987.

Miles, Margaret R. *Carnal Knowing: Female Nakedness and Religious Meaning in the Christian West*. New York: Vintage, 1989.

Mitchell, Stephen. *Anatolia: Lands, Men, and Gods in Asia Minor*. 2 vols. Oxford: Clarendon Press, 1993.

Mitchell, Timothy. *Colonising Egypt*. Cambridge: Cambridge University Press, 1988.

Montrose, Louise. "New Historicisms." In *Redrawing the Boundaries: The Transformation of English and American Literary Studies*, edited by Stephen Greenblatt and Giles Gunn, 392–418. New York: The Modern Language Association of America, 1992.

Moore, Stephen D. *God's Beauty Parlor: And Other Queer Spaces in and Around the Bible*. Contraversions: Jews and Other Differences. Stanford, Calif.: Stanford University Press, 2001.

———. *God's Gym: Divine Male Bodies of the Bible*. London: Routledge, 1996.

———. "Revolting Revelations." In *The Personal Voice in Biblical Interpretation*, edited by Inga Rosa Kitzberger, 183–98. London: Routledge, 1999.

Moore, Stephen D. and Janice Capel Anderson. "Taking It Like a Man: Masculinity in 4 Maccabees." *Journal of Biblical Literature* 117 (1998): 249–73.

Moore-Gilbert, Bart. *Postcolonial Theory: Contexts, Practices, Politics*. New York: Verso, 1997.

Moretti, J. C. "L'adaption des théâtres de Grèce aux spectacles impèriaux." In *Spectacula*, vol. 2, *Le théâtre antique et ses spectacles*, edited by Christian Landes and Véronique Kramérovskis, 179–85. Lattes: Le Musée, 1992.

Morgan, J. R. "Lucian's *True Histories* and the *Wonders Beyond Thule* of Antonius Diogenes." *Classical Quarterly* 35 (1985): 475–90.

Mounce, Robert H. *The Book of Revelation*. New International Commentary on the New Testament. Grand Rapids, Mich.: Eerdmans, 1977.

Moxnes, Halvor. "Conventional Values in the Hellenistic World." In *Conventional Values of the Hellenistic Greeks*, edited by Per Bilde, Troels Engberg-Pedersen, Lise Hannestad, and Jan Zahle, 263–84. Studies in Hellenistic Civilization 8. Aarhus: University of Aarhus Press, 1997.

Mulvey, Laura. "Visual Pleasure and Narrative Cinema." *Screen* 16 (1975): 6–18.

Reprinted in *Visual and Other Pleasures*, edited by Laura Mulvey, 14–26. Bloomington: University of Indiana Press, 1989.

Nelson, Robert S., ed. *Visuality Before and Beyond the Renaissance: Seeing as Others Saw*. Cambridge: Cambridge University Press, 2000.

O'Brien, Patricia. "Michel Foucault's History of Culture." In *The New Cultural History*. Edited by Lynn Hunt, 25–46. Berkeley: University of California Press, 1989.

Parry, Benita. "Problems in Current Theories of Colonial Discourse." *Oxford Literary Review* 9 (1987): 27–58.

Perkins, Judith. *The Suffering Self: Pain and Narrative Representation in the Early Christian Era*. New York: Routledge, 1995.

Peskowitz, Miriam. "Tropes of Travel." *Semeia* 75 (1996): 177–96.

Pippin, Tina. *Apocalyptic Bodies: The Biblical Image of the End of the World in Text and Image*. London: Routledge, 1999.

———. *Death and Desire: The Rhetoric of Gender in the Apocalypse of John*. Louisville, Ky.: Westminster/John Knox Press, 1992.

———. "Eros and the End: Reading for Gender in the Apocalypse of John." *Semeia* 59 (1992): 193–210.

Plass, Paul. *The Game of Death in Ancient Rome: Arena Sport and Political Suicide*. Madison: University of Wisconsin Press, 1995.

Potter, David S. "Martyrdom as Spectacle." In *Theater and Society in the Classical World*, edited by Ruth Scodel, 53–88. Ann Arbor: University of Michigan Press, 1993.

Pratt, Mary Louise. *Imperial Eyes: Travel Writing and Transculturation*. New York: Routledge, 1992.

Price, Simon R. F. "Between Man and God: Sacrifice in the Roman Imperial Cult." *Journal of Roman Studies* 70 (1990): 28–43.

———. *Rituals and Power: The Roman Imperial Cult in Asia Minor*. Cambridge: Cambridge University Press, 1984.

Raaflaub, Kurt A., and Mark Toher, eds. *Between Republic and Empire: Interpretations of Augustus and His Principate*. Berkeley: University of California Press, 1990.

Rajak, Teresa. "Dying for the Law: The Martyr's Portait in Jewish-Greek Literature." In *Biographical Representation in the Greek and Latin Literature of the Roman Empire*, edited by M. J. Edwards and Simon Swain, 39–68. Oxford: Clarendon Press, 1997.

Reader, William. "The Riddle of the Identification of the Polis in Rev. 11:1–13." *Studia Evangelica* 7 (1982): 407–14.

Reddish, Mitchell G. "Martyr Christology in the Apocalypse." *Journal for the Study of the New Testament* 33 (1988): 85–95.

Reynolds, Joyce M. "Ruler Cult at Aphrodisias in the Late Republic and Under the Julio-Claudian Emperors." In *Subject and Ruler: The Cult of the Ruling Power in Classical Antiquity*, edited by Alastair Small, 41–50. Journal of Roman Archaeology Supplement Series 17. Ann Arbor, Mich.: Journal of Roman Archaeology, 1996.

Richard, Pablo. *Apocalypse: A People's Commentary on the Book of Revelation.* Maryknoll, N.Y.: Orbis, 1995.

Richlin, Amy. "The Ethnographer's Dilemma and the Dream of a Lost Golden Age." In *Feminist Theory and the Classics,* edited by Nancy Rabinowitz and Amy Richlin, 272–304. New York: Routledge, 1993.

———. *The Garden of Priapus: Sexuality and Aggression in Roman Humor.* Rev. ed. Oxford: Oxford University Press, 1992.

Robert, Louis. *Les gladiateurs dans l'Orient grec.* Amsterdam: Hakkert, 1971.

Romm, James S. *The Edges of the Earth in Ancient Thought: Geography, Exploration, and Fiction.* Princeton, N.J.: Princeton University Press, 1992.

Rossing, Barbara. *A Choice Between Two Cities: Whore, Bride, and Empire in the Apocalypse.* Harvard Theological Studies. Harrisburg, Pa.: Trinity, 1999.

Roueché, Charlotte. *Performers and Partisans at Aphrodisias in the Roman and Late Roman Periods.* Journal of Roman Studies Monographs 6. London: Society for the Promotion of Roman Studies, 1992.

Rousselle, Aline. *Porneia: On Desire and the Body in Antiquity.* Translated by Felicia Pheasant. New York: Basil Blackwell, 1988.

Royalty, Robert M., Jr. *The Streets of Heaven: The Ideology of Wealth in the Apocalypse of John.* Macon, Ga.: Mercer University Press, 1998.

Rubin, Gayle. "The Traffic in Women: Notes Toward a Political Economy of Sex." In *Toward an Anthropology of Women,* edited by Rayna Reiter, 157–210. New York: Monthly Review Press, 1975.

Said, Edward. *Orientalism.* New York: Pantheon, 1978.

———. *The World, the Text, and the Critic.* Cambridge, Mass.: Harvard University Press, 1983.

Scherrer, Steven J. "Signs and Wonders in the Imperial Cult: A New Look at a Roman Religious Institution in the Light of Rev 13:13–15." *Journal of Biblical Literature* 104 (1984): 599–610.

Schüssler Fiorenza, Elizabeth. *The Book of Revelation: Justice and Judgment.* 2nd. ed. Philadelphia: Fortress, 1998.

———. "The Followers of the Lamb: Visionary Rhetoric and Social Political Situation." In *Discipleship in the New Testament,* edited by F. F. Segovia, 144–65. Philadelphia: Fortress, 1985.

———. *Revelation: Vision of a Just World.* Proclamation. Minneapolis: Fortress, 1991.

Selvidge, Maria. "Powerful and Powerless Women in the Apocalypse." *Neotestamentica* 26 (1992): 161–78.

Shaw, Brian D. "Body/Power/Identity: Passions of the Martyrs." *Journal of Early Christian Studies* 4 (1996): 269–312.

———. "The Divine Economy: Stoicism as Ideology." *Latomus* 44 (1985): 16–54.

Sherwin-White, A. N. "Early Persecutions and Roman Law Again." *Journal of Theological Studies* 3 (1952): 199–213.

———. "Why Were the Early Christians Persecuted?—An Amendment." *Past and Present* 27 (1964): 23–27.

Skinner, Marilyn B. "Zeus and Leda: The Sexuality Wars in Contemporary Classical Scholarship." *Thamyris* 3 (1996): 103–23.

Slater, Thomas B. *Christ and Community: A Socio-Historical Study of the Christology of Revelation.* Journal for the Study of the New Testament: Supplement Series 178. Sheffield: Sheffield Academic Press, 1999.

Slater, William J., ed. *Roman Theater and Society.* Ann Arbor: University of Michigan Press, 1996.

Smith, Jonathan Z. "Too Much Kingdom, Too Little Community." *Zygon* 13 (1978): 120–35.

Smith, Morton. "The Image of God: Notes on the Hellenization of Judaism, with Especial Reference to Goodenough's Work on Jewish Symbols." *Bulletin of the John Rylands Library* 40 (1958): 473–512.

Smith, R. R. R. "The Imperial Reliefs from the Sebasteion at Aphrodisias." *Journal of Roman Studies* 77 (1987): 88–138.

———. "*Simulacrum Gentium*: The *Ethne* from the Sebasteion at Aphrodisias." *Journal of Roman Studies* 78 (1988): 50–77.

Ste. Croix, G. E. M. de. "Aspects of the 'Great Persecution.'" *Harvard Theological Review* 47 (1954): 75–110.

———. "Why Were the Christians Persecuted?—A Rejoinder." *Past and Present* 27 (1964): 28–33.

———. "Why Were the Early Christians Persecuted?" *Past and Present* 26 (1963): 6–31.

Swain, Simon. *Hellenism and Empire: Language, Classicism, and Power in the Greek World, AD 50—250.* Oxford: Clarendon Press, 1996.

Tatum, James, ed. *The Search for the Ancient Novel.* Baltimore: Johns Hopkins University Press, 1994.

Taylor, Mark, ed. *Critical Terms in Religious Studies.* Chicago: University of Chicago Press, 1997.

Thompson, Leonard L. *The Book of Revelation: Apocalypse and Empire.* New York: Oxford University Press, 1990.

Tilley, Maureen A. "The Ascetic Body and the (Un)making of the World of the Martyr." *Journal of the American Academy of Religion* 59 (1991): 467–79.

Trites, Allison A. "Μάρτυς and Martyrdom in the Apocalypse." *Novum Testamentum* 15 (1973): 72–80.

Veyne, Paul. *Bread and Circuses: Historical Sociology and Political Pluralism.* Translated by Brian Pearce. New York: Allen Lane, 1990.

———. "La famille et l'amour sous le Haut-Empire romain." *Annales E.S.C.* 33 (1978): 36–63.

Ville, Georges. *La gladiateure en Occident des origenes à la mort de Domitien.* Rome: Palais Farnese, 1981.

Waelkens, Marc. "Hellenistic and Roman Influence in the Imperial Architecture of Roman Asia Minor." In *The Greek Renaissance in the Roman Empire: Papers from the Tenth British Museum Classical Colloquium,* edited by Susan Walker and Averil Cameron, 77–87. Bulletin Supplement 55. London: University of London Press, 1989.

Wallace-Hadrill, Andrew. "*Mutatio Morum*: The Idea of a Cultural Revolution." In *The Roman Cultural Revolution,* edited by Thomas Habinek and Alessandro Schiesaro, 3–22. Cambridge: Cambridge University Press, 1997.

———. "Rome's Cultural Revolution." *Journal of Roman Studies* 79 (1989): 157–61.

Walters, Jonathan. " 'No More than a Boy': The Shifting Construction of Masculinity from Ancient Greece to the Middle Ages." *Gender and History* 5 (1993): 20–33.

Webster, Jane, and Nicolas J. Cooper, eds. *Roman Imperialism: Post-Colonial Perspectives.* Leicester: School of Archaeological Studies, 1996.

Welch, Katherine. Review of Barton, *The Sorrow of the Ancient Romans: The Gladiator and the Monster. Journal of Social History* (1993): 430–33.

———. "Roman Amphitheaters Revived." *Journal of Roman Archaeology* (1991): 272–81.

Whitmarsh, Tim. *Greek Literature and the Roman Empire: The Politics of Imitation* (New York: Oxford University Press, 2001.

Wiedemann, Thomas. *Emperors and Gladiators.* London: Routledge, 1992.

Wilken, Robert L. *The Christians as the Romans Saw Them.* New Haven, Conn.: Yale University Press, 1984.

Winkler, John J. *Auctor and Actor: A Narratological Reading of Apuleius' Golden Ass.* Berkeley: University of California Press, 1985.

———. *The Constraints of Desire: The Anthropology of Sex and Gender in Ancient Greece.* New York: Routledge, 1990.

Wistrand, Magnus. *Entertainment and Violence in Ancient Rome: the Attitudes of Roman Writers of the First Century A.D.* Goteborg: Acta Universitatis Gothoburgensis, 1992.

Woolf, Greg. "Becoming Roman, Staying Greek: Culture, Identity, and the Civilizing Process in the Roman East." *Proceedings of the Cambridge Philological Society* 40 (1994): 116–43.

Young, Robert J. C. *Colonial Desire: Hybridity in Theory, Culture, and Race.* New York: Routledge, 1995.

———. *Postcolonialism: An Historical Introduction.* Oxford: Blackwell, 2001.

Young, Robin Darling. "The 'Woman with the Soul of Abraham': Traditions about the Mother of the Maccabean Martyrs." In *"Women like This": New Perspectives on Jewish Women in the Greco-Roman World,* edited by Amy-Jill Levine, 67–81. Atlanta: Scholars Press, 1991.

Zanker, Paul. *The Power of Images in the Age of Augustus.* Translated by Alan Shapiro. Jerome Lectures 16. Ann Arbor: University of Michigan Press, 1988.

Index